MBA
Management
by Auerbach

MBA Management by Auerbach

Management Tips from the Leader of One of America's Most Successful Organizations

Red Auerbach with Ken Dooley

A Wellington Press Book

Macmillan Publishing Company · New York

Maxwell Macmillan Canada · Canada

Maxwell Macmillan International
New York · Oxford · Singapore · Sydney

Macmillan Publishing Company Maxwell Macmillan Canada, Inc.
866 Third Avenue 1200 Eglinton Avenue East
New York, NY 10022 Suite 200
 Don Mills, Ontario M3C 3N1

Macmillan Publishing Company is part of the Maxwell Communication Group of Companies.

Library of Congress Cataloging-in-Publication Data
Auerbach, Arnold, date.
  MBA: management by Auerbach: management tips from the leader of
one of America's most successful organizations/ by Red Auerbach
with Ken Dooley.
   p. cm.
  "A Wellington Press book."
  Includes index.
  ISBN 0-02-504481-8
  1. Management. 2. Success in business. I. Dooley, Ken.
II. Title.
HD31.A819 1991   91-13061 CIP
658—dc20

Macmillan books are available at special discounts for bulk purchases for sales promotions, premiums, fund-raising, or educational use. For details, contact:

Special Sales Director
Macmillan Publishing Company
866 Third Avenue
New York, NY 10022

10 9 8 7 6 5 4 3 2 1

Printed in the United States of America

To my wife, Dot,
who put up with me
for the last fifty years,
and to my daughters, Nancy and Randy,
and my granddaughter, Julie,
all of whom helped
make life interesting and enjoyable.
                              —Red Auerbach

For my brother, Paul,
the greatest "sixth man"
that any family ever had.
                              —Ken Dooley

Acknowledgments

To my parents, Hyman and Marie Auerbach; my father- and mother-in-law, Dr. Edward and Sadie Lewis; Kitty and Dr. Edward Lewis, Jr.; Victor, Zang, and Johnny Auerbach; Florence, Sid, and Stewart Grossman; John and Eddie Lewis; Walter Brown, Jason Wolf, Eric Wolf, Bob Richards, Stanley Rosensweig, Sammy Cohen, Will McDonough, Joe Fitzgerald, Don Gaston, Alan Cohen, and Paul Dupee, Jr.; Bill Reinhart, Jan Volk, Dave Gavitt, Mary Faherty, Bill Friedkin, Mel Brooks, Anne Bancroft, Ray Flynn, Ted Kennedy, Joe Moakley, Bob Rota, David Stern, Tod Rosensweig, Stephen Riley, Joe DiLorenzo, Norman Knight, Mal Sherman, Paul Sann, Reid Collins, Lee Iacocca, Tip O'Neill, and Ken Dooley; to the Celtics staff and to all Celtics players, past and present—they all played major roles in my life.

And of course, my sincere thanks to David Stern, commissioner of the NBA.

—Red Auerbach

Thanks to Mary Faherty, Red's secretary, for helping me track down forty-one years of Auerbach memorabilia; Steve Curley, director of Red's basketball camp for thirty years; Dorothy Auerbach, Red's wife, for never objecting to the late-night or early-morning telephone calls; the entire Boston Celtics organization; Tom Condon, for his literary criticism; Pam McPheeters, for patiently translating hours of audio tape, and Georgene Zevnik for transcribing it; Ed Manville for keeping me on schedule; and Bill Dooley, for acting as my personal Celtics historian.

Special thanks to Brian Zevnik, whose efforts gave new credibility to the term ''agent,'' and Macmillan's Rick Wolff and Jeanine Bucek, for always being there when needed.

Finally, a special thanks to my daughters, Cynthia and Alicia, and my grandchildren, Elizabeth and Max, for supplying the enonomic motivation.

—Ken Dooley

Contents

Foreword

I USED TO HATE RED AUERBACH.

Detroit got an NBA basketball team back in 1957. The Pistons moved here from Fort Wayne, Indiana. We expected great things. We knew damn well we were making the best cars in the world then. We wanted the best of everything.

Well, we had some great basketball players—like Dave Bing and Bob Lanier. But it took us over thirty years to win the NBA championship: That guy with the cigar from Boston kept showing up and beating our brains out.

A lot of people seem to think sports is somehow not connected to the rest of the world. Somebody once referred to sports as the country's toy store. Well, it isn't.

Professional sports is a business, just like manufacturing cars is a business. That means you've got to compete on a business level with other guys who are trying to bury you. You've got to be smarter and more imaginative. You've got to think of things before they do. Most importantly, if you're running the company, you've got to be the leader. The boss.

A lot of new management theories have been passed around in the last couple of decades. Some are okay, some are crap. Red Auerbach understands what a manager is supposed to do. He's supposed to mold his people into a team and win with them.

Red's toughness and will to win were imbued within the men and teams he coached. He never asked his players to give more than they could—yet he demanded every bit of what they had, and he got it.

Red's greatest talent was knowing how to motivate men in a game situation. He would curse, coddle, enrage, or do anything he thought would make his team perform better. The results were almost unbelievable. Red would do anything within the rules to win. And if that wasn't enough, he was perfectly willing to bend those rules to give himself that little competitive edge that spells the difference between winning and losing.

Red, like me, is a son of immigrants, and one who didn't stay in the family business. It took him seven years to win a title. That isn't the amazing thing, at least to me. The amazing thing was that he could keep doing it, fifteen more times.

The way he did it is one of the key lessons of his life. He worked people hard and then convinced them they were good. They began to believe it. Then other people began to believe it. They call it "Celtics Pride"; I call it great motivation.

Back at Ford and again at Chrysler, I've tried to hire the best, promote the best, and get us all working together. That's what Red did. He is the master. He also has a realistic sense of what loyalty is all about. Many managers demand blind loyalty, then go and sell somebody down the river. Loyalty is a two-way street. Both people reach a hand toward the other. That's the only way there's any mutual respect. Red is able to be a boss without being a tyrant. That's the key. He'd listen to his people, and test what they said against what he knew. Then—and this is so very important—he'd make a decision.

Every human being makes mistakes, and Red made a few doozies. I couldn't believe he drafted a guy in the first round one year who didn't fly. It reminded me of the Edsel. But most of the time, he was right. The record bears that out.

Red was the most successful basketball coach of all time. No one else ever came close to his record, and the betting here is that nobody ever will. Like football's Vince Lombardi and baseball's Joe McCarthy, Red has become a legend.

As I went through this book, I kept finding myself saying, "Right." There's a part about dealing with the press where Red reminds managers that reporters don't know a business as well as the person who runs it. "If they did, they'd have your job. But they don't. You do." Exactly.

So, I used to hate this man, but now I like him. As you read this book, you won't find any highfalutin language or academic terminology. That's not Red. He's straight from the shoulder, no nonsense, no bull. He makes it interesting and he makes it fun.

Lee Iacocca
Highland Park, Michigan

Preface

I FIRST MET RED AUERBACH IN 1985 when I directed him in a motivational film. The more Red talked about his theories for putting together a winning team, the more I realized he wasn't just talking about basketball. He was talking about any enterprise where people are making products, where they have to compete, where they have to win. That's when the idea for *MBA: Management by Auerbach* was born.

Red's management philosophy is simple: "If there's more than one company in your business, somebody is winning and somebody is losing, just like the NBA. Somebody's got a bigger share of the market, somebody is making more money, somebody is beating somebody else.

"Take a look at your competition. What are the winners doing to win, and what are the losers doing that keeps them in the business cellar. Look at competition as a positive thing, not a necessary evil. Then develop a plan that will give you the competitive edge."

As Red described his strategy in putting together his first team—the Washington Caps in 1946—I realized he was defining Management by Objectives. He put team goals in front of individual achievements twenty years before the Japanese made it a national priority.

Many of the management techniques that are preached today—Goal Setting, Participative Management, Team Building, Conflict Reduction, Anticipating Change—have been part of Red's leadership style for forty-five years. Maybe he didn't use those titles, but he certainly practiced the strategies.

Red has all of the qualities that one would expect to find in any successful chief executive. Most of all, he knows how to sustain success. Many executives inside and outside of sports have "championship" operations. Few have been able to keep their organizations at a championship peak for any period of time. Red is one of a tiny number who have achieved championship performance for four decades.

The personal traits that have enabled him to sustain this extraordinary level of excellence are not all endearing. He can be gruff. One night we were in a Boston restaurant called Legal Seafoods. Red's lighted cigar drew the attention of a waitress who told him cigar smoking was not permitted.

"Why not?" he asked.

"Read the menu," she said.

"No, you read the menu," he shot back.

I picked up the menu. It said, "No cigar smoking in the dining room except for Red Auerbach." Really.

I think he likes people to think he's tough, but there is another side to him. In 1982 he drafted a player in the tenth round named Landon Turner from Indiana University. Turner, a great player for Bobby Knight, had been paralyzed in a car accident before the draft. Everyone knew the young man would never walk again, never mind play basketball. But because of Red Auerbach, he'll be able to say he was drafted by the most successful professional sports franchise of all time.

It didn't take long to learn that Red was a proud man and, in a quiet way, a patriotic one. It infuriates him whenever the U.S. sends an inferior team to any international competition. He's also upset when American companies don't run as well as they should and lose out to foreign competition. "We can turn those numbers around if we make a strong commitment to winning," Red says. "The first step is to get rid of the concept that being a 'sore loser' is a bad thing. Only losers accept losing, and I don't care if you're talking about a basketball game or a business contract."

Kevin McHale told me a story about Red that took place in his rookie season after a particularly tough loss to Philadelphia. Red sat down and explained in detail why the Celtics lost.

"I was shocked," McHale said. "He was able to recreate the

whole game right there on the plane. I'd played the game, but he knew more about it than I did.''

Knowledge of product is the key to the success of any organization, according to Red. That's why he always dismissed talk that he could run any other type of sports franchise. He doesn't know football or baseball or hockey. He knows basketball.

This opened up another avenue to the Auerbach personality—his great reservoir of common sense. He was stubborn enough never to let an owner take over his team, even though it cost him his first two jobs in professional basketball and nearly pushed him into leaving the Celtics. Yet he was always able to change to meet a challenge.

In his early years, he refused to talk to agents. He hated agents. He still hates agents, but now he talks to them because he has to. Unless they get in the way. Larry Bird told me about the time that his negotiations with the Celtics weren't going anywhere. Neither side would budge, and it didn't look like anything was going to get done. ''Finally, Red looked at me and said, 'Why don't you ask your agent to step outside of the room and we'll talk.' I said, 'Fine, you get your lawyer out of here and let's see what happens.' About five minutes later we had a deal,'' Bird said.

Kevin McHale told me a similar story about the time his negotiations broke down, and it was even rumored that he was going to sign with the hated Knicks. Red stepped in and the two of them hammered out a contract in a telephone conversation. Not that Kevin planned on going anywhere. Celtics have a tradition of staying with the team, no matter what the outside offer. When the American Basketball Association started, NBA players were jumping over because of the large salaries being offered. John Havlicek passed up a huge contract to stay with the Celtics. So did Dave Cowens. Not one Celtic jumped to the new league.

I was always impressed by the loyalty Red inspires, but never as much as in the past year as we put *MBA* together. We'd be talking, and he'd get a call from someone like Bones McKinney, who played for him forty years ago. They're still in touch, just as Red's in touch with all of his old Celtics.

His management techniques and record of success have created a great demand for Red as a speaker before management groups. I think those same things will make *MBA* unlike any other book on management or supervision that you've ever read.

Red talks about sports and business in the same breath, because he knows that people are people and winning is winning, whether you're wearing shorts and gym shoes or a three-piece suit.

Ken Dooley
March 1991
Old Lyme, Connecticut

Introduction

LET'S GET A COUPLE OF THINGS STRAIGHT right from the start. I don't have any magic formula for management. Never claimed to. In fact, I don't believe anyone has a patent on such a system. If they did, I'd be right there with you, banging on their doors.

But I do have certain set ideas on how to get things accomplished. Okay, some people may even claim my set ideas are set in cement, that I'm averse to change. That's their opinion. I think you only have to look at the championship banners hanging from the rafters at Boston Garden—from both my coaching and "management" days—to see the fallacy in that assertion.

Not that I don't hold strong beliefs. Far from it. But despite a certain admitted stubbornness of nature, I'm definitely willing to change. In fact, my management techniques have been re-formed and refined over the years as I learned from experience, like everyone else.

That's really the only magic formula I bring to your personal management equation. I've been through a lot over the years, and I think I have something to contribute to the "education" of today's managers.

Otherwise, I wouldn't have written this book. Period.

Point two: When you see names and dates you don't recognize, or references to events that conjure up only hazy memories, don't automatically discount them as dated. If there's one characteristic that management techniques and methods possess, it's that they're transferable over the years, with certain modifications. So keep an open mind about learning from my "aged" experiences. You never know when you'll pick up a nugget from thirty years ago that fits perfectly into a situation you find yourself faced with today.

Three: You'll also read a lot about my coaching system, and dealing with basketball players, and dealing with professional ball teams. What has all that sports orientation got to do with you and your department, office, or company? Plenty.

Again, my belief is that the moves I made on the bench, and behind it, can be applied to everyday business situations you're likely to face as you advance your career. Plus I think it's a hell of a lot easier to understand a point that develops out of a sports analogy than most of the corporate mumbo jumbo you're fed by today's business writers.

Another point to remember: I haven't always been right. I've made more than my share of mistakes, and my organization has not always been looking down from the top of the heap. But take it from me, looking up gives you a healthy perspective on just how enjoyable looking down is. It makes you want to work even harder to get to the top, to be the best you can, whether it's on the basketball court or in a conference room or poring over a computer—doesn't matter.

So whether the Celtics are in first place or last when you read this book, you'll know that I'm sticking to my managerial guns. I might be working harder, or smoking fewer victory cigars. But the management techniques I'm applying, the systems I'm working through, the type of people I'm surrounding myself with—they're constant.

The most important ingredient in using this book successfully happens to be you. It doesn't matter what the business environment is like, how quickly it's changing, or whether it's being labeled a recession or a boom economy. It doesn't matter if liberals have taken over Washington or conservatives are holding sway. It doesn't even matter whether you're the president of a Fortune 500 company or were just promoted to manager of a two-person department.

The key is your flexibility in taking what you already have stored up in your own experience bank, combining it with what's appropriate from my storehouse, and coming up with your own custom-tailored management style that works for you.

Red Auerbach

CHAPTER 1

Building Your Own Success with a Successful Organization

A PROFESSIONAL SPORTS TEAM has a great deal in common with any other business. We all have a product, with people making and selling that product. So we all need an overall goal for our product and a specific strategy for reaching that goal.

The key to any success you attain, then, is to make sure the strategy matches the goal. Some companies strive to carve out a niche in their markets. Others believe success will come only with domination of the market. That was my view. I needed to dominate my market. If I didn't dominate it, I had nothing.

The National Basketball Association as we know it today was formed right after World War II, in 1947. There was no indication it would become the success it is now. There were other competitive leagues and barnstorming teams, and no TV to speak of. Parts of the country loved high school and college basketball, but weren't used to pro basketball yet. That was the dilemma that faced us in Boston. Nobody cared about pro basketball. Everybody was gaga over the Holy Cross college team in Worcester, about forty miles from Boston. This figures into the story.

Walter Brown, owner of the Celtics, turned out to be the finest man I ever met in my life. He was a hockey man, president of the Boston Bruins. At that time, Boston was a two-sport town. Hockey in winter, baseball in summer. Some of the Boston high schools didn't

3

even have basketball teams. That was a major part of Walter's problem.

He started the Celtics late in 1946. I was with the Washington Capitols basketball team back then. The Celtics did nothing for four years. By 1950, Walter had already lost half a million dollars—imagine five hundred thousand dollars in 1950!—and all he had to show for it was a loser in a town that didn't give a damn.

So he called me.

Walter Brown was straight with me. He told me exactly how bad things were in Boston. It's a funny thing: The more he described his problems, the more I began to admire him. Most guys would try to sell you a bill of goods. They'd make everything seem rosy, then as soon as you started losing, they'd fire you and blame you for their troubles.

I've seen the same thing happen in business. You get lured into a job or project that has no chance of going anywhere. Then you get blamed for the failure. So I've got a cardinal rule when discussing a problem situation. *Give 'em the bad news first.* Then the good stuff. If they still want to tackle the job, you've got a winner.

Walter didn't operate the rose-colored glasses way, and I can't tell you how much I appreciated it. I've also tried to do the same thing myself—to be straight with people. I've tried to copy other things I learned from Walter, such as humility. He taught me a man was a man, which in today's marketplace also translates into "a woman is a woman." Walter once told me: "Take a man for what he is and what he does, and never mind anything else you've ever heard about him."

Walter the Wrathful

Don't think everything was always peaches and cream between Walter and me. Walter Brown was the Celtics' biggest fan and our best friend. He was also our worst critic whenever he let that famous temper of his get loose. But that was just the way he was, and you had to love him in spite of it.

See, we understood him, and we knew he didn't mean the things he said. After a while, it got to the point where the writers even stopped quoting his outbursts because they knew by the time the papers hit the streets Walter would have apologized and forgotten all about it.

That doesn't mean he and I didn't have our run-ins, though.

Take the Ernie Barrett situation, for instance. Ernie was six feet three inches and just out of Kansas State when he joined the Celtics in the fall of 1953. I already had Cousy and Sharman as my guards, with Bobby Dunham, another veteran, backing them up. So that pretty well took care of the backcourt.

We got off to a slow start that season and were only about .500 when December rolled around. So naturally, I'm going with my regulars, trying to get everything together. We went on the road for four games and lost a couple of them, and Barrett didn't play at all.

The next morning, I stop by Walter's office and he hits me right between the eyes: "What am I paying ten men for if you're going to lose with eight? I might as well save myself two salaries."

Now that really burned me.

"Walter," I said, "is that you talking or is somebody putting words in your mouth?"

"Nobody tells me what to say," he said. "I think for myself."

Now he's really mad and so am I.

"What you're talking about, in essence, is my handling of the team and I don't like it." We both started yelling and then I walked out and headed down the hall to my office.

Let's Do Lunch

A little while later, Walter sticks his head in my office. "Hey, Red, come on, let's go to lunch. I'm buying."

I'm not exactly Mr. Forgive and Forget. So I turned him down and we didn't talk again for three days. But Walter was a great guy and it was difficult to stay angry with him.

I can remember another time when we lost a few tough games and Walter came storming into my office bright and early the next day. "How can we lose like this with the kind of money I'm paying these guys? I'm sick and tired of it."

I've got a temper and all that. But I also can be kind of sensitive, and things like this would really hurt me sometimes. Here I was doing a solid job for him, and working harder than most people realized, and I certainly wasn't any happier about the losses than he was.

"Walter, that kind of talk isn't warranted. I don't deserve it."

"I know it, Red," Walter said. "When I get excited, I talk that way. I even talk that way to my wife."

"Walter," I said very seriously, "please remember that I'm not your wife."

Walter smiled but he got my message. I used a variation of that same message for my players. "Just remember," I used to tell them, "I'm not married to any of you."

Beantown Blues

Anyway, we had trouble back when I first joined the Celtics and I knew it. The only thing I demanded was that I run the show. I told Walter that if I didn't have complete authority over the players, I wouldn't have their respect and cooperation. He agreed completely. Walter was one of a surprisingly few bosses who lets a manager manage, something we'll get into later.

Before we even began assembling the team, I realized we were facing massive fan indifference. We had to educate our public. People weren't going to come to our games until they developed an appreciation and respect for what we could do. So the first thing we did was arrange clinics all over New England, throughout our exhibition schedule. Wherever we went, we held clinics in the morning, scrimmages at night. It wasn't easy, and we were dragging our butts by the end of it, but there was no other way to get our target audience to sit up and take notice of us.

Red Sez: No matter what your "public" is, you've got to cultivate it, whether it's customers in the marketplace, or buyers from end-use manufacturers, or maybe just your boss.

To make sure you have a finger on your public's pulse, you should have a personal pulse program that includes:

• Technical competence. You have to know your product. You have to understand your public's needs and how your product can fulfill those needs. Do you research your audience thoroughly so you fully understand what it wants and needs before you approach it? I can't stand having someone who doesn't know what I need telling me exactly what I need.

• Human relations skills. Your public should view you as being friendly, sincere, confident, and, above all, professional in your dealings with them. Perceptions are an important part of your image. So work at exuding confidence and professionalism in all your relationships.

• Persistence. If you don't sell your product/idea/project the first time around, don't give up. You're not a quitter. Look for another approach until you come up with one that works. Keep investigating until you find the right button to push.

• Credibility. Do you act quickly to correct any problems your public might have with you or your product/service? Trust disappears quickly when things go wrong. You can stop that from happening if you step in and solve problems when they are still minor. Let it be known that the buck does indeed stop here. And that you'll make changes for them on the spot.

• Accessibility. Does your audience know that you are available to it when needed? Set yourself up as the "answer person." Let it be known that no problem is too big—or small—to be laid at your doorstep, for your immediate attention.

• Action. Turn that previous saying around a little with your own philosophy of "the buck *starts* here, too." Seize every opportunity to *do* something. Learn more about your customers or competition. Speak out on subjects that you're well versed on. Be the initiator, the catalyst, to make things happen. Be proactive, not reactive. You'll stay one step ahead of your competition, and up front in the eyes of your "public."

Educating Your Public

Media people were watching these clinics, too, and that was fine with me. People believe what they read in the papers. The more intelligently sportswriters wrote about the game, the better for me. And the more fans who would come into the building. We learned this was a key part of marketing basketball in New England. The more people know about what you're doing, the more likely you are to get good press. But back then, we weren't getting good press—or bad press. We weren't getting *any* press.

The sports pages were filled with the Red Sox or Bruins or the college teams. They simply ignored the Celtics. One day I asked a sportswriter named Bill Cunningham why he never wrote a story about the Celtics. This guy was going around telling everyone that Holy Cross could beat the Celtics. "Tell me something funny about your players, and maybe I'll write a story about them," he said.

I've always had a reputation for being direct, so most of you could probably guess what I wanted to say. But I also knew that if I were going to sell basketball in Boston, I needed the media on my side. So I bit my tongue, and let him fall into the trap of his own making.

"Auerbach, those kids up there would whip your ass," another sportswriter by the name of Cliff Keane said to me. Remember, the whole area was crazy about Holy Cross. Don't get me wrong. I thought it was great that this little school could put together such a damn good team. But come on, no college team is going to beat a pro team. College and professional basketball are two separate worlds. Even the worst pro team is loaded with guys who were great in college.

So even though I knew it wouldn't be any contest, I had to make a point. I arranged a scrimmage with Holy Cross and made sure that Keane and other writers were there to see it. Then we kicked their butts.

We faced the same problem all over New England, whenever we played an exhibition. All these local towns had a team they thought could beat us. Usually, they'd have one or two ex-college players and a couple of high school hotshots, and they'd think they had a chance.

Winning Big

I had no choice. I had my guys go out and cream them by fifty or sixty points. Don't think that was rubbing it in. We could have won by a hundred! But I had to show them that the NBA had the best basketball players in the world and that we offered a clearly superior brand of ball. That was my goal, and I made sure we lived up to it, with the strategy being the lopsided wins. It's a lot tougher keeping players motivated when a team is winning big. But winning big was an economic and marketing necessity, and I made sure everyone on our team knew it.

Our attitude was a lot different than the old barnstorming teams that used to visit a town. They'd deliberately keep the games close, winning by only four or five points. This would make the locals think they could have won—even though they really didn't have a prayer—and that made them come back the next year. No one wants to get embarrassed in front of his family, and those barnstorming teams were smart enough to realize that.

But that strategy wouldn't work for me. If we beat a team from Keene, New Hampshire, by only five points, we were sunk. If they thought my product was just about as good as they could see locally, why would they come all the way to Boston to see the Celtics? I had to show them that what we had to offer was clearly superior to anything they could see locally. So we buried those local teams big time, night after night.

I wanted to sell those people, and the writers like Keane, on the idea that my product was the best one around, by a wide margin. That people had to see the Celtics to see the best. Night after night. I finally made that point.

At first I worried that people would get the idea that I was trying to rub it in. But I never ran into that, no matter how one-sided the score. Generally the other players and fans would simply shake their heads and say, "Wow, you guys really are the best. We thought we could give you a game, but no way."

Actually, we built up a real following from those scrimmages and clinics. I remember one year in particular when we held a training camp at a small town in Maine. The high school team used to watch us work out and some of it must have rubbed off, because they went out that year and won the Maine state championship. They barely had enough guys to field a team, but they beat every other team in the state. The Celtics got a lot of goodwill from the whole state. Even now, Maine and New Hampshire have special days to come to Boston Garden to see the Celtics play.

Don't Hide Your Light

If you've got a superior product or service, you have to let the public know about it. Some people are reluctant to do that, and it hurts them in the long run. For instance, every once in a while I have a salesperson call on me trying to sell me a new product or get me to switch from the one I'm using now.

I have a standard question I ask every one of them: Why should I buy your product? Now I think that gives them a great opening to show me why their product is so much better, works faster, lasts longer, or is less expensive to buy. You'd be amazed at the answers I get. Some of them even admit that what I'm using now is pretty good but maybe I should switch to them to be a nice guy. Or maybe they'll shave the price a few cents. Some of them remind me of those old barnstorming teams that just want to eke out a win. Instead of trying to bury the competition, they're content to coexist. "Let everyone make a living" seems to be their philosophy.

The ones that really turn me off don't have any idea about competitive products or the advantages of what they're trying to sell me. Those guys are out of my office fast. *If they don't have enough dedication to at least learn about the product they're trying to sell, I'm not going to waste my time on them.*

Every once in a while I run into someone who is able to give me good solid reasons why his or her product is superior to what I'm using now. They've got a good answer for every question, and it's evident that they've done their homework. They make me feel like some of the teams must have felt when we beat them by fifty or sixty points. I'm watching a real pro in action.

Red Sez: Think about it for a minute. Exactly how well do you know your product? Your company? Your industry? (And what about your subordinates? If you sent them to me, would I consider them pros?) Do you have a personal plan for staying current in your field? Here are a few ideas.

1. Study. Check out magazines, trade journals, newspapers, anything you can lay your hands on to find out about new developments in your field or new technologies that could have an influence on your product. Pay particular attention to any articles on competitive products or services. I don't know any NBA coaches, GMs—or even team presidents—who don't read everything they can on basketball.

2. Don't stop there, though. Look outside your particular field for new ideas or innovative concepts you could apply. Sports does it all the time. Basketball teams borrow training techniques from football. Baseball's Nolan Ryan takes on martial arts exercises to increase flexibility. And of course everyone knows that Bo Jackson

knows all about cross-training. You could find production techniques or marketing schemes or financial strategies that other businesses are using to advantage that apply to your situation as well.

3. Gather all the product information your company offers you—brochures, publications, new product information, notices, *everything*. Talk to managers in other departments. Pick their brains to enrich your own.

4. Keep in close contact with your company's service personnel. They'll be well aware of any problems or complaints or even new industry developments before anyone else in the company. Take advantage of your ''scouts'' in the field.

5. Do some scouting yourself. Go to trade shows and any exhibits that relate to your industry. There's no better way to stay on top of new developments. You'll also be able to pick up a lot of useful information about competitive products. No one in NBA management circles passes up the opportunity to attend the different league meetings. They're afraid someone will get the jump on them. And it happens.

The Right Stuff

Of course, you can't have a superior product if you don't build it with the best people you can get. This sounds easier than it is, whether you're talking about a better mousetrap or a better basketball team. Let's go back again to 1950, my first year with the Celtics. (If there is one thing I've learned over the years, it is that you can learn a lot from history. Many of the management motives behind my managerial moves forty years ago are still directly applicable today.)

Some say I was a marked man the day I walked into the Boston job. It was just before the 1950 college draft, and all the writers were after me to get Bob Cousy from Holy Cross. He was the fanciest player in college ball, with a whole array of behind-the-back and over-the-head passes. The pressure to draft Cousy was intense, and Walter Brown felt it.

But Cousy was a six-foot-one-inch guard, a rookie. I had no idea if he'd make it big in the NBA. Cousy at that time hadn't proved to me he had the ability. I mean, he was a great player, and they had a wonderful program at Holy Cross then and had even won the NCAA championship in 1947, the last New England team to do so. But I knew a local guy wouldn't bring more than a few dozen fans into the building, and then not for long. What brings them in is a winner.

My goal was to assemble a winning team. I closely analyzed my needs. The first one on the list was somebody to get me the ball. I had very little size. I needed a big man.

So I took a six-foot-eleven-inch guy from Bowling Green, Charlie Share. He never wore a Celtics uniform because I traded him for three good ballplayers. But in the meantime, the Boston writers treated me like I was Arnold, all right, but Benedict, not Auerbach. Through it all, Walter stayed with me. I gave him a bigger challenge in the second round. I drafted Chuck Cooper out of Duquesne. He was black, and this may have violated some kind of stupid, unspoken agreement among certain owners.

If you're a manager, you've probably been in the same situation. You need to hire or promote someone. There's pressure on you to give the job to a man or woman because of who they're friendly with, or who they know, or who they're related to. I believed this then and I believe it now. *If you don't select the best person for the job, you're making a mistake.* You're taking the easy way out and it's going to catch up with you. If you don't select or promote the best person for a particular job, you lose on two levels. You don't get the best productivity that's available to you. That's obvious. But also, everybody in the company is going to know what you did, and it's going to hurt morale.

If I knuckled under to pressure and drafted Cousy, it wouldn't have gone over with the players I already had. They knew what we needed. As luck would have it, I got a second shot at Cousy. He was drafted by Chicago, but the team folded and there was a drawing for certain players and the Celtics got Cousy.

Red Sez: As you build a strong organization—whether it's an entire company, a small department, or a basketball team—you're going to face touchy situations in hiring and especially promotions. You have to be particularly concerned today because of the legal repercussions of promoting—or not promoting—someone who's in a "protected" minority group. As far as I'm concerned, the best person gets the job. What I'm looking to do is:

1. Keep good people by making the business as comfortable and challenging as possible, with good management, good working conditions, and the opportunity to grow.

2. Be honest about a person's ability to be promoted. If the person's in the wrong job or isn't capable of handling more responsibility, level with him or her. It will save you a lot of hard feelings in the long run.

3. Encourage employees to take charge of their own development when possible. If they need more training or education, tell them.

So what do I look for in judging "promotability" in an employee? Just about the same characteristics and results I used to monitor in my players. That would include:

• Hustle. Employees who jump on projects, display enthusiasm, and take the initiative in attacking and solving problems make my job as manager (or coach) easier.

• Teamwork. Employees who pitch in to cover for each other, put the interests of the company in front of their own, work well with their colleagues and coworkers, contribute to the overall smooth running of our operations, and make a serious commitment to making the workplace a better place to work are employees I want.

• Growth. Employees who are looking to expand their skills and experience horizons, learn new techniques and methods that give them (and the company or team) an edge in the marketplace, and make a personal commitment to getting ahead by helping the company get ahead are invaluable.

• Versatility. I want employees who reflect a bunch of other "personal" characteristics, too. Like respect for others on the job, the willingness to accept (and act on) responsibility, confidence in their own abilities and in the eventual success of the projects they work on, and the resilience to face up to adversity, get knocked down, and bounce back up to give it their best shot the second time.

Dancing with Who You "Brung"

I still think the key to building a winning organization is to start with the people you have. Why is it that so many managers, after having spent all kinds of time and money hiring people and bringing them along, suddenly assume they have to go outside the company when a certain job opens up? How many times does a potentially good supervisor or manager end up sitting there and getting a gold watch and never getting promoted? Or worse still, getting fed up and going to work for the competition?

When I gave up coaching, I gave the job to Bill Russell. He was talented and he was ready. Whenever possible, as I did with Tommy Heinsohn, Tom Sanders, Dave Cowens, K. C. Jones, and Chris Ford, I've tried to stay inside the organization. If I went outside, I had to be absolutely convinced the outsider was clearly better than anybody I already had.

Again, the benefits are obvious. You get someone who knows your operation and wants to move up. And you send a message to everyone else. You tell them there's room for advancement. *If you don't promote from within, your people are going to start thinking they don't have a chance for advancement, and they aren't going to work as hard.* It's common sense.

Starting from Scratch

Of course, there are times when you don't have any choice but to go outside to strengthen your organization. Like when I put the Washington Caps together in 1946. I had gone to Mike Uline, who owned an arena in Washington and was interested in starting a professional basketball team. Uline was much more of an inventor than he was a sportsman. He had something like fifty-eight patents for various kinds of ice-making machines and he simply wanted teams to fill Uline Arena. Actually, he didn't know a hockey puck from a basketball. His plan was to simply hire a guy to run the team.

His desk was covered with applications from coaches by the time I got in to see him. "Mr. Uline," I said, "I can do the job for you."

"What makes you say that?" he asked.

"You need good ballplayers and I can get them for you," I said. "Give me an opportunity and I'll give you a team that's competitive with anybody in the league."

He bought it, and I had myself a job. But no team.

I had some very definite ideas of how to assemble a team, though. Professional basketball up to that time had been a regional sort of thing. You could go from one part of the country to another and see entirely different styles and emphases. Everyone seemed to play the game differently.

Most of the teams starting out in 1946 got their players from certain areas. For instance, the Knicks got most of their guys from New York, as did Toronto; Pittsburgh got its players from the immediate area; Chicago grabbed most of its players from the Midwest, though they were smart enough to go after Max Zaslofsky of New York and make him their ball handler.

I knew that the sources of talent were quite spread out, and I was convinced you had to have a heterogeneous group. I wanted my smart backcourt players from around New York and New Jersey; I wanted my runners and power guys from the Midwest; and I knew the best rebounders were coming from out West. *You've got to exhibit similar selectivity in business.* You may go to Rensselaer Polytechnic Institute for your engineers and Harvard for your marketing staff. It's a question of specializing.

The players from each area, in addition to having different strong points, had different attitudes and philosophies and concepts. If you could get them all thinking and working together, you'd be way ahead of everybody else. That's still a manager's job today.

Red Sez: Today I'd ask more of job applicants than just those types of assurances if I were interviewing someone for a front-office job with the Celtics or if I were a corporate manager in another business. I'd try to get inside their heads by asking:

1. Everyone has to bend the rules once in a while. Tell me about a time you had to do this. What happened? What would you do differently today?

2. Have you ever made a mistake because you

overlooked some key detail? What did you do to compensate?

3. What do you know about the Boston Celtics (or IBM or Joe's Pizzeria)? Where did you get your information? What's your impression of our "corporate culture"?

4. Why do you want to work for us?

5. What is the main thing you look for in a job? What turns you on the most/least?

6. What did you think of your last boss? Coworkers?

7. If I spoke to your last boss, what would he or she tell me about you? What would be the most complimentary and least complimentary reactions?

8. Describe a few situations in which your work was criticized. Was it fair? Did you change your work style or alter your efforts?

9. Give me an example of a pressure situation from your last job. (If they tell me about a three-point shot they made at the buzzer, I'm impressed!)

10. What are your long-range goals? What's your plan for attaining them? How are they going to contribute to this organization's goals and plans?

Selectivity in Action

It cost Uline about five hundred dollars in phone calls and a few beers at the Blackstone Hotel in Washington to put the Washington Caps together. I started with Bob Feerick out of California. He was six feet three inches, but he could play guard or forward and I knew from seeing him at Norfolk in the Navy that he was great at running a club. Plus he could shoot. And while I had him on the phone he told me about Freddie Scolari, a real good AAU guard who came from San Francisco. Feerick got Scolari to come to Washington with him.

But I wanted some New York guys in my backcourt, so I got Irv Torgoff—one of the early Long Island University stars—to come over from the National Basketball League (NBA). I picked up Buddy O'Grady from Staten Island and John Mahnken, a good six-foot-eight-inch center in the NBL.

I still needed help up front, so I chased down John Norlander at his home in Minnesota and convinced him to join us. He was only six feet three inches, but he was strong, and with Mahnken under the boards with him, he was exactly what I wanted.

There was only one more guy I had my heart set on getting: Bones McKinney from North Carolina. Bones was six feet six inches and smart. He'd played in the Army and had been around, but I found out Chicago had already made a big pitch and he was on his way there when I tracked him down. The train had a three-hour stopover in Washington, so I hustled down to the station.

"Hey, Bones," I said, "you've got three hours to kill. Let's go over to the hotel and have a couple of beers."

So we go to the Blackstone Hotel and Feerick is sitting there when we arrive. We started talking casually and then I went to work on my target.

"Bones, have you signed anything with Chicago yet?"

"No, but I told them I'd come out to see them."

"Look, Bones, you hate to fly, and you're going to go absolutely nuts taking trains all over the damn place from Chicago. At least if you're here on the East Coast you're near most of the arenas. And you're much closer to North Carolina, too."

He was listening to me, and I could see I was hitting home. I had done my homework on what they'd today call Bones' "hot spots."

"Look," I finally said, "what did those guys offer you?"

"They said they would give me six to seven thousand dollars."

"Fine. We'll match that and you can stay right here."

He thought about it for a minute, then said, "Okay, I'll stay."

But I wasn't taking any chances, so I brought him into the hotel's men's room and we signed a contract right there!

So that's how the Washington Caps were put together.

Not a bad job, either, considering that we ended up with a 49-11 record, including twenty-nine victories and one loss at Uline Arena.

Red Sez: In a hiring situation, "selling" sometimes goes both ways. You may need to convince your number one choice that this job opening should be his or her number one choice. So you probe the "hot spots" of the candidate and try to match them to the "hot spots" of the job. To do that, you have to listen to what the applicant is saying. Here are a few commonsense rules I came up with a lot of years ago to improve my ability to "hear":

1. Talk less. You can't listen if you're talking. Silence can be golden when you're picking the nuggets out of other people's conversations.

2. Don't react too hastily to something an applicant says, even if it upsets you. Keep an open mind till all the facts are in. Plus you don't want sharp candidates to pick up on your reactions and then adjust their presentation to them. You can't make an honest evaluation that way.

3. Don't interrupt. Let applicants finish what they have to say. If they're off base, let them hang themselves.

4. Focus on what they're saying. If you don't concentrate, you may end up missing some important point that might influence your decision one way or another.

5. Ask questions based on what they're saying, not just what you want to know. It lets the applicants know that they have your attention, and they better give you theirs in return.

Copying the Best

I started something with the Caps that stayed with me throughout my basketball career, including running our front office. *I studied the good teams to see what made them good.* I used to leave Uline Arena thinking, What will it take for us to win?

I'd list my club, name by name, on a piece of paper. Then I'd list the three best teams in the league name by name. I'd study the lineups, look at the matchups, and ask myself, If I coach to the best of my ability, can my club be in the same class as these teams?

If the answer was yes, I'd work my ass off to prove it. If the answer was no, I'd analyze the lists to try to figure out what I needed in a trade or draft to make my team a champion.

That's what I did in 1950, my first year with the Celtics. I started out by cutting Tony Lavelli, the great Yale player who averaged nine points a game and entertained the customers with halftime performances on his accordion. I also released George Kaftan and Joe Mullaney, the Holy Cross stars, along with guards Howie Shannon, Jim Seminoff, and Johnny Ezersky and forwards Bob Doll and Art Spector.

I kept Sonny Hertzberg and Ed Leede, drafted Bob Donham from Ohio State, and picked up Ed Macauley from the defunct St. Louis team. Andy Duncan and Kleggie Hermsen arrived from the Rochester Royals, and I also had rookies Cousy and Cooper. As you can see, one thing I've never been afraid to do is make changes. I think all good managers feel the same.

I ended up trading my number one selection—Charlie Share—to the Fort Wayne Pistons for Bob Harris, Bill Sharman, and ten thousand dollars. The money was used to purchase Bob Brannum. Harris and Brannum were two good cornermen who made substantial contributions to the Celtics for years. Sharman, of course, is generally regarded as one of the finest backcourt shooters of all time.

We lost our first three games, then reeled off seven wins in a row—an unheard-of feat in Boston at that time. After the Washington Caps went out of business, I grabbed Bones McKinney and we finished in second place, just one game behind Eastern Division champion Philadelphia.

For the next five years, we scored more points than any other team in the league. But there were no championships. Three times in a row the Knickerbockers knocked us out (1951–53), then Syracuse did the honors for the next three seasons (1954–56).

We had a lot of talent on those ballclubs. But there was one thing missing—a big man to get us the ball. All those years we had Cousy, Sharman, and Macauley together, I kept thinking there had to be a way we could do it, a way we could beat those bigger teams with our speed, finesse, and execution. But the same fact kept coming back to me: You can't score without the ball. We simply weren't able to control the ball, especially before the twenty-four-second clock came along in 1955.

Key Part for the Puzzle

People first began to notice Bill Russell during his junior year at San Francisco when his team won the NCAA championship tournament. They lost a game to UCLA early that season, then won their last twenty-six in a row. The next year they went 29–0 and won the NCAA championship again. No team had ever won fifty-five games without a loss and everybody was talking about Russell.

I made it my business to find out what kind of a guy Russell was.

Never mind the rebounding and defense and all the other things my friends kept telling me about him. I wanted to know about Russell as a person. What was he like? Was he coachable? Would he fit into a team concept? Did he take pride in his ability? Did he have a strong work ethic?

Those qualities are just as important as innate skills when you're bringing new members onto a team or building an organization. *They have got to be able to work with the people you've already got or else what the hell good will they be?*

So I asked plenty of questions about Russell and I liked the answers I kept hearing. He was very proud, very intelligent, very determined. I knew that he was exactly what the Celtics needed. The question was, How were we going to get him?

The Rochester Royals had the first-round pick, but they let it be known that Russell's asking price—twenty-five thousand dollars per year—was out of their range. (Sounds ludicrous today, doesn't it?) The second choice belonged to Ben Kerner and the St. Louis Hawks. I called Kerner and offered him Ed Macauley for the draft choice. The trade made a lot of sense. Macauley was a St. Louis boy who had gone on to a spectacular career at St. Louis University. His appeal as a gate attraction was enormous. Kerner made me include Cliff Hagan, and we had a deal. So right after Rochester went for Sihugo Green, we jumped on Russell.

Now we were ready for anything anybody wanted to throw at us. We already had the best damned scoring team in the league. The only thing that had killed us in the past was not being able to control the basketball. Russell would take care of that little problem for us.

What made the guy so special? A hundred things. Take his rebounding. He's the greatest rebounder who ever lived, and please don't give me any garbage about Chamberlain's totals. Those are just numbers. On the court, in the situations where it really counted, there's never been a man who could hold Russell's jock when it comes to controlling a rebound.

You see, every time the ball went up in the air, Russell rebounded or boxed out or did something. He was never a spectator. If he found himself out of a play, the very least he would do was box out. But usually he'd release his man and move in to dominate the boards. He reduced basketball to a science. Russell's rebounds were not accidents. He knew exactly what he was doing.

Rebounding was only part of his genius. When he got to block shots, it was a brand-new ball game. He didn't block shots the way all the other big guys used to do it. He would block the shot by reaching underneath the ball, or on its side if he had to.

Most shot-blockers are what I call shot-swatters, like Chamberlain was. They hit the ball any way they can, and it sails out of bounds or it bounces onto the floor where anybody who reaches it first can pick it up.

Russell made shot-blocking an art. He would pop the ball straight up and grab it like a rebound, or else redirect it right into the hands of one of his teammates and we'd be off and running on the fast break. When Russell blocked a shot he not only took the potential basket away from the other team, but almost always kept the ball for his own team. I'll bet that 80 to 90 percent of the shots Russell blocked ended up in our hands, whereas Chamberlain and those other guys were lucky to save maybe 30 percent.

More Key Pieces

The territorial draft rule was still in effect in 1956, allowing teams automatic rights to players who starred in nearby colleges on the assumption their natural gate appeal would be beneficial to the league. That's how I got Tommy Heinsohn, a strong six-foot-seven-inch scoring star who led Holy Cross to an NIT championship as a sophomore and then won all-American honors in both his junior and senior seasons.

We had everything we needed. Now it was just a matter of going out and getting the job done. We won eleven world championships in thirteen years, a record that's never been matched. The names changed as the years rolled by. K. C. Jones, Sam Jones, Satch Sanders, and John Havlicek came. Sharman, Cousy, and Heinsohn retired. The thing that remained constant was the method of selecting players.

It involved a lot more than having the talent to play the game or not. If I were interested in a kid, I'd talk to anyone who knew anything about him—coaches, teachers, principals, headmasters. Not about his speed or shot or strength, I wanted to know what kind of person he was. Did he get into trouble? Did he hang around with a rough crowd? Was he coachable? Those kinds of things—because as I said, I'm convinced those qualities are just as important as ability and native skills when you're adding a new member, whether to your department or basketball team.

Red Sez: It's not like I have some crystal ball I look into when it comes to choosing talent. And my system certainly isn't infallible, as evidenced by the fact that I once passed up Lenny Wilkins, the former Providence College guard who became an NBA star, even though I could have had him with a territorial draft choice. But if you asked me what I specifically look for when I hire someone, I'd list many of the same characteristics I named in the promotability area:

1. Character. That's the most important ingredient to me. It comes before size, ability, speed, strength, or any other factor. The potential worker has to be a good person on and off the court or I don't want them.

2. Dedication. I always looked for a player who would put winning in front of everything else. Same goes for a typist, a public-relations guy, a scout for my organization. They've got to have a winning attitude.

3. Adaptability. Would this person accept coaching (or managing) and put personal self-interests behind the needs of the team?

4. Compatibility. Would he or she be able to get along with the other people this individual will be working with? Again, the concept of chemistry emerges, whether you're building a pro basketball team or a professional marketing team.

Reading between the Lines

If I didn't get the answers I wanted, I wouldn't draft a kid, no matter how talented he was. Over the years, I've passed on guys with more raw ability than some of the players I picked. I also turned down a number of trades for players who had more talent than the guys I kept.

I think I see things in certain players that no one else sees or no one else looks for. It's something inside a player. When two teams are equal, or nearly equal, and they come right down to the deciding moments of a seventh game—when winning or losing is on the line—that's when the quality of the players might mean more than their talent alone.

Take K. C. Jones, who played with Russell at San Francisco. The knock on him was that he couldn't shoot or dribble. He just turned out to be one of the great defensive guards in the history of the NBA.

My selection in the 1962 draft is a good example of my philosophy in picking players. We had just won our fourth championship in a row, so of course we had the last pick. All the big names were quickly scooped up: Billy McGill, Wayne Hightower, Dave DeBusschere, Len Chappell, Terry Dischinger. I went for a kid no one seemed to be too excited about—John Havlicek. He had played on the great Ohio State teams with guys like Jerry Lucas, Larry Siegfried, Mel Nowell, and Bobby Knight. I knew that John could run and play defense. I also knew that he was a great kid, very coachable, with an attitude and work ethic that was made to order for the Celtics.

A lot of critics disagreed about his potential and even John seemed to have some doubts. He tried out as a tight end for the Cleveland Browns in 1962 and made it right to the last cut. Paul Brown, then coach/general manager of the Browns, saw some of the same qualities that I did. Fortunately, Brown was a football man. If he had been in basketball, the Celtics probably never would have gotten their all-time scoring leader and one of the greatest players of all time.

By far, the most important factor of all was that Havlicek fit the description of my type of kid: He could absorb coaching; he would listen to what you were telling him, and he'd then go out and do it: And he was a good person.

You find out about those factors by talking to people who've had a chance to observe a person on the job. Most of all, I want someone who's willing to pay the price, who's willing to work at winning, who wants to win so badly that that person will give me everything he or she's got. I want workers like Frank Ramsey, like Bob Cousy, like Bill Russell, like K. C. Jones and Sam Jones, like Havlicek. They are my type of people.

Unkind Cuts

But sometimes even my type of people just don't cut the mustard. One thing I never enjoyed at any level of coaching was cutting a player from a team. When I became head basketball coach at Roosevelt High School, I had inherited a team that had won everything in sight the year before. The problem was that most of the players were seniors so I had to build the team from scratch.

I guess I felt a little desperate, because I started checking out the hallways and intramural games for any kid who looked big enough and coordinated enough to have a shot at making my club. One particular guy caught my eye immediately. He was about six feet five inches and looked real sturdy, so I grabbed him one day in the corridor.

"Hey, boy," I said, "you look pretty strong. Tomorrow afternoon you're coming out for basketball."

He nodded and kept moving. The next day he showed up right on time and began to work out. Two days later, I had to cut him. He never would have made it in basketball, but he did okay in another sport with a smaller, harder ball. His name was Bowie Kuhn, and he eventually became commissioner of Major League Baseball.

The Celtics knew how much it killed me to make cuts, and so one year they pulled a mean joke. Actually, it was kind of funny, but I didn't think so at the time. It was at the end of training camp in 1960 and only one more cut had to be made. Either Satch Sanders, who was my first draft choice that year, or Jim Smith was going to go.

Smith was a big kid from Steubenville, Ohio, whom I had drafted a couple of years earlier. He was a free agent trying out again and he really did a wonderful job, but everyone knew Sanders was going to beat him out.

I postponed the dirty work until the last possible moment. Finally we came to our closing exhibition game and some of my clowns got a bright idea. They had convinced Smith that his only hope was to ignore me when I tried to cut him. They said I'd appreciate that kind of spirit.

So I walked into the locker room after the game and as I passed him I said, "Jim, would you step into my office, please?" I went ahead and waited. No Smith. So I popped my head out the door and yelled, "Jim." Still no Smith. Now I'm wondering what's going on. It's tough enough I've got to break this bad news to the kid. I didn't need any extra aggravation. I walked into the locker room and went up to him. "Jim," I said softly, "didn't you hear me?"

He jumped up and screamed, "No way, I won't go."

I nearly fell over. Then I happened to notice Ramsey, Loscutoff, and a few of the others with big grins on their faces. I should have guessed.

From Players to Announcers

Early on, I auditioned a number of announcers to do the radio play-by-play of Celtics games. Some of them had those very professional voices you usually only hear on radio broadcasts. Others tried to impress me with their knowledge of basketball and told me about their commitment to call an honest, objective game. Actually, they talked themselves right out of the job.

I didn't need another "coach" second-guessing me from the broadcast booth. Fairness and objectivity weren't high on my priority list, either. I was looking for a guy who was going to be 100 percent for the Celtics, no matter what he saw. I didn't give a damn about how mellow his voice was. We wanted someone to get the crowd up, to help us build a following. So I was attracted to a gravel-voiced announcer by the name of Johnny Most. Anyone who has ever heard him call a game knows that we got more than we bargained for.

If a Celtic were called for a foul, the referee was looking at the wrong game. Of course, when one of our guys even got touched, Johnny is screaming about how he got hammered. Here's a typical Johnny Most play-by play: "Bird goes up for a shot—Magic's all over him! I don't believe it. No foul." Or, "What a block by McHale! He got called for a foul! This is crazy. All he got was the ball. This ref's watching a different game." Sure, every once in a while we got complaints about his raspy voice or lack of objectivity. But no true Celtics fan would ever want anyone else delivering that famous line in the 1965 playoffs: "Havlicek stole the ball!"

After thirty-seven years as the Celtics' voice, Johnny had to step down in 1990. He had to recuperate from triple-bypass surgery, and the strain of doing the game got to be too much. If Johnny could restrain himself a little and not get too emotional during a game, he might have been able to continue. But asking Johnny Most to change his delivery would be like asking Larry Bird to cut down on his intensity. I'll always consider his selection as the voice of the Celtics to be one of the best decisions I ever made in building a successful Celtics organization. I'll always be grateful to Marty Glickman, a boyhood friend of mine, for recommending Johnny to me.

Business Connection

A lot of the techniques I used to build the Boston Celtics can be applied to a business. I guess I used some management theories without even knowing about them. Take this "management by objectives" stuff. I used that my first year in pro ball and continue to use it to this day. Look at your overall goal (winning an NBA championship), set up the strategies to get there (acquire the right human resources, translated into players), and then set objectives for each that contribute to the team's total success.

I study the good teams and try to figure out what I have to do to beat them. You pick out the leaders in your industry and then try to find out why they're beating you. Do they have better people? Are their prices, products, or services better? If you can come up with some answers you're only one step away from a solution.

The number one reason why one team outperforms another is people. I have to believe the same thing is true for business. Are you recruiting the right people? We all know about the people who look great on paper but, once they're hired, they create nothing but trouble. Sure some of them may be brilliant, just as some of the players I passed on had superstar potential. But I learned that a troublesome ballplayer can destroy the chemistry of an entire team. Maybe a little more digging, a little more groundwork, would have uncovered the fact that these people wouldn't fit into your "team's" operations.

Are you passing over a John Havlicek or K. C. Jones or Satch Sanders because you have all these preconceived notions about the type of employee you want to hire? I'm talking about the companies that set minimum grade averages or that only recruit from the "right" colleges.

I hear a lot of complaints from colleagues who tell me about all the time, money, and effort they put into training people, only to lose them to a competitor. They moan about how disloyal the employees are instead of correcting the real trouble. If a company is losing good people, it's because management isn't doing the job. There's something wrong with the pay or the working conditions or the supervision. Or maybe the company goes outside the organization for every promotion and the employees get discouraged.

I've always been amazed at how quickly management responds when there's a problem with a piece of equipment. Everything stops until it's been fixed. We'd all live a lot longer if we got the kid-gloves treatment that the average computer is given.

But people aren't expected to have problems and, when they do, they're supposed to be able to settle them on their own. The company that shows that it does care, that offers understanding and the opportunity for promotion, is going to attract and keep the best people.

Red Sez: Take a quick look at your own management style. Just how people-oriented is it? Does it contribute to, or detract from, efforts to build a strong organization? Could you improve your own management techniques, and the results you're responsible for? Maybe you could by:

> • Making a conscious effort to take more time to listen—maybe not during crunch time when a decision is due, but during your daily schedule. Get out of the office and into the trenches to find out what's really hitting the fan.
> • Going beyond listening to advising and acting. Exhibit a true hands-on attitude by doing something about what you learn. Whether it's work-related, like handling a work conflict, or personal, like career guidance, get involved.
> • Serving as the communications center for your department, so your people don't rely on the grapevine or hearsay to find out what's really going on in the organization. Make it a point to convey as much information as possible, and you'll rack up points as a "people" manager with your subordinates.
> • Taking advantage of all your employees' experience/skills/capabilities. You not only improve the chances of producing strong results from your operations, but you enhance your standing in the eyes of those you "utilize" and pour a strong foundation of loyalty for future growth.

The More Things Change . . .

I'm not saying that change isn't ever necessary. Sometimes the right chemistry isn't there, and you have to make some moves. Take the 1989 playoffs, for instance. The Celtics won the first two games against the Knicks, then lost three in a row. Jimmy Rodgers, our coach, had won ninety-four games over two seasons and he did a good job. But we needed a different kind of blend at the top because the chemistry wasn't working. So Jimmy was replaced by Chris Ford.

It's always tough to fire a person, particularly when you're talking about a Jimmy Rodgers. But sometimes there isn't any choice. A lot of companies get into trouble because they let a situation drag on. Instead of letting an employee go, they take away all of his or her authority or put that person in a nothing job. The thinking seems to be that after a while he or she will quit.

It doesn't always work that way, though. Sometimes you'll end up with bitter individuals who will poison morale around the company. Or they may just decide to take up space and grab a paycheck until they're ready for retirement. Or worse still, they cook up a case to drag you into court. No matter what happens, you lose.

Everything I've said about building an organization boils down to this: *How you select people is more important than how you manage them once they're on the job.* If you start with the right people, you won't have problems later on. If you hire the wrong people, for whatever reason, you're in serious trouble and all the revolutionary management techniques in the world won't bail you out.

CHAPTER 2

Gaining and Retaining the Competitive Edge

REMEMBER THE LATE BILL VEECK, the baseball owner? I still recall him and everything he did for baseball. Think about it. He needs to get a guy on base. Nothing in the rules says you can't send a midget up to the plate. He finds one, Eddie Gaedel. He puts him in a little St. Louis Browns uniform and sends him up. He walks on four pitches!

Okay, they changed the rules after that. So what? Veeck was a guy who was always thinking, always looking for the edge that was going to make it a little easier for his guys to win. He once had an outfield fence that he could move in and out, depending on who was up at bat. They changed the rule on that one, too, but you had to hand it to him. If you didn't, he'd grab it from you anyway.

Professional sports is entertainment, and the bottom line is selling tickets. The best way to sell tickets is with a winning team. Veeck knew that, but some years he had weak teams. So while he was rebuilding, he'd think of other ways to sell tickets. He put in an exploding scoreboard to entertain fans. Lots of these promotions you see today—bat day, hat day, towel day, or whatever—were his ideas.

He was always thinking, always looking for something to give him an advantage over the other guys. You could call it a competitive edge. I don't care if you're selling baseball tickets or shoes, a competitive edge is the name of the game today. People keep telling me that business has never been tougher than it is now. Fixed costs, taxes, labor, benefits, foreign competition, everybody's complaining about something, and they probably have a point. Things are tough. But they're not impossible.

If there's more than one company in your business, somebody is winning and somebody is losing, just like in the NBA. Somebody's got a bigger share of the market, somebody is making more money, somebody is beating someone else.

Red Sez: Take a look at your competition. What are the winners doing to win, and what are the losers doing that keeps them in the business cellar? Look at competition as a positive thing, not a necessary evil, because it:

- Encourages you to do the best job you can.
- Pushes you into designing bigger and better products.
- Gives you something to measure yourself against.
- Acts as a motivating tool.
- Forces you to change with the changing times.
- Helps you to develop an edge against those who are looking to take the food off your business plate.

Of course, just looking at competition in a positive light won't be enough to give you that competitive edge. To get a good grip on your competition, ask yourself some pointed questions about you versus them:

1. Is your product design better?
2. Can you offer a better price?
3. Do you use higher-quality materials or offer a longer warranty?
4. Do you have a better customer-service or complaint department?
5. Do you have better credit or billing terms?
6. Can you offer special delivery services?
7. What specifically do they do better than you?
8. If you surveyed your customers (which you should), what would they point to as your strength versus the competition, and vice versa. Perceptions are important!

The way competition is today, you have to know what all the players in your industry are doing and why. You have to be able to explain why your company is doing something that the competition doesn't do. Why is your product or method or service or process the best? *If you know your products or services and also know what the competition is doing, then you are controlling the tempo of the game.* You are giving yourself a competitive edge.

State of Mind

In every situation, sports or business, somebody has got a competitive edge. What is the competitive edge? Looking back over forty-five years in both the athletic and business end of professional sports, I see it as a state of mind in which you're always actively looking for a way to win. Veeck had it. So did some other guys. They'd always be looking for big wins, or small ones.

If I could make a trade to get a Bill Russell or a Kevin McHale, that's obviously a big plus. But I never overlooked the little advantages. Back when we used the center jump more, I'd keep a big beanpole right next to me on the bench with his jacket off, and send him in for every jump. It wasn't against the rules—well, eventually they changed the rules—but for a while it was a small competitive edge for me. And over the course of a season, getting the ball a few more times makes a difference. Some years, it made a big difference.

If a certain coach—not to mention any names—had a slow team and was playing a real quick, fast-break team, maybe he'd tighten the strings of the net a little. You know why he'd do that? Because if the net is tight, the ball doesn't come through it as fast after a basket. The other team has to wait an extra second or two before they can grab it and start their break, which gives the slower guys a chance to get back up the floor on defense.

If you're playing a fast baseball team, you water the infield dirt heavily. If you've got a fast team, let the grass grow to induce infield hits. The same rules apply for football and a lot of other sports.

A few years ago, the New England Patriots sent a snowplow onto the field to clear an area so their guy could kick a winning field goal. The opponent that day, Miami, had to handle the snow the best it could. Don Shula, the Miami coach, raised hell, but there wasn't anything in the rules that said the Patriots couldn't send out the plow.

My favorite part of the story was that the plow was operated by a guy who was on a prison work-release program. Right after that they changed the rule—not the prison rule, the snowplow rule.

I don't say break the rules. I do say that *every set of rules has a certain flexibility factor, and if you're always thinking about that factor and how it can work in your favor, it will.*

In 1953, I drafted all three of Kentucky's top stars—Frank Ramsey, Cliff Hagan, and Lou Tsioropoulos—even though they each had a year of eligibility remaining, due to Adolph Rupp's decision to redshirt the three while his team sat out a one-year NCAA tournament ban for recruiting violations.

Of course, every other team in the league squawked like crazy, saying they weren't eligible for the draft. At that time, the rule said a player was eligible to be drafted when his class graduated. It didn't say *he* had to graduate. Since their original graduating class was 1953, I had every right to draft them. The league immediately passed a rule preventing anyone from doing that in the future. Meanwhile, I had the three guys I wanted—another example of what can be done with a little creative thinking.

Red Sez: Every business person operates under a certain set of rules. And if my theory holds up, that means you've got a certain amount of flexibility as well. If you play within the rules, the odds are good that you'll win your fair share of the time. But if you know how to turn the rules to your own advantage, you'll do better than that. Test your rule-bending capacity by conducting a brainstorming session with yourself. Here are the rules:

    1. Don't be afraid to break new ground. It would have been easy for me to dismiss the "sixth man" concept as stupid because basketball brains like Bill Reinhart, the George Washington University coach, Joe Lapchick, the New York Knicks' coach, and Fred Schaus, the Los Angeles Lakers' coach, didn't come up with the idea. Too many good ideas get buried because a manager is afraid that it might make him or her look different than the pack.

    2. What problems might the new ideas create? Consider the sixth man idea again. I knew right away I could run into a morale problem by keeping a "starter" on the

bench. So I always made it a point to explain that it was more important to be on the floor for the finish of a game than it was to be a starter. A lot of good ideas never get off the ground because of some minor problem that should have been attended to and resolved early.

3. Be prepared to hitchhike on someone else's idea. A lot of people gave me credit for starting fast-break ball after I got Bob Cousy. That's absolutely ridiculous. I learned fast-break basketball from Bill Reinhart while playing at GWU. I used it while coaching the Washington Caps and brought it with me to the Celtics. Think back to some of the people you worked with or for. Are there some ideas that, with a little modification, could pay off for you?

4. Don't just assume there's a rule to cover a situation. When I drafted the three players from Kentucky who still had a year of eligibility left, everyone assumed I had broken a rule. I made like a Missourian. Show it to me, I demanded. The existing rule said that a player couldn't be drafted until his class graduated. These players had been redshirted, which made them eligible for the draft. The league did change the rule, but meanwhile I had my three players. So the next time someone tells you that an idea breaks precedent or violates some rule, make them prove it to you.

5. Keep an open mind and consider every angle. Don't automatically assume that what other people are doing is right for you. When I was coaching the Washington Caps, we were getting ready to play the Philadelphia Warriors, a team that featured Joe Fulks, the league's high scorer. Everyone double- and triple-teamed him but he still led the league in scoring. So I began to wonder what would happen if we let Fulks get his points but pressed the rest of the team all over the court. This was unheard-of back in those days. No one pressed a whole team over the whole court for a whole game. But we did. And it worked.

6. Don't think you have to come up with every good idea all by yourself. I remember Bill Russell called something to my attention in his first professional season. "Ninety percent of all rebounds are taken below the

rim,'' Russell said to me. So that told me that everything in rebounding is timing and position. Concentrate on boxing out and positioning and your team is going to control the boards. Listen when the people who work for you make a suggestion. A lot of business gems get overlooked because of closed management minds.

My Edge

So the competitive edge is a state of mind where you're always trying to outsmart the other guy. You try to look at your business a little differently, asking yourself how you can find ways to give yourself a little edge.

Where did I get my competitive edge?

Actually, I have to credit a lot of different sources. When I went to George Washington University, I was coached by a man named Bill Reinhart. I watched him. One of the things I admired about him was that he obviously didn't give a damn about a person's religion or color or ethnic background or any of that crap. He taught me that if you treat a person with respect, you'll get respect back. He also taught me techniques that I used every day with every team I ever coached. And I still use them when they apply in the business operations of the Celtics.

Every part of the practices that Reinhart ran was applicable to game situations. He invented the long-pass drill and concentrated on basic parts of the game, like running and catching the ball at full speed, throwing the ball on the move without curving it, and keeping your head up. Basketball is a game of instincts, and every one of his drills was aimed at training his players to react instinctively.

He also made practice fun by introducing little innovations. A lot of coaches run thorough practices but not interesting ones. Reinhart made us look forward to going to practice. Sure we were going to knock heads and work on fundamentals—but we were going to have fun doing it.

I think the most important lesson Reinhart ever taught me was not to be afraid of admitting a mistake. The university didn't have a running track, so he had us do roadwork, running through the streets of Washington. I've always felt that roadwork was a complete waste of time for basketball players. First of all, the game of basketball is confined to an area ninety feet long and fifty feet wide, and you can subtract another three or four feet from every side before you get to the actual playing area. That's a compact space, so things have to be done in a change-of-pace manner, with the emphasis on bursts of speed, not distance running.

There was another drawback to roadwork—it caused a lot of injuries. The only time I ever missed a practice in college was because of the shin splints I got from running on that damned pavement. I wasn't the only player crippled. As soon as he saw what was happening, Reinhart called the team together and ended roadwork. But he didn't simply say to stop doing it. He stood right there and told us all that he had made a mistake!

His honesty made a deep impression on me. A lot of coaches consider it a sign of weakness to ever admit a mistake. Reinhart showed me it was a way to gain respect, not lose it. For instance, when I was coaching the Celtics there were some losses which I felt I was partially to blame for. Or maybe my attitude was poor and the players picked up on it.

I'd go into the locker room after a loss like that and they'd be sitting there expecting me to jump all over them. "You know we lost that game because you played horseshit," I'd say. "But I did a horseshit coaching job, too. Let's all do better next time." And usually we would.

Red Sez: I'd like to take some potshots at a few other managerial "can't-do" myths, like admitting a mistake, that seem to be prevalent in today's business world:

- "That's much too radical."
- "Management would never buy it."
- "Why stick your neck out?"
- "We tried it once and it didn't work."
- "We need to follow the rules."
- "That's contrary to policy."
- "We don't do that around here."
- "Have you really thought that through?"
- "It's much too obvious."
- "Do you have any statistics to back that up?"

As soon as you hear any of these slipping out between your lips, clam up. Take a minute to think about why you had that reaction. Then see if you can come up with a more positive response.

Back to the Basics

Reinhart's emphasis on gaining an edge through the basics of the game never left me either. Some coaches feel that fundamentals are beneath them. Damn it, that's what the game is all about. It's amazing how many guys get to the pros and still make stupid mistakes because they've never been taught the right way to do things. A lot of my business friends tell me they run into the same thing. Their people don't know the fundamentals about sales, marketing, or whatever.

When they get new employees, they put them through these elaborate training programs to get them off to the right start. Once they're on the job, though, they're left pretty much on their own. Then managers complain about how dense they are or how they don't even know the basics about the business. It's not my fault if I can't get reliable people, seems to be the attitude of some managers.

I don't buy that argument. If I see a basketball team that is weak in the fundamentals, I don't blame the players. It's a reflection of poor coaching. *All managers have to be held accountable for the performance of the people they're supervising.*

The first coaching job I ever had was at St. Alban's Prep in Washington, DC. After three days of going through drills and getting the feel of things, I knew I had problems. So on the fourth day, I blew my whistle and called the players over to me.

"Gentlemen," I said, "everything I've taught you in the last three or four days I now want you to drive out of your minds. Okay? We're going to start over again."

Then I reached for a ball and held it up in the air.

"This thing I hold in my hand is a basketball," I began. "The object of this game is to take this ball and stick it into that hole over there. And after it goes through that hole, you've all got to work together as a team to stop the other side from putting it through the hole at the other end. Any questions so far?"

They looked at me like I was a nut, but I went into the most basic fundamentals and I continued to teach, teach, teach for the rest of that season. You could see them improving from game to game. The things they were doing wrong in the beginning—dribbling too high, not concentrating, not balancing themselves on defense—were getting better and better.

Red Sez: I've seen entire books written on "getting back to the basics" for companies. Managers can use this same philosophy to improve their own operations. You can begin by thinking back to the best team you ever played on, whether it was a pickup basketball team or your high school baseball team, a field hockey squad or a swimming team. What were the characteristics that made it a better team than others you played on? You'll probably come up with all or most of the following factors in common:

1. Goals. Good teams always have common goals. When you find that goals of certain members differ from the team's, then the team will usually do poorly. That's why teams with outstanding individual talents sometimes do poorly, while others are able to blend average abilities into championships.

2. Trust. Good teams always have a high level of mutual trust, both in the skills of their teammates and their respect for them as people. If team members have to worry about protecting themselves, either physically or psychologically, their energy can't go to team goals.

3. Communication. Good teams always have honest and open communication. They don't put personal interests in front of team interests, and they don't blame others when things go wrong. They air complaints openly and keep personal issues confidential within the team.

4. Comfort. Members of a good team are comfortable with each other and enjoy playing together, win or lose. They share knowledge with other team members and they're supportive when the going gets tough.

Hardball Connection

Looking back, I can see that my competitive edge came from bits and pieces I took from a lot of people. A man who I never met had a tremendous influence on me. I'm talking about Joe McCarthy, the late manager of the New York Yankees. I was stationed in Norfolk, Virginia, during World War II and became friendly with Phil Rizzuto, the great Yankees shortstop and long-time announcer. He told me that McCarthy believed that the way a team conducted itself off the field had a great deal to do with how it performed on the field.

McCarthy would get kids from the farms and ghettos and teach them how to dress properly and act correctly in public, how to tip in restaurants, that kind of thing. The idea made all kinds of sense to me. A guy like Joe DiMaggio looked and acted like a champion. If you could get a whole team to look and act the way DiMaggio did, they'd begin to think they were champions. You'd have a hell of a ballclub on your hands.

It wasn't any accident that the Celtics had a dress code when they traveled as a team—shirts, ties, and jackets were mandatory. In every time-out I'd inspect my team to make sure there were no shirttails hanging out, no uniform straps twisted and turned. It was all part of the image. My team looked good, looked crisp, looked confident.

I even had certain rules for my huddles that gave us a psychological edge. *No Boston Celtic ever sat down during a time-out.* I wanted to show contempt for the other team. They had to sit down. They were tired. They needed rest. But we were in superb physical condition. The Boston Celtics were not tired. The Boston Celtics did not need rest. We were ready to run right back out there and chase them off the court.

I wanted the other team to look over at our huddle and see how strong and fresh and confident we were. I wanted them to think about that the whole minute they were sitting there. I wanted it to bother them, to distract them, to embarrass them.

It's the same thing in business. *If your people look good and know how to behave with class, the whole organization will have the look of a winner.* Then they'll start thinking like a winner. Then they're going to win.

Red Sez: Some people will scoff at this idea, call me oldfashioned, say it just doesn't work that way anymore. Even IBM doesn't demand white shirts on all its managers today. But it's not the actual clothes that count. It's the attitude that accompanies them.

Here are a few ways to work in a winning attitude—for yourself and for the people you manage:

1. Enjoyable. Win or lose, members of a winning team enjoy working together. Enjoyment adds motivation and trust in the team.

2. Nonthreatening. Members of the team should not be nervous about making honest mistakes, nor should they be reluctant to offer ideas, opinions, or feelings.

3. Mutually supportive. Team members should always be ready to help each other.

4. Rewarding team performance. When the team plays well, everyone wins.

Sixth Man

My search for a competitive edge gave me the idea for the sixth man concept. One year I took a look at my starting five and decided they could hold their own with any team. The problem was that two or three other NBA coaches could make the same statement.

All around the league, everybody starts his best. Suppose I don't start my best. Suppose I start 80 percent of my best. Now after five, six, seven minutes go by, it's time to substitute. Their 100 percent is getting tired, and so is my 80 percent. In goes their sub and in goes my sixth man. What happens? *They've decreased their proficiency while I've increased mine.*

Psychologically, as soon as you pull one of your five starters out of the game, the other team is going to let down just a bit. That's when I wanted a guy like Frank Ramsey or John Havlicek to get out there and run them into the ground. It didn't work every night, but it worked often enough so that a number of teams tried to copy it. Sometimes other teams would try to hold a starter back in response. Then I've got them. I'm controlling the tempo, the play. They're following me. I'm in their heads. I've used my people to beat their people.

"Utilizing human resources." That's what the theorists would call it. I call it managing people. It gives you an edge. You don't send your best production person out to sell a customer on your product. You send your best salesperson.

But what if you know the client is worried about meeting schedules, hitting deadlines. Maybe you double team them with a sales-production combo. It gives you the edge over your competition who are merely sending in their salespeople. That's managing your team well.

Pregame Edge

I had a routine I went through before every game, looking for that little extra that would give us a win. I'd start by taking a close look at the officials. You've got to realize one thing when you're talking about referees. You can be the best coach in the world and have the best-prepared team in the world, but if you don't get your fair share of breaks—by that I mean an even distribution of calls—the referees can destroy you.

Everything being equal, one team might be six or eight points better than another. How many lousy calls does it take to turn a game around? Is it a travel or not a travel? Is it a charge or a block?

I'll never forget a clutch game the Celtics had in Minneapolis one year. We're three points up with fifteen seconds to go and we've got the ball. The Lakers call a time-out and the whole joint is jumping because they hardly ever lose up there. They lost only eighteen home games in six seasons. With their narrow court and big guys like Mikan, Pollard, and Mikkelsen, you never had a chance. But we were going to win this one.

All of a sudden the referee blows his whistle: "Technical foul on Boston!" He said we took too much time in the huddle. Apparently he yelled over to us and we didn't hear him because of the crowd. So he makes this terrible call. The Lakers made the technical and Mikan scores and sends the game into overtime. We end up losing.

I had another incredible situation back in the 1947 playoffs when I was coaching the Washington Caps. We were facing Chicago in the opening round. We had beaten them five times out of six in the regular season, so there was no question which club was better. One of the refs was Pat Kennedy, a fabulous guy who always had the game under control. I don't know who the other ref was but he made eleven straight calls against us.

Chicago had a big guy named Gilmur who just grabbed one of our key players, Bones McKinney. Bones couldn't pass, couldn't cut, couldn't move. Pat looked at me, kind of embarrassed, when the other guy started making those calls. What could Kennedy do? I blew my stack something awful, and that jerk never worked in our league again. But the damage was done. We lost the series.

Personal aside: Some of you may be shaking your head and saying "I thought the Lakers were in Los Angeles and the Caps were a hockey team." You're right. But as they say, history repeats itself. The point

is, these incidents helped mold the way I managed later in my career—
when the Lakers were in LA and the Caps were exchanged for Bullets.

Explaining the Edge

Anyway, that's why I made it my business to know all I could
about every referee, to study him, to analyze his personality, to an-
ticipate the way he might call a game. Referees became a big part of
my pregame talks. Suppose, for instance, the Celtics were on the road
and I found out Sid Borgia's doing the game. I would talk about him
in our locker room.

"We've got Borgia tonight. Don't challenge him. He's going to
give us a fair shake. He's tough on the road. So don't aggravate him.
If he blows one, let him have it. But that's it. Don't keep it up. Don't
try to make him look bad. He's not going to give us the next call just
because you bitch and moan. Borgia doesn't operate that way. He likes
to think he's in charge. Let him be in charge. He likes action under the
boards, so don't be afraid to bang."

Now Borgia was a good, tough official. But they weren't all like
him. Most of your referees in those days were frustrated jocks. Give
them a whistle and a little bit of authority and they think they're big
shots. I just didn't want them taking their frustrations out on me or my
ballclub. I never expected to get a call reversed. But I did think a little
preparation was important. And I was convinced that my tirades against
the refs would help swing the next call my way.

There was another good reason why I wouldn't let a referee get
away with a bad call. A coach delivers a message to his players when
he backs them up when a referee blows one. In Bill Russell's third
game with the Celtics, the referee called goaltending, and I came
storming out onto the floor, arguing like mad. It cost me a technical
foul but the expression on Russell's face told me that it was worth it.
He knew that I'd be 100 percent behind him and the rest of the team.

That type of thinking isn't restricted to a basketball court. The
worst thing that can be said about any manager is that he doesn't back
up his people. Think about it. How many times have you heard employees say that they'd do anything for their boss because they know
he or she is behind them? I'm not saying to support them right or
wrong. But give them a fair hearing and, if they're right, fight for
them. There's no better way to promote teamwork.

I was always a firm believer in the team concept. For instance, some coaches had the team come out on the floor while they walked to the bench. Not me. We came out as a team. Of course, once I was on the bench before the game I didn't pay much attention to the Celtics. I'd always concentrate on the other guys when they warmed up. You'd be surprised how much useful information you can pick up that way.

For instance, if I spotted a guy limping or otherwise hurting during warm-ups, you can bet we'd go at him right away. Sometimes a team would try to hide an injury by not having a guy warm up or start. But we were ready to take advantage of him if he came off the bench. Going at a player who's not 100 percent won us a lot of games over the years. It all goes back to preparation—and teamwork.

Red Sez: It's easy to talk about teamwork in sports because the benefits are so obvious. But teamwork can be just as much of an edge in your workplace. Try playing coach for a minute. What would you do to promote teamwork?

How about:

- Being frank and open with communications.
- Discussing complaints openly and objectively.
- Keeping personal issues confidential within the team.
- Not blaming each other when things go wrong.
- Not putting personal interests in front of team interests.
- Sharing resources with other team members.

Almost any group of workers can be thought of as a team with the supervisor as the coach. Most people like to feel they are part of a team because it makes them feel more secure. If the team approach to work is stressed, each employee is going to feel that it's important for him or her to make a contribution. Which will make you, the manager, look all the better.

Like any other team, some players will be better than others. It's up to the coach to make sure that each member plays up to his or her ability. If the coach develops the right team spirit, other team members may give a little push to employees who need assistance or prodding.

If you're dealing with a "rookie," it might be a good idea to assign him or her to a veteran—a mentor, in business jargon—who will get the newcomer off to the right start. If you're dealing with members of your "team" who are not performing up to their abilities, have them work with others who are. The slower "players" will pick up some of the techniques and motivation that will improve their abilities.

Another Edge— The Strategic Foul

My study of the referees gave me the idea for the strategic technical foul and, later, the strategic ejection. Sometimes the game would start and my team would be flat. So I'd make a substitution and nothing would happen. I'd start juggling the lineup and nothing would work. We're flat and there's no way we're going to win.

So I'd find something to gripe about. I'd yell and scream and jump and the crowd would get going and everybody would get excited. Sometimes that would snap us out of it. If not, then I'd go for the ejection. The ref would run past our bench and I'd yell, "No wonder you're working such a horseshit game. You're not hustling!"

You tell a referee he's not hustling and it's like waving a red flag. He'd just glare at me. "What the hell are you looking at me for?" I'd say. "The game's out there!"

I can see he's getting very close to letting me have it. So the next time he runs by, I yell, "Did you get my message? It still goes."

That's it. Technical foul.

I'd just sit there staring at him. Next time down the floor I get on him again.

"Didn't they teach you guys anything about rabbit ears? You don't know anything about what's happening out there because you're too busy listening to me instead of watching the game."

Bang! Technical foul. I'm out of the game. But I didn't go quietly. That wasn't part of the plan. I'd run out onto the floor, yelling and waving my arms and getting red in the face. Bob Cousy would rush over and grab me, and sometimes Russell would pick me up off the floor. By now, I'm raising holy hell. The crowd is screaming at the referees, the other team is all upset, and my own guys are suddenly motivated as they see me getting kicked out.

But the important thing is that we won 80 or 90 percent of the games I was kicked out of. I never had the ego to believe that they went out and won it for dear old Red. They wanted to win in spite of me, just to show they could do it. I didn't care about that. All that mattered to me was that we won.

Me versus the Refs

I'll never forget the day I was coaching in Washington and the ref runs by our bench and yells, "Technical on the Washington bench."

I asked him who the foul was on.

He said, "Scolari."

"That's great," I said. "For your information, Scolari's not even here today. He's in bed with a cold."

The ref looks at me like he was going to cry or something. But did he say he was wrong? No way. He said, "Well, someone on the bench said something so the foul still goes."

What happened was that he heard someone in the stands saying something but, rather than admit his mistake, he just got stubborn. Whenever people asked me if I didn't feel sympathy for referees, I tell them stories like that.

My best run-ins came with Sid Borgia. Personally, I thought he was a great official. I'd put him, Pat Kennedy, and Earl Strom up at the top. Sid was a damned good commonsense referee. But he was not hired to be a commonsense referee. He was hired to enforce the rules as they were written.

Sid came up with the "forced walk" interpretation. It made sense. He was 100 percent right in his thinking, but 100 percent wrong in his calling. A referee is supposed to enforce the rules, not write them. I'd tell him this over and over, but we'd still have forced walks and forced backcourts every time Sid worked.

The fact that the rule about walking was changed is proof that Borgia was right. But he was wrong at the time he made the call. He admits contact took place. Then he says it was not enough contact. What's that supposed to mean? The rule didn't say anything about how hard you had to hit someone. What's hard enough? What's too soft? No harm, no foul? How hard do you have to push to make someone walk?

I'd say, "If there's contact, call it. And brushing someone is a form of contact." Sid wanted to judge each case by itself, and that's the problem with officiating. There's too much judgment on the part of the referees.

Fun and Games

I think the funniest thing that ever happened involving officials was one night in Boston when Borgia made a couple of bad calls. In those days, once you called a time-out, you could walk onto the floor and talk with the refs.

So I went out to midcourt, looked at Sid, and said, "How can you be so bad? You're the worst incompetent I've ever seen."

He looked at me and said, "Same to you!"

I turned back and went at him again. I really let him have it. I must have thrown half a dozen insults at him.

He looked at me again and said, "Same to you—in spades!"

Now I'm laughing to myself, but as soon as I get back to the bench, I start thinking, "Wait a minute. He had the last word." So just before play resumed, I called another time-out and headed back to midcourt. Now the crowd is on its feet and roaring, thinking some big strategic move is taking place. Another time-out. Auerbach must really have something on Borgia now.

"Sid," I said, talking very gently now, "you've got to be a stupid man."

He looked shocked. "What's with you?" he says. Before I was yelling and jumping around, but now I'm talking very soothingly to him.

"You and I have been fighting and feuding all these years," I said. "While you're out on this court, I have no use for you and you've got no use for me. We're enemies. But you've just saved me $350. If you hadn't said, 'Same to you in spades!' I would have cussed some more and you could have hit me with a technical. Then I would have gotten madder and you could have thrown me out. But you didn't do that. Now, Sid, how does it feel knowing that you have just saved me—your enemy—all that money?"

Then I stamped my foot real hard, turned around, and walked away. The crowd went out of its mind and Borgia didn't know what to do.

The Last Word

It all goes back to the concept of competitive edge. A lot of coaches go along with the Grantland Rice aphorism that goes something like this: "It matters not that you won or lost, but how you played the game." It's a nice poem, but the philosophy is bullshit. So is that baloney about losing coaches building character.

It *is* important whether you win or lose. As long as you keep score, you've got to have the idea of winning. I've always wanted my players to believe that. Winning is important.

I don't say be dirty or vicious. I've never played an injured man, and I've never wanted to see anyone hurt. But I'd bend any rule in the book to help win the game!

If you go to war, you go to win. If I was asked to give my life for my country, I'd take General Patton's suggestion—make the other son of a bitch give his life for his country. From the beginning, basketball was a war to me. I wanted to be successful. That meant I wanted to win. Same goes for the way I run the front office.

Society tells us it's bad to be a sore loser. That's a lot of garbage. Being a sore loser is not a bad thing. Only losers accept losing. I've drummed that into the minds of every team I've ever been connected with.

As you can see, there are a lot of things I did over the years to give the Celtics a competitive edge. Some of them cost me dearly, like the seventeen thousand dollars in fines I was hit with during my coaching career. But those extras translated into a few points in each game that made the difference between a winning and a losing season. I take a look at the sixteen world championship flags hanging over Boston Garden and I know I wouldn't change a thing.

Business is as much a war as basketball. You've got to be thinking, comparing your operation with your competition. If they're beating you, you've got to do something. You've got to find out what they're doing, then beat them at it.

Start with the fundamentals. Don't ever let your people forget them. Every once in a while you should stand in front of your employees, product in hand, and say, "Ladies and gentlemen, this is a ————. I want you to forget everything you think you know about it, because we're going to start with the basics."

CHAPTER 3

The Psychology of Winning

A LOT OF WRITERS AND COACHES hung that "poor loser" tag on me early in my career. Are they right? Is Red Auerbach a lousy loser? Does he have to win at everything? As I've said before, yes and no. If you're talking about basketball, emphatically yes.

But did I have to win at everything? Of course not. The concept of winning was not basic to my whole personality. I play handball. I play tennis. I play racquetball. I play those games to win, sure. But I don't cheat or go into fits of rage if I'm beaten. I'm happy to get a good workout. I'm realistic enough to know that, in this life we live, if you hit one out of two, or one out of three, you're doing pretty well. Winning has its place. That place in my life happened to be on a basketball court.

Vince Lombardi is frequently quoted as saying that "winning is the only thing." Actually, what he said was, "Winning is not everything—but making the effort to win is."

That Lombardi quote sums up my attitude about winning. I teach my players not to accept the philosophy that being a sore loser is a bad thing. Only losers accept losing. A player—or employee—who gives his or her all, who is willing to pay whatever price it takes to succeed, is a winner regardless of who wins the game or what the standings are at the end of the year, or whether a particular project succeeds or not. The only losers to me are the individuals or teams that should win—and don't.

Take the San Francisco Warriors in 1964–65. They had Chamberlain, Thurmond, Attles, Rodgers, Hightower, Meschery—all those good players—and they only won seventeen games all year long! Now that was absolutely ridiculous. They even had a good coach in Alex Hannum, but he couldn't control that group. It was as though each player said to himself, "It doesn't look like we're going to win, so I might as well get my points." They just weren't willing to pay the price, to play with their hearts and blood and guts. And it showed in their performance.

Remember that when we started winning championships, there were only eight teams in the whole NBA. With eleven men on a roster, that meant that the eighty-eight best players in the world were thrown together. You want to talk about fundamentals?

That's why I get upset when I hear the old Celtics couldn't compete in the NBA today. Maybe today's players are bigger and faster and everything else, but modern teams can't compare with those old St. Louis, Syracuse, and Philadelphia teams when it comes to being fundamentally sound. And we beat them all.

Not only were those teams deep and sound, but they always saved their best efforts for the Boston Celtics. There were no soft touches. After a while it seemed like the whole world was against us.

Some people think winning comes easy. That's especially so if you happen to be lucky enough to win a lot. But to really appreciate winning, you've got to know what it's like to lose. Losing makes you appreciate winning. Believe me, I did my share of losing. It started with my first coaching job at St. Alban's Prep School. And it continued as the Boston Celtics scored more points than any other team in the league between 1952 and 1956, but without gaining a championship. We were the fastest, highest-scoring bridesmaids during those pre-Russell years.

Red Sez: Don't blow away the notion of learning how to win from a losing experience. I won a lot of basketball games during my coaching career. But I lost a lot of games, too. It's a lot more fun when you're winning. The feelings are all positive—excitement, stimulation, challenge, reward, delight, motivation, and anticipation. The feelings can be negative when you're losing—stress, anger, procrastination, rejection, and resentment. I say "can" because they don't have to be. You can learn a lot from losing.

Ending up on the wrong side of the score taught me a lot during my career. That's how I learned that I would never win a championship until I got a guy like Bill Russell. It also told me what I would have to do to rebuild after John Y. Brown (former owner of the Celtics, and former governor of Kentucky) almost destroyed the team. You can learn from your losses, too, providing you take the right approach. Here are the reactions you have to avoid:

1. Denial. "This can't be happening to me."
2. Guilt. "It's all Jack's fault. He should have known better."
3. Group-think. "Let's form a committee to study the problem to make sure it doesn't happen again."
4. Withdrawal. "We just won't get involved with that type of project again."
5. Projection. "If it hadn't been for Al there wouldn't have been a problem."
6. Avoidance. "We won't compete in that area again."
7. Panic. "We have to do something!"
8. Omnipotence. "I'll have to do this on my own, because I'm the only one who can handle it."
9. Disbelief. "I don't believe this is happening."
10. Depression. "Why do these things always happen?"

Lighting It Up

It always surprised me to pick up a paper and see myself described as arrogant. People assume I'm flamboyant and outgoing, but actually I'm a little bit of an introvert. A lot of stories about my arrogance started with the victory cigar. Let me explain how the cigar thing got started. It had nothing to do with winning at first, but was intended to irritate Maurice Podoloff, the NBA commissioner when I joined the Celtics.

I wasn't a big college coach when I entered the NBA, so it was tough competing against Joe Lapchick, Ole Olsen, Eddie Gottlieb, Honey Russell, and giants like that. So if I did anything, Podoloff would fine me, but he'd only give Lapchick a reprimand. Lapchick used to light up a cigarette and relax whenever the Knicks had a game in the bag. So cool. So confident. It was that New York smugness type of thing.

Podoloff didn't mind it if Joe smoked on the bench, so he couldn't very well object if Auerbach did it, too. But I never smoked cigarettes. Besides, what expresses contentment, relaxation, and celebration any clearer than a big, fat cigar?

So I started puffing away and there wasn't a damned thing they could do about it. If Podoloff got upset when I sat back and lit up, beautiful. That just made the cigars taste sweeter.

Then, of course, the thing caught on with the public and I was trapped. It became a big image. That wasn't the idea in the beginning, but I liked it. It allowed me to tell my starters that this game is all over, so I could send in the subs. When I started winning championships, the governor was coming out of the stands to give me a light. Once it caught on the way it did, I couldn't back off.

A lot of people didn't like it. One night we had a game in Cincinnati and I found out the management there had passed out five thousand free cigars to its customers. It was a big, clutch game, back when the Royals had guys like Oscar Robertson, Jerry Lucas, Bob Twyman, and Wayne Embry, and they were our biggest rivals in the East. The arena was sold out. They thought they were going to run all over us and then have five thousand nuts blowing cigar smoke in our faces.

I gave my guys a speech that night that got them so hopped up they raced out there and ran them off the floor in the first five minutes. The only guy who lit up a cigar that night was me.

Not all Celtics appreciated the significance of the cigar. Cousy used to say that it helped increase fan hostility, and we usually had enough of that already. Granted, it increased the other team's intensity 100 percent. But it had a pretty good effect on my team, too. They didn't want to suffer the humiliation of blowing a game after I had already lit up.

Red Sez: Part of the psychology of winning is instilling confidence, pumping up your employees to give you an effort at or near (or even above) their best—even when you're in a losing situation. You may not be able to light up a victory cigar in your office, but you can avoid the negative aspects of losing if you take the right attitude, starting with acceptance. As in, *It happened and now it's time to take steps to prevent it from happening again.* It's important that you take steps to boost your own self-confidence and the confidence of the people who report to you. Here's how to do it:

1. Evaluate employee reactions. Regardless of the nature of the loss, employees will have fears, arguments, rationalizations, personal opinions, and doubts. Try to resolve as many of these negative reactions as possible by substituting attitudes such as challenges, rewards, stimulation, and rejuvenation.

2. Add flexibility. In any loss situation, a manager has to be more flexible. Some managers take the opposite approach and end up with a bunch of robots who are afraid to make a decision or take an action. These are the times when you should be looking for more input from employees, not less. Nothing will rebuild an employee's self-confidence faster than a manager who listens to him after a mistake has been made.

3. Consider new methods. Maybe the loss was the result of old, inefficient methods. Consider every setback as a possible signal that change is in order.

4. If the loss results in new methods, make sure you fully explain them to employees. Some managers understand the reasons for the change completely, but they don't explain them to the people who have to carry them out. Make sure all employees' questions, doubts, and uncertainties are answered before you make the changes.

5. Expect an impact on performance. Some managers expect overnight results from a change or new method. Sometimes performance actually goes down immediately after changes are made. It's like introducing a new play in basketball. You can't expect overnight results. But as the team gets used to it, execution will improve.

Coaching against Coaches

One thing I never did was knock another coach's strategy or players. Check the records and you'll never find me quoted as saying some other coach did a lousy job, or such-and-such a player stinks.

Hundreds of times someone in New York would ask me: "What's the matter with the Knicks?" I'd always answer: "Hey, I've got my own problems. Do you want to know what's wrong with the Knicks? Go ask the Knicks."

I never went out of my way to embarrass anybody. If we got a twenty-point lead, sure, I'd want to make it thirty. But I wouldn't try to beat someone by fifty or sixty points, as a lot of teams have done. Once I felt we had a safe enough lead, I'd just tell my guys to keep playing hard, maintain their lead, keep the game out of reach. There's a big difference between staying in command of a game and trying to humiliate someone. Once my guys had complete command, I was satisfied. The killer instinct was satisfied. I've got him down and I'm going to make sure he stays down, but I'm not going to kill him ten times.

The same mentality applies to most business situations. Once you've beaten down your competition, you're not going to score any extra points by putting him out of business. In fact, drub your competitors too much, and before you know it, you'll get a reputation in the business community as a corporate bully. Now, while there are some executives out there who might actually enjoy that reputation, it's my experience that you're going to risk a positive image with your clients, customers, and fans when you come across as the hard guy.

That doesn't mean I wouldn't take advantage of another coach if I detected a weakness in him. Take Freddie Schaus, the Lakers' coach, who was very knowledgeable about the game.

I always felt Freddie could be disturbed and ruffled. Every time I made a move that worked, I would make sure Freddie was aware of it. We drove Schaus to the point of distraction. He was so worried about what I was going to do, what new thing I was going to come up with. Most of the time it was nothing. I just wanted to play the ball game. But we would let them think we were coming up with something unusual and Freddie would get so excited he'd start thinking about me instead of thinking about his own ballclub.

That was fine with me, since I always operated on the theory that I'd rather have them adjust to me than me adjust to them. And it usually worked out that way.

Red Sez: Being able to adjust is a necessary attribute of winning in today's business world. Some managers and organizations thrive on change while others are buried by it. Here are factors that helped me accept change:

    1. Challenge. I never looked at change as a threat but as an opportunity to better myself or my team.

    2. Curiosity. I always had a healthy interest in new things, new methods.

    3. Letting go. It's easy for a manager to get so wrapped up in a certain way of doing things that he or she doesn't want to change. It's always more comfortable to deal with the old and familiar. But in today's marketplace, that kind of thinking can be deadly.

    4. Self-confidence. Change sometimes means that we have to switch from the role of a veteran to a rookie. A manager who can't make that switch comfortably is going to end up on the bench. Bill Walton was able to adjust from his role as a franchise player to a bench player, and he made valuable contributions as a result. It's always easier to adapt to new situations, learn new rules, and accept new realities if a manager has the right self-confidence.

    5. Willingness to ask for help. There are few managers who don't need some help in the face of rapid change. A manager who is able to accept help instead of struggling against it will adjust to change with a minimum of stress and struggle.

One other thought on "coaches." I never really enjoyed all that talk about my being a coaching genius, either. Sure the praise and tributes were nice, and I appreciate them. But they were also potentially destructive. One of my biggest concerns as a coach was making sure my guys didn't get fat heads with all of their success. There had to be some kind of proper perspective maintained or else we'd have been buried in our press clippings.

That went for the coach, too. That's one of the reasons I was so careful not to hang around the locker room talking with writers after the game. Too many coaches got caught up in this "I . . . I . . . I" business: I did this. I did that. I saw that happen with Al Cervi back in the fifties, when he was coaching Syracuse.

He made the mistake of using the first person too much when he had some great teams. One year the players got fed up with it and voted him out of a playoff share. The vote was ten to one. He started yelling about it on an airplane, so Dolph Schayes stood up and said, "I just changed my vote. That makes it unanimous."

Cervi was a good coach. He was a tough guy from the old school and he really knew how to motivate, but he never gave his players enough credit. Finally they rebelled. I learned a good lesson from that experience.

Learning from "Killers"

I also try to learn from people who impress me, the ones who have that killer instinct, that inner drive, the self-starters who have the burning desire to succeed. Every player doesn't have the natural tools of Larry Bird to work with, and every employee you've got isn't going to be the president of the company.

If someone does a lousy job at one thing because they're lazy or uninterested, they'll probably do a lousy job at something else for the same reasons. But someone with drive who doesn't get in one door will get in another, even if they have to knock it down. I'll tell you one of the best examples I know of.

Early in my Celtics coaching career, we had a kid who kept sneaking into the Garden to play. Our owner Walter Brown had the crew throw him out for a while, but he finally relented. He said if the kid wanted to play this badly, let him do it.

The kid went to South Boston High and was all-state. He'd hitch-hike down to New York, to Harlem or the Bronx, to find the best players to play against. He figured if he could play with New York's best, he could play with anyone—pretty solid thinking, especially then. He wasn't tall or fast, but his reputation as a player spread around the New York playgrounds.

Going Places

The kid developed into a terrific shooter. He went to Providence College and played for Joe Mullaney's great teams, with guys like John Thompson and Johnny Egan. He got better. He was MVP when Providence won the NIT in 1963. Syracuse drafted him in the fourth round, but he entered the service instead of the NBA. The Celtics got him for a second-round draft choice in 1964.

He had a good camp. It got down to two players for our final roster spot, the kid or Larry Siegfried of Ohio State. It was close. I always had a rule that I'd pick the best players available for my team, no exceptions.

I was tempted to break the rule in this case, because I wanted this kid to be a Celtic. But I couldn't. Any way I looked at it, Siggy was going to contribute more to the team. He was bigger, a better inside player, and that's what we needed.

I was straight with the kid. I told him I wanted to keep him, but I couldn't or everything I stood for for all those years would have been meaningless.

The kid appreciated the fact that I was straight with him. I let him know that I realized that he had given me everything he had to give. When a guy does that, he's not a loser, I told him. The kid said it was okay, that he was at peace because he knew he had given his best, and if that wasn't good enough, he was going to do something else.

I had a lump in my throat as big as a basketball when he said goodbye that day. But I also knew that he'd find something where his best would be good enough. He did. He became the Hon. Raymond J. Flynn, Mayor of Boston.

No Dirty Tricks

Over the years, I've been blamed if the visitors' locker room is too hot or too cold, if the visiting team loses its luggage at Logan Airport or gets stalled in Boston traffic. I'm thankful that the power outage at Boston Garden in 1990 occurred during a hockey game or I probably would have been blamed for that, too.

Okay, the visitors' locker room is too small and the Garden should be air-conditioned. But to suggest I pull any dirty tricks to give the Celtics a competitive advantage is ridiculous. If the temperature in the Boston Garden hits a hundred degrees, as it did in a playoff game against the Lakers in 1984, it's not seventy degrees for one team and thirty degrees for the other.

Maybe the Garden doesn't have some of the modern touches of other NBA arenas. But it doesn't have any of the gimmickry, either. Celtics fans won't be subjected to rock and roll blaring from the speakers, no cheerleaders or characters dressed as ducks, chickens, or other animals trying to incite the crowd as long as I'm around. Hey, you don't see IBM or Federal Express selling their products or services with chickens. To my way of thinking, the team makes it on its own, or forget it. I think a lot of that stuff is demeaning to the game.

I've also heard a lot of complaints about our parquet floor, which was built in 1946. Some players claim that the floor is softer than most so you have to dribble harder to make the ball come up. Others say it's tough to do a lot of fancy dribbling on it because of the dead spots. This is the same floor Bob Cousy operated on, so I don't pay too much attention to those complaints. As far as I'm concerned, if the Celtics do move to another arena, the parquet floor goes with us.

Getting Floored

Of course, an incident at Boston Garden in the fall of '90 gave critics new ammunition to add to their long list that the floor gives the Celtics an unfair advantage. A game between the Celtics and the Atlanta Hawks had to be postponed when referee Dick Bavetta ruled that the condensation seeping through the floor made it unsafe.

Atlanta's Duane Ferrell slipped and fell to the floor early in the game and Bavetta stopped play while the condensation was wiped up. After a delay of nearly a half hour, play was resumed. But the Hawks' Tim McCormick lost his footing and the game was postponed. Now I didn't have any quarrel with Bavetta's decision. The floor was slippery and too dangerous for play to continue.

Here's what really caused the postponement. A late-November heat wave brought a record-high temperature of seventy-four degrees the day of the game. The temperature was sixty-seven at game time and the relative humidity was 85 percent, according to the National Weather Service in Boston. The Boston Bruins had played a game in the Garden earlier that day, and the temperature caused the ice underneath the floor to melt. This created the condensation which led to the slippery conditions. Those are the facts.

In a few years, critics will be questioning why only the Atlanta players were slipping and sliding. It's already started. Right after the game, Tim McCormick, one of the Atlanta players who slipped, said, "I'm really impressed with Red Auerbach. I thought I heard about all his tricks, but climate control, that's one I never expected."

Now I know McCormick was only kidding. But give it a few years and the whole incident will take on a life of its own. Another arrow in Red Auerbach's arsenal of dirty tricks. All I can say in my own defense is that I'd have to be pretty stupid if I did push a magic button to water the floor. The Celtics were ahead, 37–22, when the game was stopped. When the other team has lost eight in a row and it's down by fifteen, getting a game postponed is not a strategic ploy.

There was another factor to consider, too. Larry Bird needed just six points to reach the twenty thousand career mark when it was called. He would have joined Kareem Abdul-Jabbar, Jerry West, Oscar Robertson, and John Havlicek as the fifth man to score that many points and also ring up five thousand assists. Representatives of the Spalding Company were there to hold a ceremony in which it would take the ball that Bird used to hit his twenty-thousandth and give it to the Hall of Fame.

This wasn't the first time wet floor conditions caused a postponement. On Christmas Day in 1971, we were scheduled to play in Cincinnati Garden, but because of wet floor conditions, the game was called before it was started. Of course, our postponement will go down in history as the first NBA game ever called on account of nice weather.

For years I've been accused of keeping the Garden a hothouse for opponents by purposely keeping temperatures uncomfortably high. Los Angeles fans still complain about the playoff game when Kareem Abdul-Jabbar had to take oxygen so he could continue to play. Did they think the air was better on the Celtics' side of the court? Ridiculous. But those stories get started and you can't stop them.

Winning through Negotiation

Through the years, a lot of stories went around about what a tough, shrewd negotiator I was, and down deep inside they always hurt me a little. I wasn't being shrewd at all. I was trying to watch the money because we just didn't have that much dough to work with. As far as I'm concerned, there's no such thing as a great negotiator. Everything depends on circumstances.

For example, it was a joke to say that I ''negotiated'' a lease with the Boston Garden. I'd go into the office and they'd tell me the terms. ''Take it or leave it'' was the message I got.

They knew they had us behind the eight ball. There was no building in Providence, there was no building in Worcester. We had no place to go. So our negotiation was from total weakness. We had nothing going for us. Of course, later on, when things did change, I refused to even talk to the guy who pushed me into a corner all those years. So whenever you're negotiating from total strength or total weakness, keep in mind that situations and circumstances do change.

I learned that the hard way after announcing in 1967 that I would not deal with agents or would not let them sit in when I was negotiating with my players. Okay, it was a stupid comment. But I wasn't the only general manager in sports who felt that way about dealing with agents.

There's a great story involving Lombardi when he was still the general manager of the Green Bay Packers. One of his players walked into a negotiating session with an agent. When Lombardi asked who the man was, the agent said he was there to "protect the player's interests." Lombardi excused himself and left the room. He came back a few minutes later and explained that the agent would have to do his "protecting" in Philadelphia, because the player had just been traded there.

Of course, I finally had to deal with agents even though my personal view of them has never changed. One of my first experiences involved an agent who was representing a kid who wasn't even a high draft choice. He started out by telling me how this kid was going to help the Celtics win another world championship. I didn't say anything. Then he started outlining a package that included incentives for X number of points and X number of winning games.

That did it for me. "If making my ballclub isn't enough incentive for this kid, I don't want him." Then I threw them out, and the next day he signed with another team. It was okay with me. This guy was an example of a bad agent as far as I'm concerned. He really didn't have the interests of the kid at heart.

Determining a Winner

One of the best negotiation stories I've ever heard involved Cornelius Vanderbilt, reportedly one of the richest men in the world, and J. P. Morgan, the financier. While on a cruise across the Atlantic together, Vanderbilt mentioned he was interested in selling iron properties in Michigan. Morgan had just acquired steel mills and he was looking for raw-material sources. So he offered $60 million for the property and Vanderbilt accepted immediately.

Morgan was delighted with the deal because he had been prepared to go to $80 million for the property. Vanderbilt was equally happy because he told friends that he would have accepted $40 million. So this was a case in which both sides could claim a victory. Most negotiations don't end that way.

That doesn't necessarily mean there has to be a clear-cut winner or loser in every negotiating situation. I think a negotiation settlement should be like a trade—if it doesn't help both sides, it's not good. Of course, I always felt that if one side was going to get the edge, it might just as well go the Celtics' way. Here are the principles I used that got me players like Russell, Cousy, and Havlicek and helped me sign Parish, Bird, and McHale to long-term contracts.

1. Prepare early. The tempo of a basketball game is usually set in the first fifteen minutes. A team that gets off to the right start has a good chance of winning. That means that you have to know the other team thoroughly and understand what it is capable of doing. It also means that you have to know which weaknesses you can exploit.

All these techniques apply to a negotiation session. If you do your research properly, you'll know the total circumstances of the other party, which individuals make the decisions, and what they are likely to accept. For instance, how dependent is the other party on your services? Do they have alternatives open to them? How do your services compare with the competition?

2. Let the other party make the first bid. This gives you the information you need to go to the other extreme. Even if the offer is better than you expect, ask for a little more. But don't get greedy. A lot of potential deals that would be beneficial to both sides are blown because one party tried to gain too big an advantage.

3. Remember that power swings both ways. I have a friend whose company was totally dependent on one supplier for a key ingredient. The prices went up even as the deliveries slowed down. At one point, my friend was ready to chuck the whole thing—just stop production altogether. I told him to hold on, that circumstances change. A few months later, he found another supplier and those other guys were out the door the same day. Of course, if you're bargaining from a position of strength,

name your deal and hold out for it. But try to make some small concessions that will at least give the other party the idea that they're gaining something.

4. You don't have to be disagreeable to disagree. I admit that I didn't always follow that rule. Like the time I threw a player and his agent out of my office after I lost my temper. There are times when a little irritation or anger can actually help in a negotiation session. But you shouldn't let it get out of control or it will undermine your judgment. The easiest thing in the world is to storm out of a bargaining session. The toughest is to have to crawl back on your knees.

5. Never take anything for granted. I learned this point during my early years of basketball. I put it to good use when we negotiated with Ben Kerner to get Bill Russell. Ask even the most avid Celtics fan how we got Russell, and he'll tell you we gave up Ed Macauley and Cliff Hagan for St. Louis's second pick. That's only partially true.

Rochester had the first pick, and if they took Russell, all of our great plans would go right out the window. Now Les Harrison, the Rochester owner, had already said he had planned to pass on Russell and take Sihugo Green instead. But Walter and I decided we should have something a little more concrete. Walter controlled the Ice Capades at that time, and he knew that Harrison wanted to bring them to Rochester. So Walter offered the Ice Capades for two weeks a year in return for Harrison's pledge not to draft Russell. So in a real sense you could say we got Russell for Macauley, Hagan, and the Ice Capades.

6. Maintain your integrity. Okay, remember my reputation for being a tough, abrasive bargainer. I don't reveal my hand all at once, because if I do some agent is going to try to take advantage of the Celtics. If I have some special clout, I'm going to use it. But no one can ever say that I'm not trustworthy. If I make a commitment in a bargaining session, I keep it. I expect the same treatment on the other side. When I'm negotiating with people for the first time, I'm more interested in judging their honesty than uncovering any weakness in their posi-

tions. Reaching an agreement with a person who can't be trusted means nothing.

7. Use silence as a weapon. There's one statement that can be made about all the agents who ever lived: They like to talk. So I let them. That way I pick up problems in advance, pinpoint areas I can rebut, and assess the relative strength of our positions. Then I can modify my position based on what I've just heard. It's been my experience that the person who talks least, who forces the other party to give him feedback, is in charge of the relationship.

So what do you do when you run into others who listen more than they talk? Take control of the negotiation and try to put them on the defensive. But reveal as little of your plan as possible. Try to avoid arguments and ask the other people to explain their positions fully. Then give them yours.

8. Don't gloat, no matter how happy you are with the completed deal. Likewise, I never deliberately tried to show up another professional basketball team by running up the score. Amateur teams were another matter because I had something to prove. But in the professional ranks, there's always another game next week, next month, next year. With good draft choices, a weak team today can become a powerhouse tomorrow. So I always made it a point not to go public with my delight over a final score or a deal or a contract.

A few years ago, I watched Merv Griffin and Donald Trump on national television explaining how each had gotten the best of the other in a business deal. I remembered thinking at that time that they both sounded like losers.

9. Don't try to do everything at once. A lot of deadlocks result because both sides take an everything-or-nothing approach. Identify your most important demand and try to get a commitment on it, then move on to the next one. Try to trade concessions. If you can reach a series of small agreements, you might be ready to attack a major disagreement.

10. If it's your final offer, make sure the other side knows it. If word gets out that your "final" offer

is only a negotiating ploy, you'll never be taken seriously again. That doesn't mean there isn't room for some minor concessions, but you have to stand firm on your major issues.

The worst example of this kind of bargaining in professional sports involves baseball. I read about teams that refuse to give more than three-year contracts or refuse to insert a no-trade clause. Then, when there's a danger of losing a star player or the opportunity of signing a free agent from another team, all these principles go out the window. Don't think that agents don't take notice of these games and act accordingly.

The same principle holds true for business. If negotiators get the idea that your "final" price is a bargaining tool or merely an attempt to get a feel for the market, they won't take you seriously.

Going Out a Winner

It would have been easy to retire after the 1965 championship. No one would have blamed me. Yet it bothered me. Would people say I was quitting while I was on top? Would they say I got out when the getting was good?

Throughout my career, I operated with the idea that I didn't give a damn what anybody thought or said about me. I was me. Take me or leave me. I let my record do my talking.

But after nineteen years in the league, I did care. They could call me anything they wanted—a lousy loser, a poor sport, an egotist—anything they felt like calling me. But I didn't want to be called a quitter. That was very important to me.

So I made a decision. I would quit. The time had come, but not while I was on top. They would never say that about me because I would never give them a chance to. I announced that I would retire, but I announced it one year ahead of time. I said 1966 would be my final year on the Boston bench.

Freddie Schaus and the Lakers knew it.

Jack McMahon and the Royals knew it.

Richie Guerin and the Hawks knew it.

Every team in the league knew it. They each had one more shot at Auerbach. There were no guarantees that I would go out a winner. Cousy, Sharman, Ramsey, and Loscutoff were gone. Heinsohn had just retired. We were getting old fast. We had seven straight championships in our pockets, eight out of nine altogether. No one could possibly predict what would happen in 1966.

That Championship Season

I got a lucky break at the beginning of the '66 season when I was able to pick up Don Nelson. Every other team in the NBA turned thumbs down when his name appeared on the waiver wire, but I knew he would be right for the Celtics. He went on to give us eleven outstanding seasons.

We held on to first place through the holiday season and on into the dead of winter, but the Philadelphia 76ers remained just a step or two behind. In early March, we met head-on and the 76ers swept a home-and-home set, finally jumping into first place. Neither team lost again, and the final records were Philadelphia 55–25, Boston 54–26. For the first time in ten years, the Celtics were not Eastern Division champions.

That meant playing a preliminary series against Cincinnati, a best-of-five affair. The Royals won games one and three, but twice we fought back to even the count. Sam Jones came through with thirty-four points in game five and we wrapped it up, 112–103.

Our much-heralded best-of-seven showdown with Philadelphia was a clinker. We routed them in five games, winning the first two by margins of nineteen and twenty-one. Then we lost the opening game of the championship series with Los Angeles in overtime. Right after the game I ordered all my players to report to a news conference the following morning downtown. Speculation was rampant that the new Celtics coach would be announced. Who would it be?

His name, it turned out, was Bill Russell. The next night we clobbered the Lakers by twenty points to square the series. Freddie Schaus refused to talk to the writers because he said his team should have gotten more press from its opening game victory. The papers, of course, had ignored LA's win and focused on Bill Russell being named our coach. Schaus even suggested that I did it deliberately, so his team wouldn't get the credit it deserved. I couldn't believe that he would think me capable of such an underhanded act. Meanwhile, we went on to win the series in seven games.

Incidentally, I didn't have to light the victory cigar myself that night. Massachusetts Governor John Volpe did it for me. After a quick round of handshakes in the locker room, I left the Garden, closing the door on twenty years of coaching. The important thing was that I closed it as a winner.

CHAPTER 4

Discipline: Key to Celtics Tradition

YOU CAN'T PICK UP A NEWSPAPER today without reading about some ex-employee suing his company because he was fired improperly. Wrongful discharge, they usually call it. "You fired me but, according to the rules, I was only supposed to get suspended," is one of the arguments you hear.

"Bill Smith got only a written warning, but you threw the book at me for breaking the same rule."

"The rule says I'm supposed to get another chance before you fire me."

"Paragraph 4b under Rule 1012 says I'm only supposed to get a written reprimand."

Most of these people end up getting their jobs back, in addition to a pile of money for pain and suffering.

I've always been against having too many written rules. The more you have, the more susceptible you are to misinterpretation, confusion, or outright unfairness. Let me give you an example. Kevin McHale, one of the best players on the Celtics, got stuck in tunnel traffic and missed a flight. Now there is a rule that players can be disciplined for missing a team flight.

So I was asked what we should do about Kevin. Absolutely nothing, I answered. Let me explain. Kevin McHale is a great kid who would never do anything deliberately to hurt the team. So he got into a situation he had no control over. Sure the rule says we can fine him.

And he certainly makes enough money to take care of it. But the point is, it's annoying for a player to be fined, particularly for something he doesn't feel is his fault.

No one gives more to this team than Kevin. His attitude, his dedication to the Celtics and the game, are obvious to anyone who's ever watched him play. So what do you do when a guy like Kevin breaks a rule? Of course you mention it to let him know that you're aware of what's going on. But you don't talk about fines or suspensions. Not to a guy like Kevin McHale.

Red Sez: Don't get the idea that I'm antidiscipline or anything. A quick poll of my former players will knock that notion flat. I'm all for discipline, especially when it's done by someone who wields authority correctly. To do that, you must:

1. Keep yourself in check. Losing your temper will only make the situation worse. I was supposed to have a legendary temper, but I never let it cost me a game. It's only human to get angry. But a good manager, like a good coach, knows how to control his or her temper and when to pick the right spots for expressing it.

2. Tell them what they did wrong. When I was playing for George Washington University, I was benched for three games without any explanation. I had no idea what I did wrong. I learned a valuable lesson from that experience. I vowed as a coach to always let my players know exactly what they did wrong and what they could do to correct the situation, the same as I do as president in the Celts organization.

3. Let employees ventilate. Don't interrupt while they're letting off steam. You might get some useful information that will help you understand the situation better.

4. Listen but don't respond immediately. Try to hear what's being said, not only the words, but what's being said between the lines. Don't appear judgmental. If you get in a shouting match, nothing will be accomplished.

5. Stand your ground. Being patient and listening doesn't mean that you should be passive. Some employees are at their best when they know they are clearly in

the wrong. Let them tell their side. Then, if they're
clearly in the wrong, explain why and spell out what you
intend to do about it.

6. Allow for exceptions. Maybe there is a legitimate
reason why the rule was broken. If that's the case, consider changing the rule or policy.

7. Be consistent with your discipline. If you slap
one person on the wrist for breaking a rule and throw the
book at another, you're going to create a real morale
problem.

8. Make the penalty fit the crime. If it's a serious
offense, you've got to impose a serious penalty. But
don't come down too hard on what amounts to a trivial
offense.

Some managers back themselves into a corner with a series of
written rules that don't leave any margin for decision making. "You
will be suspended for breaking rule 19, and violating rule 101 means
instant discharge." You see this a lot with college coaches. They come
up with a rule that players missing or reporting late for practice will not
start or even play in the following game.

So a team goes into a big game and has to play without its best
player because he was late for practice. And it might not have been his
fault. That's what happens when you cast all these rules in stone and
don't allow any margin for error.

Of course, I recognize that a business has to have rules to function. People have to report to work at certain times and give notice if
they are going to be late or absent. They're expected to meet performance standards and get along reasonably well with the people they
work with and for. Basic rules have to be in place to cover these
situations and they have to be enforced fairly. A company can get in
a lot of trouble if it enforces rules inconsistently or writes confusing
rules that nobody understands or that employees aren't even aware of.

*But I particularly object to rules that don't give any margin for
interpretation.* For instance, a manager gets upset because a few people in the department are coming in late or not at all. So he or she
makes a public announcement that the next person who's late or absent
is going to get the book thrown at him. You know what usually
happens. The most reliable person in the department, the one with the
best attendance and attitude, gets a flat tire on the way to work.

This manager loses either way. If he lets the person off the hook because of a prior record, he's going to have a tough time disciplining anyone else for the same offense. If he throws the book at the worker, he's got a good chance of losing a valuable employee.

Pick Your Spots

There are certain rules that have to be enforced, no matter what the situation or the person. I remember one game in particular when Bill Russell was coaching, and we were playing San Francisco at Boston Garden. There was a terrible snowstorm, but both teams and a few people—myself included—were able to fight our way through it. The only one who could not make it just happened to be one of the most intimidating players in the history of basketball—player-coach Bill Russell.

I came down out of the stands to coach, and we built up about a fifteen-point lead with a minute to go. At that point, Russell came walking into the Garden. He broke into a big grin when he glanced up at the scoreboard and saw that we had the game under control. Right after the final whistle, Russell walked up to me, smiling, extending his hand for the victory shake.

"Where the hell were you?" I shouted at him.

"Did you look outside?" Russell asked. "There's a blizzard out there."

"Havlicek walked four miles through that blizzard to get here," I yelled. I let him have it in the dressing room.

At that point, Don Nelson came up and reminded me that there were rookies listening to the general manager publicly reprimanding the coach. "Besides, we won," Nelson said.

"Let them hear it," I yelled. "The coach has the main responsibility to get here. Everyone else made it except him. Winning has nothing to do with it. He was supposed to be here and he wasn't."

Red Sez: The same goes for any manager in any business. If you expect your employees to "be there"—under even the worst conditions—then you have to be there, too. That goes with the territory.

Sometimes it's tough to "be there," not just physically but mentally. You avoid certain tasks that you don't particularly like. You put off projects you feel uncertain about. You allow yourself to procrastinate when a job doesn't contain specific, immediate requirements. Work on overcoming those bad habits by:

1. Tackling your hardest job first. Usually when we're faced with a number of projects to work on, we take the easiest or the most rewarding one first. Try it the other way around. Start with the job you really don't want to do. Once you get it out of the way, everything else will seem easy.

2. Working at a steady pace. When we feel pressed for time, we usually rush and that's when mistakes occur. Plan your activities and list them in order of priority, based on their urgency and importance.

3. Meeting wisely. A lot of time is wasted at meetings, both the structured types and the informal drop-ins. Ask yourself what's accomplished at these meetings and if the time could be better spent working individually.

4. Providing plenty of feedback, both positive and negative. We all like to tell people they're doing a great job, or they're getting a raise or promotion. Negative feedback is something a lot of managers avoid because it's harder to do. If you handle it fairly and focus on the problem, you give employees the chance to learn from their mistakes.

5. Listening to employees. The best question I ever asked as both a coach and a general manager—and even now as president—is: "What do you think?" Put down what you're doing when somebody comes to you with a suggestion or a problem. Even if you can't resolve it for them, the fact that you listened will help.

6. Letting people know it's okay to make mistakes. Employees have to feel free to come to you when they make mistakes. If they aren't allowed to talk about them freely and learn from them, you won't find out about small mistakes until they've grown into huge problems.

I know it's supposed to be a bad practice to discipline anyone in public. But one thing I can tell you for certain. My little speech made an impression on both rookies and veterans alike. And Bill Russell never missed or came in late for another basketball game.

Sure, I could have made the message a little stronger by hitting him with a fine. But that would have turned a guy like Russell off completely. By the way, we didn't have any rule that said, "In the event of a snowstorm all players are expected to report to any game as scheduled, despite any hardships." As smart as Bill Russell is, he probably would have gotten around it by saying he was a player-coach so it didn't apply to him. And if that didn't work, he would have argued that a blizzard is not a snowstorm.

The point is that some companies have rules on the books that are that specific. From what I've seen, *The more written rules a company has and the more specific and inflexible they are, the more likely it is to be hit with a lawsuit from some employee who claims the company didn't follow the right policy in dealing with him or her.* It's sort of mind-boggling when you think about it.

I mean some of these people don't deny that they deserved to be disciplined or even fired. They're just saying the company used the wrong rule to do it. The moral: Have rules that are adaptable enough to take in all the circumstances of any particular situation.

Back in the Beginning

I'm frequently asked when and how I developed my philosophy on discipline. Actually you'd have to go back to my first year in pro ball with the Washington Caps after World War II. Right from the start I was determined that if I was going to be fired or unsuccessful, it was going to be because I lacked the knowledge or the ability to do the job. It wasn't going to be because of some spoiled athlete who wouldn't do what I told him, or wanted to take over the ballclub. There was just no way I was going to let that happen.

So my first concern—yours, too, if you're a manager—is *how to get these guys to do what I say*. I knew what they were thinking. They're better ballplayers than I am and as a result they thought they knew more about the game than I did.

I had to impress on them that I knew what I was doing, so I gave them this little speech.

"Look," I'd say, "my job is to coach you guys, and I've made a study out of it. That's my job—to know what's going on out there. And I've had some experience at it. You can't see everything out there, but I can. If you have suggestions, give them to me. If you spot little ways to take advantage of the players out there, tell me and I'll make sure you get the ball. Let's use all the knowledge we've got on this team. But remember one thing: *I make the decisions. All you make are suggestions.*

"I know you guys are better players than I am. If I were better, I'd be playing. But I'm not. My job is coaching, and I work damned hard at it. I work twenty-four hours a day. All I want you to worry about is staying in shape and playing the game. And you've got to think about trying to beat your man and remembering the plays. Let me worry about everything else, because I can see the overall picture.

"If I tell you something, I have a reason for it. If it bothers you, ask me about it—after the game! I'll listen. And I'll prove to you that I'm right. Or, if I can't, I'll back off. I'm not stupid. But I am the boss, and I don't want you to forget that for a minute. I hired you and I can fire you."

Now I know this language is a little tough for the average manager to use. I didn't have to worry about labor unions or unfair labor regulations or all of this employment legislation. But the principle remains the same. If you're a manager, you've been in this spot. You'll have people who think they can do your job better than you. Well, you should listen and get the best out of them, but not let them run over you. You can't. If you do, you may as well chuck the whole thing. I've never seen an effective coach or manager who lets the people he's supposed to be directing call the shots.

Red Sez: It's vital to have a two-way communication system to elicit feedback and give out directions. You can create a strong process to make it clear you want input, but reserve the right to make the final decision, if you:

1. Stay flexible. Steer clear of setting down policies or rules that are so hard-and-fast as to be unworkable. If someone breaks a rule that seems unfair, consider changing it.

2. Keep people informed of changes that might affect them. A lot of discipline problems are the direct result of employees not understanding new rules or procedures.

3. Accept responsibility for others. If you want to be a leader, you have to be accountable for the actions of

those you lead. Be willing to accept some of the responsibility for the failure of an employee.

4. Show personal dedication. The best leaders are those who are themselves hardworking and totally committed to their work. You lead by example. A manager who refuses to break a rule himself is a lot more likely to have employees exhibit the same behavior.

5. Exhibit confidence. A coach who shows doubts to the players is going to lose control of the team very quickly. Every player, every subordinate, every employee has to understand that you have the responsibility for the final decision.

Luckily, I didn't have too many problems in those early years. And when I did, I dealt with them directly. When I was coaching the Washington Caps, I had a player by the name of Matt Zunic come storming back to the bench after I sent in a substitute for him. He threw his jacket and screamed, "What the hell did you take me out for?"

I let him cool off for a few minutes, then I spoke.

"I'm going to tell you this just once. What you just did doesn't go here. I could take you out of the game for a million reasons. When you come out, I just want you to sit down and shut up." That was it. I never had any more trouble with him.

Matt and I had played together in college, and he probably felt that he could say those things. We became very close after that incident and still are to this day.

I had another incident when I was coaching the Tri-Cities Blackhawks in the National Basketball League. We were playing the Anderson Packers, and I substituted for starting forward Warren Perkins. When he got to the bench, Perkins objected to my giving him hell about mistakes he had made. I threw him off the bench and suspended him for the game.

As I told the press later, I already had six thousand coaches in the stands. I sure didn't need another one on the team. By the way, Perkins started the next night, and I never had another problem with him. Or any other member of the team. The message got across.

Don't get the impression I reduced my players to automatons. I always listened to suggestions. Many times one of my players would come to me during the game and say, "Red, I think it might work better if we did such-and-such." When a guy had a suggestion to make, I'd consider it. Sometimes we'd try it and other times I'd say no. *But I always gave them an explanation when I turned it down.* If I were thinking of a new play, I'd discuss it with them at practice. *I never kidded myself into believing that I had all the answers.* I respected their knowledge of the game.

But when the time came to make a decision, when the game was on the line, the responsibility belonged to me and nobody else. Somebody had to be the one who said, "This is the way we're going to do it!" If I left it up to my players, I'd have five different answers.

From High School to College to Business

I've had that same philosophy at every level I've ever coached or managed at—high school, college, or professional front office. There can only be one coach, one leader, on a team. I remember one night the Celtics were playing lousy and I was mad. Willie Naulls had just joined the team, and I jumped on him about not boxing out. "I tried to, but I got caught in a switch," Willie said.

Everyone on the team waited for my reaction. "I don't want to hear any speeches from you," I shouted at Willie. "I told you to do something. If you can't do it, then sit down. I don't want to hear 'why' from you. I don't care why. And I don't want talking in this huddle unless you're asked to talk."

I knew it was a pretty strong put-down, and I felt bad as soon as I said it. Willie didn't mean any disrespect for me. But I had to get him started on the right foot.

After the game, I took Willie aside in the locker room. "When I tell you something in a huddle, I don't have time to go into any long dissertations. We've only got sixty seconds to get things straightened out. I told you that you weren't boxing out and you gave me an excuse. That stuff might go on other teams, but not here. That's why I had to give you hell."

Willie said that he understood and a few months later he proved that he did. We were playing in Providence and had a three-point lead with ten seconds to go. In the huddle, I called for a semi-zone (which was semi-illegal) to make the other team shoot over our heads. There was no way we were going to lose. The guy Willie was guarding went up for a shot and Willie went with him. He had his hands at his side, and he shouted to distract the guy. The shot went in and the referee called a foul. So the game is tied in the last second and we lose in overtime.

I got all over Willie after the game. Now I know that he thought the referee had blown the call, and he wanted to set me straight. The important point is that Willie didn't say a word. He kept his mouth shut and listened.

Red Sez: The art of ''correction'' is a prime management skill. It requires tact, toughness, sensitivity, and a keen analytical mind to decipher what each different situation calls for. When I'm in my correction mode, I:

1. Pinpoint the problem early. Too many managers let things go, hoping that the situation will correct itself. That doesn't happen. Little problems grow into big ones.

2. Describe the exact behavior that's bothering me. I'm always amused by the coach/manager who says a player/employee has an ''attitude'' problem. What does that mean? It's a lot different to say, ''I don't like your attitude about practice. All that false hustle doesn't impress me at all.''

3. Describe the effect of the behavior. ''If I let you loaf during practice, how do you think it's going to affect the team?''

4. State the standard I expect. ''You're getting tired at practice because you're carrying too much weight. I expect you to be at the weight we set for you by opening game.''

5. Ask why the problem exists. Is there a reason why the player/worker has a behavior problem?

6. Have the person look for solutions. You can probably come up with answers yourself. But it's a lot more effective to have the employee participate in the process. ''Do you have any ideas on how to prevent this from happening in the future?'' is a lot more positive than saying, ''Why haven't you . . . ?''

7. Set a plan of action. Discuss the possible solutions and decide on a plan. Then summarize it so future expectations are clear. ''The first thing you'll do is take off those extra pounds.''

8. Give the employee credit for wanting to do well. This is the key to the whole critical approach. If you can, cite past behavior showing the employee's commitment to doing the right thing: "Your hustle and good physical condition are the two things that got you on the team in the first place."

Different Discipline

I had a similar situation in 1955 with Arnie Risen, one of the most gentlemanly players who ever played the game of basketball. Arnie had come from Rochester where Les Harrison was the owner-coach. Actually, he was much more of an owner than he was a coach. The players used to form a circle and not even let Les in. So the team ran itself during huddles.

His first game with the Celtics, Arnie walked into the huddle and began to talk. The other guys looked at him in disbelief, then waited for my reaction. I didn't even raise my voice. "Arnie, I want to tell you something. You guys did things a little differently in Rochester. We have a simple rule for the Boston Celtics that's not hard to understand. You play. I coach. In other words, keep your mouth shut in the huddles."

On the surface, it probably sounds like I was a lot easier on Risen than I was on Naulls. The same message got through but it was tailored to the situations and personalities of the individuals involved.

K. C. Jones once said Willie Naulls didn't know there were four other men on the floor until he came to the Celtics. Now Willie was a great player, a five-time all-star with the New York Knickerbockers. He was used to doing his thing, so I knew there was only one way to get a message across to him—strong and clear.

Risen was a quiet, sensitive guy, about as different from Naulls as you could get. He was also coming from a team that didn't demand a great deal of discipline. If I had come on too strong with Arnie, I might have turned him off completely. Like on the first road trip that Arnie made as a Celtic. He ordered a cocktail in the dining car (we traveled by train in those days). The other players all looked at me, because I didn't allow mixed drinks on a road trip. (Think about that for a minute. Can you imagine a coach today telling a superstar what not to drink and how not to dress. I believe the best still do. But that's another story, one about leadership.)

I called the trainer over and gave him a message to take to Arnie. "Finish the cocktail but never order another one when you're traveling as a Boston Celtic. Anything other than beer or soda from now on, and it's an automatic fine."

The situation never came up again. Now I could have made a big deal out of it and used Arnie as an example. But he just didn't know the rule. I think it all boils down to this: *A manager has to know when to be tough and when to be reasonable,* when to speak softly and when to use the proverbial big stick you carry—your position as manager.

Another time Bill Russell approached me after a tough game against the Knicks.

"How about letting me drive back to Boston instead of taking the team flight?" he asked.

"Why?" I asked in turn.

"I'm still keyed up from the game. The drive will relax me so I'll be able to sleep."

"Okay for this time," I said. "Now give me your ticket. I'm not going to let you drive and turn in the ticket."

A few months later, Bill approached me again. "Don't even ask," I said before he could get a word in edgewise. "You're flying with the team tonight." Bill smiled and never said another word.

He got my message very clearly. He had asked for a favor, and I gave it to him. But this time Bill knew that I had a good reason for turning him down. I couldn't have a bunch of guys asking to make their own travel arrangements after every game. I couldn't have two sets of standards.

Red Sez: A lot of times a thorny management situation boils down to a case of communication—or more precisely, miscommunication. I let Risen, Naulls, Russell, and indirectly all the rest of my "subordinates" know just what I wanted from them. As a manager, you've got to do the same for your team. Start by:

1. Recognizing that communication is a two-way street. You have to receive messages as well as send them. Most communication breakdowns happen during the receiving process. A manager becomes preoccupied with his or her own thoughts and reactions and doesn't really hear what an employee is trying to say.

2. Becoming an active listener. You not only have to hear the message, you must respond to it. If you just

sit there silently, you give employees no sign that you understand. Without some reaction from you, they can't be sure that you've received the message accurately.

3. Accepting the fact that you and the employee may have strong feelings on the subject. If you let emotions take over, both of you will stop listening while you mentally prepare yourself for the next rebuttals. Good listening requires reasoned, constructive responses. If one of you is going to lose your temper, let it be the other person. Sometimes the simple act of letting him or her blow off steam resolves the problem.

4. Providing feedback. Repeat what the employee is telling you in your own words. Don't make a simple tape-recorder response. Use your own words to reflect your understanding of his or her words. This helps the employee gauge how well you have understood and forces some mutual reflection on the message.

5. Getting more information. The best way to do this is to avoid closed-ended questions that start with ''did you,'' ''will you,'' or ''can you.'' Questions that begin with phrases like these almost always lead to one-word answers: ''Yes,'' ''no,'' or ''sometimes.'' Ask open-ended questions such as ''tell me about it,'' ''give me the details,'' or ''please explain.''

Discipline in Different Shapes and Forms

There are lots of different discipline situations that have shaped my system. I got a job at a reform school during my senior year at George Washington. I had been working for the NYA—National Youth Administration—a program set up to help kids get through school, or at least keep them off the streets. Then a new program opened up. The NYA wanted three or four young men to work about twenty-five hours a week at this place called the National Training School, which was really a reform school.

I learned a lot from that job, especially about how to get along with people. They were supposed to be kids, but a lot of them lied about their ages when they got picked up, so instead of going to penitentiaries they ended up out there. We had some guys who were older than we were.

There were six "companies" with about sixty to eighty guys each. Four were white and two were black. One of the black companies was run by a guy named Mr. Burns, and after a while I made it a point to study that man. He'd growl at them and yell, yet you could see that it wasn't because he was mean or didn't like them.

When the other companies went somewhere, say to a local swimming pool, everyone would be smoking and talking tough and have their shirttails out. But Mr. Burns would go somewhere with his kids and they were neat and well-mannered. He'd be all by himself with around eighty of them, while other companies had two or three helpers to keep the kids in line.

Why? Because he was fair with them. If he thought one of his kids was getting a bad deal, he'd go up to the superintendent and say, "Let's open up this kid's case again." The kids in his company actually had keys to the place. That would have been impossible in any other company, but he trusted them and, in turn, they gave him their respect.

Kids from other companies were always trying to run away, but none of Mr. Burns' kids ever did anything like that. If they did, the rest of the kids would have killed them when they got back. That's how smooth and nice things went in his company, even though the kids were no different from any of the others when they first arrived at the school.

Mr. Burns showed me what a man can do if he's fair and honest with his people, if he treats them with respect and goes to bat for them when they deserve it. That's the essence of discipline.

People Aren't Things

Every once in a while I get a question as to how I "handled" my players. *You handle things, not people.* Bill Russell was once asked how people as different as the two of us ever managed to get along so well.

"What Red and I shared is, I think, the most essential ingredient in any relationship," Bill said. "We shared a mutual respect. He knew I was a man and I knew he was a man, and that's the way we treated each other. He was the coach and I was the player. That's the way this game is set up. There are coaches and there are players. I understand his function and he understood mine, and we worked very well together.''

Bill's answer summed up my relationship with almost all my players. And the ones it didn't apply to usually weren't members of the Boston Celtics for very long. That's why I made it clear from the day that a player joined the Celtics that discipline was a very big thing with us. We just didn't want any loudmouths, complainers, or dissenters like they have on other teams.

If the respect isn't there, discipline won't be either. I don't care how many rules you have or how many fines you hand out. An organization can't be successful if it has to constantly make and enforce rules. In all my years with the Celtics, I fined only four players, three of them for the same violation—insulting my intelligence.

We had just finished a long road trip on a Saturday night. I planned to get up at dawn and fly home to Washington and then meet the club at practice on Monday morning. The team was supposed to fly home later Sunday morning. Some of them had other ideas, however. As I walked across the hotel lobby early Sunday morning, I spotted three of my players sitting in a coffee shop with three ''ladies.'' When they saw me, they wanted to crawl under the counter.

One of them introduced me to the three ladies, and then explained they were all on the way to church. I told them how commendable I thought that was, said goodbye to the ladies, and said I would see them at practice on Monday.

When I got to practice, I knew everyone on the team had been told about the incident. So whatever I decided was going to affect more than the three players involved. I called the three ''churchgoers'' into my office and told them I wasn't going to fine them for breaking curfew. It was the last night of a long road trip and a little relaxation might have been called for. They all smiled and relaxed. ''But I am going to fine all three of you for insulting my intelligence,'' I growled. ''Now get back on the floor and go to work.''

I'll even name the guy who got my fourth fine. I had a dumb rule that you couldn't eat pancakes on the *day* of a game. We played Syracuse at the Boston Garden on a Saturday night and then took a flight to Syracuse for a return game Sunday. I walked into a restaurant in the wee hours of the *morning* and there's Sam Jones, one of the great shooting guards of all time, sitting at the counter eating pancakes. It turns out that Russell and K. C. Jones had also ordered pancakes, but theirs hadn't arrived.

"Those pancakes are going to cost you five bucks," I said to Sam.

"Okay," Sam says and starts to eat.

"Take another bite and it will cost you another five bucks," I said. While this was going on, Russell and K.C. were frantically signaling the waitress to cancel their pancake orders.

I took Sam's five dollars more as a joke than a fine. Of course, he still says I was wrong, because it was two A.M. when he ordered those pancakes. So he was eating pancakes the night after the game. It didn't matter to me. I just wouldn't have been happy if he ate them after he knew I was in the room. It would have been flaunting a rule right in my face.

I still say that you can have effective discipline without a hundred rules. The best discipline comes from respect: respect for the team, for one another, for the coach; in a business, for the workers, the supervisors, the managers, the entire department. My players weren't expected to love me. I just wanted them to respect me. If you get their respect, everything else comes more easily. If you can show your employees that you know what you're talking about, discipline comes naturally. People will follow someone they respect.

Red Sez: As the famous brokerage ad might be paraphrased, a manager must get respect the old-fashioned way, by *earning* it. So start earning your team's respect by:

> • Showing your confidence in them. There are two maxims I never believed in. The first is, "If you want it done right, do it yourself." The other is, "It takes longer to show someone else how to do it than to do it yourself." There might be some truth in the second one, at least the first time around. But following either one of them for any length of time leads to the "do-it-yourself" syndrome. Besides provoking a stress situation, a do-it-yourself manager doesn't do much for the confidence of his or her "players." If they don't have confidence in themselves, they won't have any confidence in the coach, either. Without confidence, there can't be respect.
>
> • Following through when you make a commitment. Nothing destroys a manager's reputation faster than breaking or postponing a promise. It affects not only the

player that the promise was made to, but every other
member of the team. "If he let so-and-so down, he'll
likely do the same to me" is the thinking of most players. Making a commitment that's beyond your authority
is even worse. In that case, you lose the respect of both
your players and your boss.

• Listening carefully. Make sure you understand
what the employee is saying. Don't interrupt or make any
decisions while he or she is still talking. Then tell them
what you can do, what you can't do, and the reasons
why. Don't be pushed into a fast decision that you might
regret later.

• Being accessible, honest, and straightforward. Try
to keep your workers as informed as you possibly can,
particularly in times of stress. In basketball terms that
might mean rumors of impending trades or other deals. In
business it might mean layoffs or reorganization. Of
course, you can't give away company secrets or reveal
information you don't have yourself. Just be aware that
the grapevine comes up with scenarios that are usually a
lot worse than what's happening. Be clear with employees about what you can or can't say or do.

• Not playing favorites. Nothing causes a coach to
lose respect faster than playing favorites. It affects every
element of the team's performance, because people tend
to judge everything in light of that relationship. If it's
necessary to give one player or employee special treatment, let the rest of the team know why. For instance,
Bill Russell used to hate to practice and, admittedly, I
used to take it easier on him. But all the players knew he
was the guy who had to give us forty-five tough minutes
when the real game started. So the other players looked
on it as a good business decision, not an example of favoritism.

• Letting people know it's okay to make mistakes.
It's the sign of a good manager when employees can
come to them with a mistake. There's no better way for a
player to learn than by talking over a mistake with the
coach. Show me a coach whose players come to him with
their problems, and I'll show you a coach who has the
respect of his team. Same goes double for a manager.

Special Discipline Problems

Do you discipline a player who loses his temper and ends up probably costing his team a big game? That's exactly what happened in the fall of '90 when Roger Clemens, ace pitcher for the Boston Red Sox, got ejected in the second inning of the fourth and final American League playoff game with the Oakland Athletics.

Clemens was chased after allegedly cursing plate umpire Terry Cooney over disputed calls. I couldn't fine Clemens any more than I could have gone after Dave Cowens, one of the most competitive centers to ever play for the Celtics. Clemens and Cowens are both emotional, competitive people who tend to be perfectionists. They try to get every aspect of their games just right and when an umpire or an official tells them they're doing something wrong, they get frustrated. Usually they get angrier at themselves than they do at anyone else.

Don't get me wrong. I'm not justifying what Clemens said or did, but somebody has to be the cooler head in a situation like that and it ought to be the umpire. When Clemens yelled the first time, Cooney should have turned his back and resumed his position behind the plate. That's what a great umpire would have done, particularly in a playoff game. Then if Clemens continued, he should have been ejected.

But Cooney was obviously afraid he'd look bad if he turned away, so instead of giving the player a chance to cool down, he reacted immediately. The best referees in basketball—guys like Sid Borgia or Earl Strom—would always walk away after calling a technical, giving the player or coach a chance to unwind, rather than forcing a confrontation.

From what I understand, the bad blood between the Red Sox players and the umpiring crew had been building since the second game. By the start of the fourth game tempers were taut, triggers were tight, and anger was deep. Each side was looking for trouble when Clemens took the mound that day.

It's the old story of familiarity breeding contempt. If you assign the same umpiring crew throughout a series, you're asking for trouble. With a pennant on the line, it's natural for a team to get angry when a close call goes against them. Usually a few personal barbs are directed at the individual umpire who made the call. So he gets a little upset about what he hears and erupts at the first comment.

Both the National Basketball Association and the National

Hockey League rotate their officials during the playoffs to prevent emotions from building from game to game. Tonight it's Jack Madden calling the Celtics-Pistons, tomorrow he's calling the Hawks-Jazz. So if Madden makes the charging call with one second left on the clock, wiping out the winning basket, he doesn't have to deal with the team he made the call against the next night. A new crew of officials does and he's doing a game in another part of the country. Usually teams will not see an official who made a deciding call against them for three or four games. Rotating officials is only common sense.

Red Sez: Personality conflicts aren't restricted to sporting events. They happen more than they should in business. An employee doesn't get along with his boss for any number of reasons. But management decides to look the other way and let the situation correct itself. Then one morning there's an explosion—usually over some event totally unrelated to the original problem—and somebody ends up getting fired or quitting. How many companies have lost valuable employees because they refused to step in and correct a situation that could be resolved with a simple transfer?

Some managers refer to people they can't get along with as "problem employees." Usually the problem that's causing the friction doesn't have anything to do with job performance. It may be tempting to let these people go, but I can think of four good reasons why that would be a mistake:

1. They must have useful skills. If they didn't, why were they hired in the first place? Maybe you should take a look at your hiring practices if you end up with too many "problem" employees.

2. The problem behavior can be changed. Maybe a transfer to another department would do the trick. I was always concerned with the way my players got along, both on and off the court. I had a system of rotating roommates, a policy I started during my first year of coaching in Washington. I wanted the players to get along with each other, and I was also determined to avoid any cliques from forming. That stuff can kill a ball club quicker than anything else I can think of.

3. There aren't too many perfect employees, just as there aren't too many perfect coaches or managers. Being

able to work with a problem employee is good training for any manager.

4. A manager sends a morale-boosting message to all employees when he's able to "salvage" a problem employee.

"Frankenstein Meets the Werewolf"

Speaking of problems between a manager and an "employee," a reporter made me laugh when he used that phrase to describe the possible outcome of Wilt Chamberlain, the player/employee, and Red Auerbach, the coach/manager, ending up on the same team. Actually, I've been asked that question many times in my career. Would I have been able to coach Wilt Chamberlain?

I always liked the answer that Joe McCarthy gave to a similar question when he took over as the Red Sox' manager. He was asked how he expected to get along with the sometimes temperamental Ted Williams. "I never met a .400 hitter that I couldn't get along with," McCarthy said. Of course, Joe ended up coaching Ted, while I never did coach Wilt.

Except once, early in his career when he was on my team at Kutsher's resort at an all-star game. We were playing this other club and two of its players were eating Wilt up. We were behind at halftime when we went into one of those rooms and I started talking.

Chamberlain wasn't even listening. He lay down on a bed and covered his head.

"Hey," I yelled, "you sit up and listen!"

He said, "I'm sorry. I played so badly I wanted to hide my head in shame."

I said, "Okay, you've hidden your head. Now sit up and listen."

Even in those days, he had his own mind. I tried to explain to him how to guard a pivot man properly, but he insisted on doing things his own way. He was only a high school kid, but he had his own theories and nobody was going to change them. I remember thinking that someone was going to have a tough time trying to coach him.

Then he got big money early when the Globetrotters persuaded him to quit college, and from that point on there was no such thing as anybody telling Wilt what he was going to do.

If I could have had him before he quit school, before he got the big money and the no-cut contracts, that would have been a different story. Eddie Gottlieb was one of the greatest men in the history of this game, but he spoiled Wilt badly. For years, Wilt often didn't travel with the rest of the team. There was no disciplinary control whatsoever. Wilt did whatever he felt like doing.

Different Strokes for Different Folks

Under those conditions, he and I never would have lasted a day together. If I could have had him before he went to the Globetrotters, and if no one interfered with my authority over him, I think I could have disciplined him. But we'll never know. Chamberlain was a giant among giants. I'll never take that away from him. I'll tell you something else about him—he was a damn decent guy, too. Every year he made it a point to get up to Kutsher's for the Maurice Stokes Benefit Game, and one year he even flew back from Europe just to participate in it.

Chamberlain was a lot like Freddie Schaus, the Lakers' coach, in that he always seemed to be worried about me. I unnerved him and he didn't like that. One night I was arguing with a referee and Wilt suddenly walked over to me and said, "That's enough out of you."

Immediately, Russell stepped between us. "If you're going after Red, you've got to go through me," Bill said.

Chamberlain flexed his muscles. "Look at this arm!" he yelled.

Russell glared at him and didn't back down an inch. "I don't give a damn what you've got," he said. "You've still got to go through me if you want Red."

Bill was madder than hell and Wilt knew better than to push it any further. I've always maintained Chamberlain is the strongest man in the world, but I wouldn't want to bet on who'd walk away if he and Russell ever mixed it up. I don't have any question as to who was the better ballplayer. It wasn't even close. Russell was better because he played with his head and he had the bigger heart. He was the better athlete, too. And I know he was more disciplined.

CHAPTER 5

Motivation Mandate: You Can Only Win One for the Gipper Once

REMEMBER THAT FAMOUS MOVIE when the dying football player, George Gipp, asks Knute Rockne, the Notre Dame football coach, to tell the team to win that big game "for the Gipper"? The story goes that Rockne used it to inspire Notre Dame to a famous come-from-behind victory over Army several years later. It probably did work—once. My question is: What did Rockne do for an encore? He could only ask his team once to win one for the Gipper.

That's why I've never been a big believer in those inspirational locker-room talks before a big game. First of all, there are too many "big games" in the course of an NBA season. No matter what the message is or how eloquently it's delivered, not too many games are won or lost in the locker room. If your players aren't sufficiently motivated at that point, nothing you can say or do is going to make much difference.

How did you keep your players motivated? That's the number one question I get when I speak before management groups. Managers must have the idea that I used some sort of magic formula to roll up sixteen world championships, nine as coach, seven as general manager and president. Maybe they think they can use it to turn a losing situation into a winning one—overnight!

There are a lot of books and seminars that promise to do just that. Five easy lessons to turn a bunch of underachievers into winners! "Use these techniques and you'll get your group working harder, better, and happier," is the usual message. I don't believe any of that stuff. *First of all, you can't motivate a team or a group. You have to motivate an individual.* We're all too different. What gets one person going can turn off another. There's also no quick fix when it comes to motivation. It's a gradual process that starts in the initial recruitment of an employee or a player and builds throughout a career.

A for Attitude

I was starting guard for George Washington until we played Ohio State and I ran into a big, tough guy by the name of Hull. I thought I was pretty tough, but this guy took me into the pivot, leaned on me, and hooked me to death. I shouldn't have been playing him in the first place.

All of a sudden, I went from being a starter to being our twelfth man. One game goes by and I don't get in, then another. I didn't know what my coach was thinking, but I knew it wasn't my place to challenge him. I didn't say a word, but I worked like hell in practice.

Finally, we got up to playing Army and they had a guy named Brinker who was their hotshot. Out of the clear blue sky, Coach Reinhart says to me, "All right, you take Brinker." So I took him and I shut him off. After that, I was back in the lineup and no one ever said a word about what had happened.

I thought that was a good lesson: Shut up, keep working, and your chance will come again. Most athletes today don't have that kind of attitude. If they get benched, they sulk or demand a trade. In the long run, they end up hurting themselves much more than the team.

That's why the key to motivation as far as I'm concerned is attitude. If a player doesn't have the right attitude, he isn't going to play for the Boston Celtics. Period. Attitude is always more important to me than ability. It tells me if he is going to be my type of player or not, if he can absorb coaching, if he will listen to what I'm telling him, and then go out and do it.

Like I've said a million times, I made it my business to find out what kind of attitude Bill Russell had before I drafted him. Never mind the rebounding and the defense and all the other things I kept hearing about him. I wanted to know about Russell as a person. I asked plenty of questions about Russell and I liked the answers. He was very proud, very intelligent, very determined. All this added up to a great attitude.

Red Sez: It's not easy to get a good handle on an applicant's or a current employee's attitude. You have to read between the lines of a résumé, ask key questions in an interview, look for certain activities and reactions on the job. When I'm trying to judge attitude, I probe areas like these:

1. The person behind the person. An internal investigation. I ask: Tell me about yourself. The way a person answers this question tells me a lot about him or her. I want to know about early years, work experience, and recent times. But most of all, I want to get a feel for the person.

2. Homework. I'm impressed with a person who does his or her own investigating, who knows the history of our club and its traditions. A friend of mine told me about an interview he'd had with an applicant for a sales position. He said the applicant talked for nearly twenty minutes about why he wanted to work for the company. Finally, when my friend could get a word in, he asked what products the guy wanted to sell. It turned out the applicant didn't have any idea because he knew nothing about what the company actually manufactured.

3. "Creativity" in following orders. I ask: Do you take everything at face value, or can you run "options" off formal "plays"? This kind of question definitely puts the applicant on the spot. But it's the kind of behavior-oriented question that will tell you a lot about attitude. I get a little nervous about applicants who tell me they never break the rules under any conditions.

4. Why the person wants to play (work) for us. Over the years, I've had some interesting responses to that question. One young lady told me she wanted to work for the Celtics because her boyfriend worked on the next street and he'd be able to drop her off.

5. Strong and weak points. The answers to your probing about this will give you a good idea about the applicants' attitudes. Do they think they already have all

the answers and probably won't be "coachable"? Or are they so lacking in self-confidence that they're a major long-term project?

6. Former work relationships. A big red flag goes up in my mind when an applicant spends a lot of time putting the knock on his last coach or boss or coworkers. I usually get the feeling that I'll be the topic of conversation at the next job interview.

Goal Setting

A player or worker can have the best attitude in the world and still not get the job done if he or she doesn't know what's expected. That's why I've always considered goal setting an important part of motivation. Team goals always came first with me. For instance, I knew that I would never win an NBA championship until I got someone who could get that ball off the boards and into Cousy's hands. I knew that Russell would do that for me.

Goal setting and role setting go hand in hand. So do corporate and individual goals. Before Bill Russell even put on a Celtics uniform, we defined his role for the Celtics, what we wanted his goals to be so they'd fit with our goals. I knew that he was concerned about scoring, because there was a lot of talk going around that he didn't shoot well enough to play with the pros. At our first meeting, Bill admitted that he was worried about his shooting.

"Bill," I said, "I've got all the firepower I need with guys like Cousy, Sharman, and Heinsohn. We need a guy to get us the ball. I don't give a damn if you ever score a point." So Russell went out and controlled the boards, and we won our first NBA championship.

I set a goal for Bob Cousy early in his career that I think helped turn him from a flashy, uncontrolled player into the greatest fast-break guard of all time. I got the idea after watching Cousy's first practice as a member of the Boston Celtics. His passes were hitting guys in the head or bouncing off their chests or just missing their fingertips.

Finally, I took Bob aside: "If you are going to play for me and do the things for this team that I think you can do, you've got to start making sure those guys can hold on to these passes of yours. Remember, I don't care if you pass with your head. Just make sure they catch it. The prettiest pass in the world is no good if someone doesn't catch it. And nine times out of ten, if a pass is not completed, it's the fault of the passer.'' So my first goal to Cousy was very clear: Don't pass the ball unless someone can catch it.

Red Sez: You've got to be able to set several types of goals. You've got departmental, corporate, team, and individual. That last one gets subdivided even further. You help set goals for each individual who works for you. And you also have to set your own individual goals as a manager. To do this better, take a crack at these points:

1. What are your lifetime goals? What do you stand for, what do you want to accomplish? My number one goal before I ever walked to the sidelines to take over my first team was to be a winning basketball coach.

2. What are your time-priority goals in groups of years? When I took over the Celtics in 1950, it would have been ridiculous for me to expect to win a league championship that first year. So I set up incremental goals over the next few years and won my first championship in 1957.

3. List your top-priority goal for next year. In 1955, I realized that the Celtics couldn't win a league championship until we got a center who could get us the ball. So I set this as a top priority and got Bill Russell. The rest is history.

4. Set short-range goals for next month. It's a lot easier if you can meet them on a monthly basis, rather than making a big push at the end of the year. If you have to carry over a goal from one month to the next, give it a top priority.

5. Set lower-level goals for next week. These are the ones that are relatively easy to accomplish if they are attended to in a timely fashion. They create a lot of problems if they're put off too long. Try to spread them over the whole week. Then check them off each day.

6. List your goals for tomorrow. Look them over before you go to bed, then review them early the next morning. Check off the goals as you meet them, transfer the ones you don't meet to the next day. Then don't attack any other goals until you've finished up with the carryovers.

The Team Concept: Motivating Factor

It's during those first meetings with a new player that I instill the concept that victory belongs to the group, not the individual. Here's a set talk I deliver to every new Celtic, whether he's just entering the NBA or he's been around for a while.

"Have you ever seen our team play?" I ask. "You can tell a lot about a team that way, and I'm not talking about talent right now. If you're going to be a champion, you've got to feel like one, look like one, and act like one. Then you'll play like one. That means paying a price to play here. We're smart enough to know when you're giving us false hustle. As soon as we spot it, we'll get rid of you because we have no time to go into the whys and wherefores.

"But if you have the desire to give us the best you have, you're going to get all kinds of help here—not just from me and from your coaches, but most of all from your teammates, because they want to win, and they'll do all they can to improve you so that you can help them win. That's the whole concept we have here, and you'll be aware of it right away."

There's no better way to build the team concept than to encourage players to help each other. There's supposed to be an unwritten rule in sports that veterans don't help rookies take their jobs away. I always pushed the idea of players helping each other. Veterans were made to realize that rookies could actually prolong their careers by taking some of the burden off them.

When Sam Jones first joined the Celtics, both Cousy and Sharman had reason to regard him as a threat to their own security. Yet they both helped Sam learn the system and gave him little tips. They realized that if either one of them got hurt, Sam could give them some rest. Ramsey did the same thing when Havlicek came on board, even though the papers were warning that a new "sixth man" had arrived.

Mentoring and Motivation

Don't get the impression that the veterans tried to make things too easy for the rookies. Some of the toughest battles I've ever seen on a basketball court took place behind the closed doors of Celtics practices. One year, we had a rookie by the name of Steve Kuberski learning the ropes from Bailey Howell, a veteran forward. Now Bailey probably could have lectured Steve about the demands of playing forward in the NBA. But instead of warning Steve about how physical it could get, Bailey beat the hell out of him every day in practice.

After a week of merciless poundings, Steve finally got the message—he leveled Bailey with a vicious forearm. It was a little tough on Bailey, but it brought a smile to my face—I knew as soon as I saw Bailey hit the deck that Steve was going to be okay. When the season opened, he didn't have any surprises about the amount of punishment he'd have to take and dish out.

That mentoring system was also a good motivational tool. I always tried to match up players in practice who were vying for the same job. So I'd play Sharman against Sam Jones or Cousy against K. C. Jones. Okay, everyone knew that Sharman and Cousy had a lock on those starting jobs. But they still had to go out every day and prove it to K.C. and Sam in practice.

Ramsey and Heinsohn used to go at each other in practice, too. Sure, sometimes tempers would get a little short, but I never let things get out of hand. It was only natural for players to take practice less seriously the more we won in league games, so it was a good way to motivate the team, to get them keyed up.

Practice was also time for learning, planning, developing, and communicating. If we were going to work on a new play or a certain pattern, I'd explain exactly what I had in mind. Do you understand what we are going to do? If you don't, ask questions. This was the time I looked for player input—not during the last thirty seconds when a game was on the line. Communication is everything in coaching. It's not what you say that counts. It's what they hear and absorb that really matters.

Red Sez: Mentoring can be just as effective for industry as it is for basketball. Nothing can get a new player or employee off to a better start than being coached by a veteran—providing you select the right ''coach.'' Here's what to look for:

1. Knowledge of the subject. A coach must have a thorough knowledge of the subject being coached if the rookie is to learn. There is no other way. That doesn't necessarily mean that a coach has to be a star performer.

Sometimes stars make the worst coaches just as some excellent mechanics make lousy supervisors. On the other hand, some ordinary players make excellent coaches.

2. Ability to communicate. Coaches can know all the moves, but if they can't communicate their knowledge, it means nothing. A good coach has to be able to explain the subject and follow it up with understandable feedback.

3. Patience. This ranks right up there with knowledge and communication skills. Every player being coached learns at his or her own pace. A coach who tries to rush a student can do serious damage. Watching Kevin McHale working with Ed Pinckney and Joe Kleine is a case in point. Pickney and Kleine are both talented ballplayers, but McHale is one of the great "inside" ballplayers of all time. He's got some moves that just aren't teachable. But he works patiently with those guys, hour after hour, offering encouragement and feedback. You can watch their improvement from game to game.

4. Measuring ability. A good coach has to be able to evaluate the skill level of the person he or she is supposed to train. This means starting from where the player is, rather than where a coach thinks that person should be.

5. Ability to coach in more than one mode. Some people learn better by being told how to do something, while others have to watch it being done or go through it themselves. Sometimes a coach chooses the method he or she likes best and the player doesn't get it. That doesn't mean that the player is dumb. It just means that the wrong coaching language is being used. That's why it's safer to use more than one coaching method. For instance, if a coach is teaching one of your employees a new production process, he might give him reading materials, show him a video of the process, then have him go through it himself.

6. Responsibility and good judgment. You should give your "coach" the responsibility of getting your new player off to the right start. If he or she does the job, there should be some sort of reward. Coaches can also be invaluable in helping you determine if you've made the right hiring decision. Sometimes they pick up signals that

tell them right away that this person is not right for the team. Listen to them.

When the Going Gets Easy

Getting new players off to the right start is important. It's also a lot easier than keeping them there. The toughest kind of motivation is the grinding, day-to-day type, especially when your team is doing well. I was especially concerned, for example, with motivating my players against the easier opponents on our schedule. It's the weaker teams you've got to be motivated against. The big games are self-motivating. You preach against overconfidence all the time, yet it's going to happen now and then.

Rather than repeat the word over and over until they get tired of hearing me say it, I wouldn't mention overconfidence. I'd find a different approach. "Look," I'd say, "you guys are already chalking up this win, but you're not going to win it on paper. If you get out there and really pour it on, you might wrap it up by the third quarter and then we can take it easy. But if you don't, you're going to wind up playing forty-eight hard minutes. The choice is yours."

Of course, the more successful your team is, the greater the chance for overconfidence to set in. When we were winning all those championships, I had a standard opening speech I used at training camp each year. It went like this: "Gentlemen, you are the world champions. You've heard all the accolades all summer long. You've had the prestige. You've had a good time. But now everybody's out to knock your jocks off. It's unfortunate but true. They're all out to get you.

"Now if you want them to get you, just try living off last year's reputation. This is going to be an even harder year because every team in the league is after us. They got all the hotshots in the draft. We got the last pick. So now they think they are as good as we are. We know what it is to be world champions. They don't. So what we have to do is go out there, meet them head-on, and say, 'You're damned right we're the world champions, and if you want this title you're going to have to take it from us.' "

Red Sez: As a manager, you have different motivation dilemmas than trying to combat overconfidence or defend a championship ring.

But the theory is similar. You prepare your team to succeed by motivating them to do their best. One key personal concept in your program involves individual networking. You start by:

1. Being visible. As managers move up in their careers, there is much more for them to do—travel, meetings, additional responsibilities. The pressures mount, so the number of people they interact with gets smaller and smaller. Finally, they become almost invisible and isolated from the people they are trying to manage. The best way to beat this problem is to make a conscious effort to stay in touch with all of the people you manage. Just walking through the department and letting them know you are accessible will usually do the trick.

2. Explaining decisions that affect them. Sometimes employees are the last ones to learn about decisions that have an impact on their jobs or working conditions. Regardless of the nature of the changes, employees are going to have fears, doubts, questions, rationalizations, and personal opinions about them. I never really bought the management argument that employees can't accept change. If they're given the reasons for change and enough time to adjust, they will feel a lot less threatened.

3. Providing feedback. To be effective, feedback should be given as soon after the event or situation as possible. If I didn't like the performance at a certain game, I didn't wait for the next practice to make my feelings known. Telling someone he did a "lousy" job doesn't tell him anything. Explaining "lousy"—you didn't box out or you took too many low-percentage shots—pinpoints the problem. Even positive feedback loses some of its bite if it's generalized. For instance, saying "you had a great game," doesn't mean as much as "you protected the ball and hit the open man."

4. Making it applicable. Feedback must concern behavior over which the employee has some control. For instance, for me to get on the guards for not controlling the offensive boards would be ludicrous. Yet some managers climb all over employees who had nothing to do with the actual problem.

Tailor Your Approach

So how do you motivate your people to give you their best? Do you do it through yelling, reasoning, pride, psychology? All of the above? It depends on the situation and it depends on the person. *I made it a point to study my players, to analyze them to determine which ones would respond to which kinds of motivation.* Some you whisper to, some you berate. There are some players you can motivate without saying a word.

Let me give you an example. In 1959 we were playing a very weak New York Knicks team. Gene Conley was playing as a backup to Bill Russell at that time. A number of Gene's relatives came to the game, so I knew he expected to get a lot of playing time.

The first period went by, and we built up a big lead. By the third period, we were way out front. Everyone is playing, even a rookie by the name of Gene Guarilia. But not Conley. He sits on the bench, and I know he's fuming. Finally, with about two minutes to play, I tell Conley to go in so Russell can get an ovation. He's so mad by this time that he can't even look at me. After the game, Conley just stormed off to the locker room. I asked him if he wanted to go out for Chinese food after the game, and he told me what I could do with my fortune cookie.

The next night, Wilt Chamberlain and the Philadelphia 76ers come to town. Conley is still angry with me for embarrassing him in front of his family and doesn't have a word to say during warm-ups. So I play him thirty-five minutes, and he belts Chamberlain all over the court while Russell picks the boards clean. After the game he smiled at me. "Why didn't you tell me that you wanted me rested and angry for Chamberlain?" he asked. Of course, if I had, it never would have worked.

Sometimes a player like Sam Jones would be having a great game, so I'd pull him out after we'd built up a big lead. Sam would get so angry that he'd go out the next night and play even better. Other nights, Havlicek would be sitting on the bench, just itching to get in the game. I'd glance over at him every once in a while, and just as he'd start to get up to go in the game, I'd look away. Usually, he'd get in the game after six or seven minutes. But on certain nights, I'd keep him sitting for a period and a half. He'd really be angry when he finally got in the game. So he'd take his anger out on the other team, which was what I was after in the first place.

The point is, different strokes for different folks. Develop your own arsenal of motivation techniques, but then apply them judiciously to individual situations, not indiscriminately across the entire work-force.

Hitting the Right Motivation Levers

It's nice to see an inspired team pouring out onto a basketball court or a playing field before a big game. But if all that "fire" comes from a locker room talk, it's going to get doused before the game is over. A lot of eloquent messages are delivered in losing dressing rooms, too.

I'm not saying that the right kind of talk can't get a team motivated to produce better. I used to change my pregame talk according to the game, the situation, the standings, a whole lot of things. Sometimes I'd talk for two minutes, sometimes eight, sometimes ten. I'd change the inflections as I went along. Sometimes soft, sometimes hard, sometimes a combination. But one thing I never did. I never spent any time talking about how strong the other team was. I wanted my guys to feel invincible.

I remember the opening night before a playoff series against Philadelphia in 1965. That was a great team, with guys like Hal Greer, Wilt Chamberlain, Chet Walker, Luke Jackson, Johnny Kerr, and Larry Costello. Our regular series ended up tied at 5–5 and more than a few people predicted the end of our championship era. I could feel the tension when I walked into the locker room before the first game. So I put my hands on my hips and glared at the team. "If you guys are nervous, think of how they must feel having to play us. You guys have won six championships in a row," I said. End of pep talk. We went out and won.

Actually an overconfident locker room is a worse motivational problem than an apprehensive one. After knocking the 76ers out of the playoffs that year, we got ready to meet the Los Angeles Lakers in the championship series. Now the papers were working against me. Elgin Baylor, the great forward for LA, had injured his knee and was out for the series. Even the California papers were predicting that we would win in a breeze.

When I went into the locker room before the first game, everyone was wisecracking and fooling around. Obviously, they had all been reading the papers, so there was no question that the Celtics had already won their seventh championship in a row. The games themselves were merely a formality. I really let them have it. I told them that if they didn't smarten up, we were going to get our heads handed to us by the Lakers. They were still a hell of a ballclub, even without Baylor, I told them. And they would probably play a whole lot harder to make up for his absence. You could feel the atmosphere change when I finished. So we went out and won the first game, 142–110, and brought the championship back to Boston in five games.

The point is that every game is a separate entity. *Every management motivation problem is a different animal. You get your message across in a different way, depending on the circumstances.* Sometimes I wouldn't say one damned thing before a big game. They'd think, Gee, Red doesn't want to talk about this one. Let's show him how we can do it anyway.

Two of the best pregame talks I ever gave had nothing to do with basketball. We were playing St. Louis in the championship finals in 1960. On the night of game seven, I walked into the locker room and couldn't think of a thing to say. Then I saw Russell drinking a cup of tea, his big hands wrapped around the little cup with his pinky stuck up in the air.

"Before we start on the intricacies of this ball game, I want you all to look at Russell," I said. "He thinks this is a tea party. Will you look at Mr. Russell's little pinky? Isn't he delicate? Aren't we lucky to get his lesson in etiquette?" Then I gave an eloquent speech on the proper way to drink tea. So we went out and won the game by nineteen points.

The year before, we were getting ready to play Minneapolis in the championship series. I walked into the locker room before the first game with absolutely no idea as to what I was going to say. Then I spotted Bill Sharman eating his pregame chocolate. He was just like Russell with the tea. Every night the two of them had their piece of chocolate and cup of tea.

"Tell me," I began, "has anybody in this room ever been offered a piece of chocolate by Bill Sharman? I haven't. Have you Ramsey? Have you Loscutoff? How about you, Heinsohn? See what I mean? He sits there every night eating his chocolate, getting energy like Mr. America, and he's never offered a piece of it to any of his teammates. He's got to be the cheapest guy who ever lived."

I carried on about that piece of chocolate until someone banged on the door and said it was time to go. "See what you did?" I yelled at

Sharman. "You've made me lose the whole impact of my pregame talk with your damned chocolate bar. Now we've got to go out there and play and I never got to say what's on my mind. Okay. Get out there. Maybe you'll know what you're doing anyway." So we went out and won the championship in four straight games.

Red Sez: You don't have to be a great speaker to be a great motivator. But it helps! Not that I consider myself to be a great speaker. I was always at my best when my speeches were delivered extemporaneously to a referee during a game. Ask Sid Borgia or Mendy Rudolph. I was never at a loss for words with those guys. I didn't care how many people were in the stands or watching on television.

It's not the same when I'm asked to speak to management groups, something that happens frequently today. Here a few speaking tips that helped me over the years:

1. Don't worry about being nervous. The trick is to let this nervous excitement work for you. Flowing adrenaline tends to make for dynamic speeches.

2. Be overprepared. If you're supposed to speak for twenty minutes, have enough material for thirty. Having more than enough will allow you to be more selective in the material you're going to use.

3. Pace yourself. Some speakers take off like a fast-break basketball team. They might think they're scoring a lot of points, but they're leaving the audience behind. Others talk so slowly that the audience's twenty-four-second clock runs out.

4. Look your audience in the eye and maintain eye contact throughout your speech. This will involve your audience and give you a more effective presentation.

5. Don't read your speech. Try putting key words on three-by-five-inch cards. This will force you to talk to your audience instead of reading to them.

6. Practice with a tape recorder. Try to avoid a flat, dull monotone that will put your audience to sleep.

7. Find out about your audience. Who are they and why are they going to be there? What do they expect you to give them?

8. If you make a mistake, mispronounce a word, or

just plain stumble, don't worry about it. Sometimes you can even make a joke about it.

9. Try to inject a little humor. I spoke to one management group on the subject of competing in today's tough marketplace. I told them I had a one-word answer to all of their problems with foreign competition—cheat. Then I explained the tricks of tightening and loosening the basketball rims and watering the grass depending on the speed of your baseball team. A little amusement can go a long way in making your points.

Using the Competition to Motivate

The subject for some of my best motivation talks came directly from my opponents. When I was coaching the Washington Caps, we went into New York and lost to the Knicks. After the game, Joe Lapchick, the Knicks' coach, told the reporters that his team won because it was better conditioned. The next day, the headlines in the Washington papers read:

BETTER CONDITION BEATS CAPS!

I didn't say anything to either Lapchick or the press. But when the Knicks came into Washington for the next game, I plastered the walls with the stories knocking our physical condition. I also made it a point to bring up Lapchick's comment in my pregame talk.

"If there's one thing we're not, it's a poorly conditioned team. We're in great shape. But the only way we're going to shut him up is to go out there and run them off the court. Now get out there and show them." We did just that. We flattened them by thirty points. So whenever another coach or player took a shot at us, I always featured it in my motivational moves.

Red Sez: Sometimes it's not easy to find a focus for dealing with motivation. I used competition as a positive thing, not a negative. Here are five reasons to tie competition to motivation:

1. Competition encourages you—and your subordinates—to do the best you can. Nothing motivates a player more than going against someone who is bigger, stronger, or better. The same is true in business. Nothing motivates managers more than going up against tough competition. Remember how successful that "we're number two but we try harder" was for Avis. So maybe you have to shave your price or beef up your quality or deliver your products faster. Not having to compete for a lot of years is what got our automobile business in so much trouble.

2. Competition gives you something to measure yourself against. Practice and preseason games will tell you something about your ballclub. But not enough. When the season starts, when winning or losing means something, that's when you evaluate a ballclub. Your "season" starts when one of your salespeople calls on a customer. All of the research and development, all of the training, all of the advertising mean nothing if he or she doesn't walk out with an order. Compare your products to the competition's. How do they hold up in terms of price, quality, service, delivery, and customer confidence? How can you use the answer to motivate your people?

3. Paying attention to the competition will help you develop a winning edge. In athletics we use scouts to check out our competition and help us put together a game plan. Managers should check out competitive products the same way, looking for weaknesses that will encourage a salesperson to show how his or her products are superior. Why will your product do something that a competitor's won't? Why is a lower price misleading when things like quality or benefits are considered? Can you offer special incentives that encourage your people to go out and beat the competition?

4. Competition acts as a motivating force. If another player or manager slammed the Celtics, I used to post it on the bulletin board. I'd use that same technique if I were running a company. If we lost a big account to the competition, I'd want everyone to know about it. More importantly, I'd ask for suggestions as to

how we could prevent that from happening again. If a consumer magazine knocked my product, I'd make sure the people in my company who were making it read every word. Then I'd look for positive steps to turn that reputation around.

CHAPTER 6

Performance Appraisal, Training, Motivation: Key Combination

"PERFORMANCE APPRAISAL is easy for you," one of my business friends once said to me. "All you have to do is look at the stats to know how each of your players is doing. I wish we kept box scores on our employees. It would make it a lot easier to pick out the ones who are producing and the ones who aren't. It's a lot harder to judge performance in the business world."

Maybe that does sound like the way to do it. Add up the minutes played, field goals, foul shots, assists, rebounds, and blocked shots and you'll have an accurate idea of a player's production. Right? Wrong. Dead wrong.

Stats are the most overrated thing in sports as far as I'm concerned. You may feel the same way about your business. There are too many factors that can't be measured. You can't measure a ballplayer's heart, his ability to perform in the clutch, his willingness to sacrifice his offense or to play strong defense.

See, if you play strong defense and concentrate and work hard, it's got to affect your offense. But a lot of players on a lot of teams only point at offense. Like in baseball, they say, "I hit .300 so I should get X amount of money."

I've never paid much attention to how many points a guy scores. When did he score them? Did he score them during garbage time, when a team is so far behind or ahead it doesn't really matter? Did he score them when the game was on the line? Did he score them against good opponents? There are so many factors. There's really only one stat I was ever concerned about: When this guy's in the game, does the score go up in our favor or go against us?

Red Sez: Call them intangibles or extra contributions or whatever. Every manager in every business should have a way to pinpoint and evaluate employee contributions that don't have numbers attached to them. Your system could include:

• Rewarding extra effort. There are people who go beyond their job descriptions to contribute. Maybe it's not reflected in their production records, but it can have a positive effect on the whole department. They'll do anything to win and really kill that "It's not my job" thinking that is so typical today. Recognize their efforts and find a way to reward them. I had a guy like that in Bob Brannum on one of my early teams. We had a lot of team speed that year, and a lot of our opponents tried to cope with it by leaning, holding, and shoving. If they got away with it, our speed would have been neutralized. Brannum's job was to stop the manhandling. He was the only guy I ever knew who would get mad before a season started and never smile again until it was over. No one wanted to mess around with him. No one. He never got much ink in the papers, but I always let him know how much I valued his contribution to the team.

• Recognizing positive thinking. People with a can-do attitude have a motivating force on everyone. Positive thinkers can handle the normal and abnormal upsets that occur in business. They always find the good side of a bad situation and look for something that can be done. It may not be easy to assess this quality in terms of performance evaluation. But try to find a way because this type of person is invaluable. Larry Bird once described M. L. Carr as the soul of our 1984 championship team, even though he played a backup role.

• Letting them take risks. People who succeed have to take risks. This means they have to be willing to make mistakes. It also means that you have to be willing to let them make mistakes. Don't break the spirit of this type of employee by lowering his or her evaluation.

• Showing pride in their success. If your people do a good job, let them know about it. Sometimes all you have to do is stick your head in the door of their office and tell them it was first-rate. Other times, you might want to take five minutes and tell them why you think what they did was outstanding. Guys like K. C. Jones and Satch Sanders hardly ever got recognition, yet the jobs they were doing out there were fantastic. I convinced each one of them that his best contribution to winning came through his excellence in certain phases of the game.

Individual Accomplishments versus Team Success

Take a guy like K. C. Jones. He wasn't much of a scorer and there was never anything impressive about his stats. But every time I put him in the game, we'd build up a lead. And the other team's leading scorer would suddenly be struggling.

We had a rule on the Celtics. I didn't want anyone to bring his statistics in with him when he sat down to negotiate. (Okay, I was a little stubborn on this point.) I didn't want to see them or hear about them. For one thing I never really believed in them. A lot of statisticians cheat on things like rebounds and assists, trying to build up the guys who play for their home team. So what do the numbers mean if that sort of thing is going on? What is a steal? What is an assist? If a guy gets a rebound and hands it to another guy who then dribbles down the floor, shakes and bakes, and makes a basket, do they give the first guy an assist? For what? But some teams do.

Another bad thing about statistics is that you get so caught up in them, so worried about records and things like that, you end up forgetting about the game. This happens all the time in sports and it's wrong.

I'll give you an example. One day Gene Conley and I were listening to the World Series while driving in Maine. Early Wynn was pitching for the White Sox and in the first three innings he got a 9–0 lead.

So I turned to Gene. "Get him out of there," I said. "Bring in somebody else and then come back with Wynn again tomorrow. That way you get to use your ace twice in a row." Made sense to me.

Conley said they can't do it because Wynn wouldn't get credit for the win. "What's more important?" I asked. "Winning this one game and having a pitcher add to his record, or winning the Series?"

Wynn stays in the game and by the fifth inning he's ahead, 11–0. "Take him out now," I said. "He gets credit for the win and he'll be able to come back a lot sooner, maybe on a couple days' rest, for the last game of the Series."

"You can't take him out now," Conley said. "He's got a shutout going." As Steve Martin would say, "Well excuuuuuse me!"

So Wynn stayed in the game—and ended up hurting his arm. He started two more games but was ineffective, giving up big early leads and being knocked out early. *That just strengthened my belief that the win comes first, every other statistic a distant second.*

Red Sez: Does your performance appraisal system allow you leniency in giving weight to numbers? It should. But there are pitfalls, one of the main ones being subjectivity. How do you judge "unmeasurable" characteristics like initiative and judgment? Make a list of all the people who report to you and ask the following questions:

What can this person do that no one else can?

What does this person do better than anyone else?

What would happen if this person stopped doing the job? Do you have someone who could take it over immediately? Would the work be as good?

Does this person control the work of others? You can have four talented ballplayers, but if you don't have a good point guard to make the plays, you're in trouble.

Is this person committed to the organization?

Does he or she like to help others succeed or is this one a loner who likes to do his or her own thing?

Is this person willing to put him- or herself on the line? There are certain ballplayers who want the ball in their hands for that last shot that determines who wins the game. There are other talented players who simply can't take that kind of pressure. The same holds true for business. Individuals who can't handle a pressure situation shouldn't necessarily be penalized. But those who can should be rewarded.

Records Made to Be Broken

The only record I was ever concerned about was wins and losses. When I was coaching the Washington Capitals we were playing the Providence Steamrollers, who would have been the equivalent to the NBA's LA Clippers in the late 1980s. We had fifty-nine points by halftime and a good shot at breaking the record of 117 set earlier by the Minneapolis Lakers. Our leading scorer, Bob Feerick, had twenty-four points in the first twenty-eight minutes and probably would have broken Carl Braun's mark of forty-seven in the BAA (Basketball Association of America), precursor to the NBA.

So I pulled Feerick and the rest of my regulars out of the game and let the bench finish up. After the game, Harold Kease, a Boston sports columnist, asked me why I pulled Feerick out of the game when he had a chance to break the scoring record.

"I'm not interested in individual records," I told Kease. "I'm interested in winning ball games."

"Wasn't Feerick unhappy about coming out?" he asked.

"Guys who are interested in individual statistics won't play for me for very long," I told Kease. That comment was made over forty years ago. But it's as true today as it was then. Look at the record. The Boston Celtics have never had the league's top scorer. We won seven championships without ever placing one Celtic in the top ten.

People would always ask me how the Celtics won all those championships without ever having a player lead the league in scoring. My answer is that you can count the players who've done it on one hand: Michael Jordan, Chicago Bulls, 1991; Kareem Abdul Jabbar, Milwaukee Bucks, 1971; Joe Fulks, Philadelphia Warriors, 1947; George Mikan, Minneapolis Lakers, 1949 and 1950. So scoring wasn't a big factor to me when I evaluated a player. There were a lot of other things I considered before drafting or signing a player.

My Rating System

So no Celtic got rated according to how many points or rebounds or assists or anything else he might have compiled. *Each man was assessed according to how well he did what we asked him to do.* What was his contribution toward making us a better team? That's all I cared about. In our system, the guy who set the good pick was just as important as the guy who made the shot.

Or take players like K. C. Jones and Satch Sanders. If they could stop people like West and Baylor from getting their normal quota of points, wasn't that worth as much as if they each scored twenty and let their opponents score fifty? Every man on our team had a job, and every man's job was recognized and appreciated when it came time to discuss performance and contracts.

"Your salary depends on what I've seen with my own two eyes," I'd tell a player. "Until the day your statistics can tell me how many points were scored in the clutch and how many came in garbage time, I don't want to see them." I promised Bill Russell during our first contract negotiation that we would never discuss statistics, and we never did. I never once saw him looking at the sheets to see how many rebounds or assists he got. All he cared about was winning.

Red Sez: You'll get better bottom-line results if you can convince your employees that they will be rewarded for "doing the little things" to accomplish the goals, measurements, and objectives you've laid out for them. To get the participation and commitment of employees in setting goals, you should:

• Give plenty of advance notice. People need time to think about what they are expected to accomplish. If you set unrealistic goals or put too much time pressure on a person, it's going to backfire.

• Give them all the essential information they need to do the job. This could involve equipment, functions, people, and new products or services. Make sure they have a complete understanding of what you want accomplished. As a benefit, they may give you a perception of the job that you were not even aware of or come up with innovative ideas to make it work even better.

• Have them state the goals clearly and concisely. Do they agree with them? They might come up with alternatives that could be an improvement. Don't set too many goals. There are just so many things that a person has time to do. Don't include routine activities that they are expected to perform as part of their normal jobs as goals.

• Set a time frame. Make sure you agree on a realistic schedule that the person will be able to live with. Making it too short may result in too much pressure, too long and the person might not take it seriously. Then follow up. Make sure you follow up on every goal you assign. If you don't, you'll give the impression that you weren't that serious about them in the first place.

Total Commitment

Okay, I've told you about the things I don't consider when evaluating a player's performance. Now let's get into what I do look for. My type of player has to be totally dedicated, totally involved, totally prepared to sacrifice whatever is necessary in order to win. That's more important to me than talent, size, or speed. It's one of the reasons I think the Celtics are a cut above everybody else in their desire to win.

Respect and discipline are absolutely essential, as I've discussed in other chapters. My type of player has to be coachable; that means he's got to be ready to put aside personal goals for the sake of the team. *They have to be knowledgeable.* There are certain things I expect every Celtic to know. During the last five minutes of play, they must know the score, they must know how many time-outs are left, they must be aware of how many fouls have been called against them and the other team, too. They must be aware of what's happening at all times out on the floor. Committing a stupid foul and costing us a ball game does stay in my memory when I'm evaluating a player's performance.

When I made a similar comment to a friend, he told me I was practicing another management technique called critical incident evaluation. You've probably done it yourself. You make notes when something positive—or negative—occurs involving one of your employees. It becomes part of his or her scorecard or personnel file.

Performance as a Reflection of Attitude

A player also has to have the right attitude about winning. By that I mean he has to be a poor loser, a lousy loser.

Remember I mentioned earlier about Vince Lombardi and his quote, ''Winning is not everything—but making the effort to win is''? Well, his teams exemplified that. The bread-and-butter play for the Green Bay Packers under Lombardi was the power sweep, sometimes called the Lombardi sweep. There wasn't anything spectacular about it, but it almost always gained yardage. As soon as the guards would pull, the defense would start screaming, ''Sweep, sweep!'' But the execution was always so perfect that they couldn't do much about it. I think Lombardi liked that play because it required all eleven men to play as one to succeed, and that's what ''team'' is all about.

Red Sez: One of the hardest parts of performance appraisal is segmenting individual accomplishment from team results. As you've surely deduced from your reading, I preach the value of teamwork until I'm blue in the face. But you've got to appraise individuals, too. So here are some ways to judge individual employees within the framework of the team:

- Be specific. Exactly what contribution does the person make to the team? What would happen if this person weren't a member? Where would the person be missed the most? Is there something this person is doing that could be improved? Sometimes this is more difficult than it seems. For instance, critics used to say that Don Chaney couldn't shoot or rebound. But the score always went up in favor of the Celtics when he was in the game.
- Does the person fit in with the team? Don't get compatibility confused with ability. Some players with super talents never would have made it with the Celtics because they were more ego-oriented than team-oriented. It's no accident that no member of the Boston Celtics has ever led the league in scoring. Not all employees have the personality traits or the necessary interpersonal skills that allow them to become good team members.

For instance, an individual who places a high value on independent action may have difficulty in accepting compromises that may be required for the good of the team. That's why you have to pick your team members with extreme care. It's also the reason I traded Bob Mc-Adoo, a real scoring machine. Retraining or transfer may be the best answer for those who don't fit into the team concept.

• Don't make unfair comparisons. There aren't too many Birds, Jordans, or Ewings out there. Judge the person on what he's doing, not on what others are doing. Your main concern here is what his contributions to the team are.

• Don't consider the record only. I've had teams with losing records where every player is making a contribution, when the team is playing up to its ability. Coming down hard on players under those conditions won't accomplish anything. This is the time you have to consider making a trade, changing or retraining employees.

Getting back to Lombardi, take a look at the record and you can see what he accomplished in a relatively short time as head coach. In his first year, he turned a 1–12 team into a 7–5 team. In the next seven years, the Packers won the conference championship five times and finished second twice. They won four or five playoffs for the league championship. He was also the winning coach in the first two Super Bowl games.

A number of sportswriters and even a few ex-Packers have told me that I remind them of Lombardi. Of course, I take that as a real compliment because I consider Lombardi to be one of the greatest coaches of all time. He was tough on his players because he was tough on himself. He wouldn't accept excuses or compromises, yet he never demanded more than a player was able to give.

Recognizing Reality

Being able to recognize, accept, and utilize a person's ability is the mark of a good coach or manager. But so frequently in sports, a kid is touted as another Cousy or Bird, so he's thrown onto the starting team and told to go out and save the franchise. Usually he ends up getting burned so badly that he's never able to live up to his legitimate talent level. I always felt I had the right to demand every bit of ability that a player had to offer. But it's wrong to expect more than a person can possibly give.

Unfortunately, some coaches and managers don't recognize when a person is giving everything he or she has. So a player or an employee is pushed beyond his ability level and everyone ends up losing. The mark of a good coach is identifying the strengths and weaknesses of an individual and tapping them accordingly. In basketball terms, it might mean training him as both an off-guard and a small forward. While he may not be outstanding at either position, you've doubled his value to the team.

Managers could use this cross-training technique successfully. More than one mediocre athlete reached stardom after being switched to another position. Bob Lemon, former Yankees manager and outstanding pitcher for Cleveland after the second world war, never would have made it to the majors in his former position as an outfielder. Fortunately, a coach recognized his great arm and made him a pitcher. Maybe you have a few people around who are never going to make it as engineers but could really do a job for you in sales. Listen to them. Especially if they're complaining.

For instance, an employee comes to the boss and says that she's unhappy with the job. Too often, the boss cuts her off, gives her a fast pep talk, and sends her back to work. Actually the boss missed a wonderful chance to find out what's really going on. When people feel so strongly that they are compelled to go to the boss for a face-to-face meeting, they are going to tell it like it is. Maybe she doesn't feel that she can work with someone else in the department. Maybe the reason for her substandard performance will come out. Maybe she's simply not right for the job and no amount of training is going to improve it. Maybe a transfer or retraining would resolve the problem.

You may not think the problem is as serious as the employee does, but that won't do the employee much good. She has a problem, and she won't tell you about it if she thinks you're going to belittle it or tell her she's wrong. Listen to what she has to say and try to act on it. One criterion for judging the performance of any coach—or manager—is whether or not he or she gets the most out of the available talent, whether it's mediocre or outstanding.

Teaching to Improve Performance

Lombardi was also a teacher. He could communicate an idea to his players and explain it so that they understood it. That's why plays like the Lombardi sweep worked time and again. You had to be smart to play for Lombardi. In a split second a player has to read and react to the move of his opponent. The ability of his players to cut the right way, block the right man, pick up the blitz—those are the reasons for the championships. Most managers are looking for the same thing— employees who know how to close a sale, how to choose the most cost-effective vendor, where to go for the best price on material.

I know another thing we had in common. Neither one of us was impressed with frills or gimmicks. I've never been much into Xs and Os and all kinds of fancy diagrams. Keep it simple. That was my rule. You have one move away from the ball, a little pick, pop a little shot, very simple. But timing was everything. In all my years of coaching the Celtics, we had just six plays, with options off each setup. So altogether there were twenty-six plays we could run.

One thing that I always emphasized was that a play does not have to succeed to be good. We never force plays. If one didn't work, we tried something else. The play is merely a beginning. If it works, great. If not, go to the options. A play might be good just because it opens up something else. If your play doesn't work, do you hold the ball and panic? No. The idea is to have continuity. Keep moving. Try something else. A good team should never panic out there.

If you took the shot and missed, that wasn't the important thing. Anybody can miss a shot. What was important was executing properly so that you at least got a good shot away. Failing to execute properly in a situation like that was the biggest mistake you could make on our team. That's why we worked so hard on execution. We wanted to know what we were doing at all times so there would be no panic or confusion when a big play was needed.

Psychology and Performance

The bread and butter of our offense, of course, was the fast break. Our first thought was always to run, run, run, to get the ball down the court as quickly as possible. That meant every Celtic had to be in top shape physically. Lombardi once told his players that "fatigue makes cowards of us all." I never put it that eloquently, but anyone who ever attended a Celtics camp knew how I felt about conditioning. I was always convinced that if you left training camp in great condition, you could steal a lot of games early in the season while the other guys are playing themselves into shape. Believe me, the Celtics always left camp in good shape.

I'd use little forms of psychology to keep them going. Like they'd be scrimmaging real hard and real long and I could see they couldn't go much more.

"Okay," I'd say. "Is everybody tired? Beautiful. Now we're really going to get in shape. Let's see twelve more baskets!"

The groans would erupt up and down the line.

Sometimes I'd ask them if they were tired and they'd say no.

"Really?" I'd tell them. "Great. Let's do forty more!"

Red Sez: I love reading about psychological ploys, mind games, smart moves. Both sports and business have their share. One of my favorites took place when I was coaching the Washington Capitols in 1946. We all traveled by train in those days. There were only ten players to a team, a perfect number since there were exactly twelve berths in each Pullman car, six uppers, six lowers. Of course, a problem developed about who would get the lowers.

If I assigned them to the top six players, I'd be opening the door for complaints about who was more valuable, who should get more money and playing time, and so on. I thought about it, then came up with an idea. I explained that the upper berths were four inches longer than the lower ones, so the big men should have top priority. "The short guys should be willing to make the sacrifice so the tall players wouldn't be cramped," I said, looking up from my full five feet ten inches.

The ruse worked great for about five months. Then Bones McKinney, who was six feet seven inches, told me that he thought the uppers and lowers were the exact same length. I denied it, of course, but Bones brought along a tape measure on our next trip and the scam was over. Meanwhile, I'd had almost six months of relative peace, and we all got a good laugh out of it.

I used another little psychological trick my first year of coaching at Roosevelt High School. About thirty kids were excused from my gym class for physical reasons. They all had doctors' notes, but the real reason most of them got excused was that they just didn't like the class.

Well, I liked my job and I worked hard at it, and I was sure these kids would like the program if they gave it a chance. So I went to the football and track coach, Artie Boyd, with an idea and got his permission to go ahead with it.

"Do you take a bath at home?" I'd ask each kid who handed me an excuse to get out of my class. He'd say yes, of course. "Good," I'd answer. "That means you have no problem taking a bath or a shower. Right?" They'd agree with that.

"From now on, then, every one of you who's excused from physical education can sit here and study or whatever else it is you do while the group is in gym class. But twelve minutes before the class ends, I want you to report to the rest of the group, get undressed, and take a shower with them."

You know what? Within a week only one kid was still being excused from class. The rest of them were out there shooting baskets or running or whatever. They figured if they had to change their clothes and shower anyway, they might as well go out and play.

Training to the Top

In essence, players' reactions to training didn't matter. Whether they were tired or not, I was going to push them harder. Some of them got sick and fainted, but that was their problem, not mine. Every year, at the end of the season, I'd warn them what to expect at the next training camp. "If you get sick, it's your fault. If you faint, it's your fault. If you come in overweight, it's your fault. We're only going to have a month to get ready, so you'd better be in shape the next time I see you."

In order to play our kind of basketball, a Celtic has to be in better shape than the next guy. If he gets tired, his game is hurt. Take shooting. It's a matter of touch. The man goes up, releases the ball, and follows through in one fluid motion. If he's tired, his hand gets a little shaky, his control is off, his timing is gone. There's a lot of difference between shooting when you're fresh and shooting when you're exhausted. My teams were trained to run, to press, to beat the other guys' brains out with their hustle.

That's why my training camps were so tough. The only way to get in that kind of shape is hard work. Lots of hard work. And that's what I gave them. The whole idea of professionals playing themselves into shape is absurd. Only one person could really get them working hard enough so that it would do some good. Me. Lombardi had the same philosophy. I always liked the comment that Willie Davis, the great Packer defensive end, made when he was asked what kind of practices Lombardi ran. "He treats us all the same," Willie said. "Like dogs."

My favorite training camp story came in 1961, the year Carl Braun came to us to finish up his career. About the third or fourth day after we got started, Ramsey came up to me and said, "You must be getting soft, Red. This is the easiest camp we've ever had."

That bothered me. Was I really slowing down? Was I getting softer in my old age? Was I too preoccupied with other duties? I began asking myself some of those questions. Then Braun almost collapsed on the court and I felt better. He moaned to one of my veterans: "This is worse than all twelve of my New York camps put together."

Training Troubles

I remember one time I was coaching in the annual Maurice Stokes Benefit Game up at Kutsher's Country Club and Ray Felix of the New York Knicks was on my team. About five minutes after the game started, he grabbed hold of one of the support posts and vomited. I looked over at him and ignored it. "Get back in the play!" I yelled.

That night my wife, Dot, really got angry with me. "How can you be so callous?" she said. "You didn't even go over to see if Ray was okay."

"Dot," I told her, "that man ate seven pieces of pie at dinner! He's a professional athlete, and if he's that stupid, then let him vomit. Let him get as sick as he wants to. There's no way I'm going to hold his hand."

To play the kind of ball I wanted, my teams had to be conditioned.

That's why my training camps were so tough. The only way to get in that kind of shape is hard work. Lots of hard work. And that's what I gave them. Human nature being what it is, most players don't like that system. Athletes would much rather play themselves into shape.

Take baseball players, for instance. As far as I'm concerned, they live in the past when it comes to training. They've had training camps down there in Florida for seventy years now and nothing's changed. Sure, you need warm weather. I'll buy that. But not this stuff where players take their wives and their golf clubs and spend their afternoons sitting by the pool and their evenings in the local nightclubs. Are you trying to get into shape or are you trying to run a country club?

In my mind, that's ridiculous. I've even heard of situations where baseball players were singing in those nightclubs during spring training. You can bet that no Celtic ever felt like singing after a day in our camp.

Tips on Training

No one expects you to run that kind of boot camp in training your subordinates. But the key concepts—preparation, more repetition than the competition, and honing basic skills to their highest level—are very similar when it comes to you training your employees, or me training my players.

Here are some training strategies I like best:

• Train in "chunks." People learn best when information is presented in small bits. Don't try to cover large areas at once. Always break up subject matter into units that can be mastered quickly. When I teach "fast break," I do it this way:

—The ideal fast break occurs after we rebound. You make the outlet pass, you fill the lanes, your trailer follows you down. But you want to be ready to fast break all the time, not just when the situation is perfect.

—Lift up your head before you release the ball, so you won't throw it away.

—Make sure you don't curve the pass. You waste a fast break if the passer curves the throw and it sails out of bounds.

• Provide short-break benefits. All training should have built-in rewards. Sometimes I'd shorten the practice if everyone worked hard and picked up what I was trying to teach them. Other times, I'd single somebody out who was doing the job. Just remember that any training program that relies on only long-term benefits to motivate trainees is headed for failure.

• Performance is part skill, part motivation. Which part is missing? If a player lacks a basic skill, some training is required. On the other hand, if a lack of motivation is causing the problem, a different solution is called for. A good manager has to be able to spot the differences.

• Don't expect immediate results. If you do, you're going to be disappointed. It usually takes time for a person to be able to put the training into use.

• Is it more cost-effective to train a present employee or replace him with a new one? In most cases, you'll find that retraining employees is a lot cheaper than hiring replacements. It's also a morale builder. Of course, there are times when you have to go outside the organization to get fresh input. But there's nothing better than developing your own talent, whether you're talking about a basketball team or a box company.

• What are the time considerations? Do you need this player or employee right away or can you take a little time? We were able to bring Sam Jones and K. C. Jones along very slowly because they were playing behind Cousy and Sharman. Our 1990 top choice, Dee Brown, got a lot of time for a rookie because we needed a fast point guard. Again, it depends on the circumstances.

• How are you going to follow up on the training? A lot of training dollars are wasted because of improper follow-up. Even the simplest training program shouldn't be considered a one-time event. We can follow up our training at the next practice. It's a little more difficult for a company, but you have to find a way to do it or you're wasting your training dollars.

Talent, Training, and Teaching

I have another story about ability that applies to every sport, every business. Some people are born with a natural talent that can't be taught. In terms of shooting a basketball, I'm talking about guys like

Bill Sharman, Sam Jones, Oscar Robertson, Jerry West, and Larry Bird. Now you can improve any player's shooting style and adjust his rhythm and release. But you can't turn a K. C. Jones or a Don Chaney into a Larry Bird or a Kevin McHale, any more than you can give Dee Brown Bob Cousy's peripheral vision. So you should concentrate on the things that can be improved and accept the others.

I had a friend who ran a meat packing company. He told me about this one employee who knew more about meat than anyone in the plant, so they decided to move him into sales. The problem was that he didn't like selling. They sent him to Dale Carnegie courses and spent a lot of money to teach him selling skills, but nothing worked. Meanwhile, they really missed this guy's work on the production line.

Finally, he got so frustrated that he quit and went to work for a competitor—in his old position. The company should have accepted the fact that the guy was never going to be a salesman and let him do what he did best. *He should have been judged on how he performed his particular job, with his talent tapped to the fullest in that specific position.*

I'm not saying that people can't be taught new skills. For instance, defense in basketball is something that can be taught. It means work. You play defense until you get the ball. Suppose we're in a full-court press, working hard, and the other team pulls off a series of perfect moves and scores. What then? You work harder, because you know eventually you're going to make the other side tired. You're going to wear them down. Then they start throwing bad passes and missing easy shots. You've got to outlast them.

If you check, you'll find out most great sports teams were great defensive teams. I don't care what sport you're talking about. No matter how powerful you are and no matter how good your players are, there is no substitute for that getting-down-to-the-ground-and-sacrificing type of defense. If you can get good players to do that, they become great. If you can get great players to do that, then you'll have superstars.

Performance Appraisal and Motivation

I always looked on a performance review session as a great motivational tool, particularly when it involved bench players. It was important for me to convince these individuals that their contributions were appreciated—no matter what the fans and writers were saying.

Take a player like Jim Loscutoff. He was much better than people gave him credit for. He could shoot and he was pretty fast for a guy his size. But there's only one ball in the game, and I already had guys who could put it into the hole for me. I needed Jim to set picks and box out. He was great at that, but who the hell ever writes stories about setting picks? It's not a glory job, but it's necessary.

Or how about Gene Conley? I wanted him to go out there and get the ball whenever Russell needed a breather. That's all. He had to appreciate his role and his limitations while at the same time appreciating Russell's greatness. It took a certain type of personality to do what we asked him to do. Guys like K. C. Jones and Satch Sanders hardly ever got the recognition they deserved from the fans or the press.

So it was up to me to convince each one of those players that his best contribution to winning came through his excellence in certain phases of the game. I knew that if I could convince every member of my team of that, we would have a fabulous team.

Red Sez: Take a look around your department. Do you have "bench players" who make valuable contributions that go unnoticed. You can make them feel like more valuable members of the team by:

1. Looking for small, easily measured factors in the employees' jobs. Set small goals and recognize them when they are accomplished. Avoid discussing shortcomings unless they are doing damage.

2. Providing as many opportunities for advancement as possible. Remember that some employees are not assertive about wanting to get ahead. So they simply go out and find another job when they feel they have reached a dead end. Of course, some employees never want to advance into management. They're willing to trade authority and money for comfort and job security. It's up to you to be able to recognize these people and reward them in other ways.

3. Being honest. If you have one management opening, and three employees are competing for it, level with them. Pick the one you think is best for the job, and then

tell the other two why. If you drag it out, you'll end up with three unhappy people.

4. Tying the reward to the job. Factors like loyalty, friendship, or congeniality should never be considered in this type of incentive system. You are talking about rewards for performance only.

5. Offering your personal assistance when you know you can help the employee. By the same token, let the person make as many decisions about the work as possible.

The Color of Money

As I said before, I always tried to watch the money because we just didn't have that much to work with.

People kept comparing us to the Yankees, but there was one big difference. After every season, the Yankees would go out and buy someone like Johnny Mize or Catfish Hunter or Reggie Jackson or Dave Winfield. The Celtics couldn't do that. We had to depend on what we got out of the draft and on any older players we could convince to postpone retirement. The most I ever spent for an older player was the six thousand dollars I paid to Cincinnati to get Wayne Embry. We simply didn't have any cash reserves to go to if we came up short. Believe me when I say we were winning world championships some years when we didn't have a dime in the bank.

That's why I made sure that every one of my players knew that his salary was totally dependent on his performance, what I believed to be his contribution to winning. I'm sure it's more difficult in industry to measure this contribution and turn it into dollars. I'm looking at twelve players. You may be looking at hundreds, even thousands. Some of you have union considerations or federal or state laws regulating compensation.

But I still think there can be a way to reward good performances and penalize substandard ones. I don't think you can do it by using the categories on some of those performance evaluation forms that some companies use. You check off a series of boxes and you're supposed to end up with a fair evaluation of an employee's performance. To me, that sounds too much like evaluating a basketball team from the box scores.

I'd rather go the goal-setting route. I always tried to set some goals for a player during an evaluation session. Again, I'm not necessarily talking about points, assists, or other stats. You may have to deal with actual sales results or production numbers. But there's more. Sometimes with me it'd be something like weight. Take Tommy Heinsohn. He played in college at 235. I told him in our first session that I wanted him to come in at 218 and he did. That extra mobility more than made up for any lack of bulk under the boards. I've tried to set those types of personal goals for all our players.

There are certain guys you don't have to set goals for because they are self-motivated. Take Larry Bird. He's the most highly self-motivated athlete I've ever seen. He is continually setting goals for himself and achieving them. He's the true professional. He doesn't only think of the game during the seven months of the season. He thinks all twelve months. His great anticipation on the floor might very well come from his preoccupation with the game.

So what do you do with a guy like Larry? Show him that you appreciate his efforts, that you are aware of the high standards he sets for himself and what it does for the game. *Try to use his example to motivate others to higher performance levels.*

Do you have any Larry Birds on your payroll, men or women who give their all every day? Do you show them that you appreciate their efforts? Every once in a while, I hear about a real valuable employee, one who can never be replaced, being stolen from a company. It's not until that employee's gone that the company is even aware of his or her value.

Red Sez: If this happens to you, I think you should take a close look at your performance review system and the managers who are carrying it out. It's failing in the motivational aspect. Keep these points in mind when appraising your own appraisals or planning a training program to teach a performance review system to other managers:

1. The main point is not to make managers "comfortable" with evaluations. They must understand that performance appraisals are critical, decision-making situations. Their choices are going to affect the company's future and the lives of all their employees. A certain amount of anxiety about doing the job right should be expected.

2. Look at how, not just what. While job standards are important, beware of criteria contrived simply to make the appraisals appear more objective. In many instances, the employee's enthusiasm, attitude, and effort are as important as quantitative achievements. Take a player like M. L. Carr on our 1984 championship team. His enthusiasm and desire to win motivated everybody, whether he was in the game or on the bench.

3. Pay attention to the employee's input, particularly if the performance is not up to expectations. Sometimes there are good reasons why people don't live up to what's expected of them. A simple change or better understanding of their roles can make the difference between marginal and outstanding performance. Some managers make the same mistake as basketball coaches. They fall in love with their own voices and don't get any feedback about steps they could take to improve the system.

CHAPTER 7

Age: Call It Experience
Loyalty: Take Advantage
of It

IT SEEMS THE RULES of the game have changed in corporate America. A lifetime of hard work, achievement, and dedication no longer guarantees a place in a company's plans. "Reductions in force," "downsizing," "efficiency programs"—they all seem to be aimed at the older worker. I'm told that age discrimination lawsuits are the hottest area of employment discrimination around today.

I guess that's why a number of companies have come up with special programs to get rid of older employees—legally. I read about one company which decided it could save a lot of money by cutting some of its older, higher-priced talent that it simply decided wasn't cutting the mustard. So they put together a generous early retirement program to solve the problem.

Of course, they had to offer the package to everyone, not just the ones they wanted to get rid of. You can guess what happened. Some of their best people grabbed the money and ran, while a lot of the deadwood is still on the payroll today. That company shot itself in the foot; it's still suffering from that decision, and probably will for years to come.

The most surprising part of the story to me was that top management offered the deal in the first place. If anyone ever came to me with a plan that would place me in jeopardy of losing my most experienced players to weed out a few who weren't producing, I know who'd go

124

out the door first. Does a company really think it can save money by dumping its most experienced personnel?

Call It Experience, Not Age

I learned a number of years ago just how valuable older employees can be to an organization. Okay, I run a basketball organization, not a manufacturing or service company. And my older employees are in their thirties, not in their fifties, sixties, or seventies. But the principle remains exactly the same: *Who's in a better position to analyze the competition, come up with new ideas, and train new employees than the person who's been around for a while?*

Let me give you an example. I went into the 1957 season with players like Bob Cousy, Tom Heinsohn, K. C. Jones, Sam Jones, Jim Loscutoff, Bill Russell, Bill Sharman, Ben Swain, and Lou Tsioropoulos. But one of the main reasons we won our first championship that year was because of a thirty-four-year-old guard that nobody else wanted. I'm talking about Andy Phillips, a great playmaker who the Fort Wayne organization decided was washed up. I knew I had the premier backcourt in the league with Cousy and Sharman. But I wanted the steadying influence of a veteran, and Phillips fit that bill perfectly.

Two years earlier, I talked Arnie Risen, a former Rochester player, out of retirement. Arnie did a great job as Ed Macauley's backup. But he did his most valuable work for the Celtics during Bill Russell's rookie year. Risen had been around the league and he knew a lot of the little shortcuts, the tricks you pick up after a while. He knew the habits of the big men Russell had to face. It was a beautiful thing to watch the two of them working together.

Red Sez: Take a close look at your own operation, where it is right now and where it's headed. Are you taking advantage of all the experience at your fingertips? You can better utilize your human resources by realizing:

• People don't become obsolete. Equipment and methods do. It's just as easy for a thirty-year-old to be caught with obsolete skills as it is for a worker of sixty. Age and obsolescence often are found together, but that doesn't mean one causes the other. Of course, you don't want to be stuck with a work force of people with obsolete skills. The solution is to improve the skills, not discard the people.

• It's a lot more expensive to train and develop a younger worker than it is to give the job to an older, experienced employee. Older workers may be at the peak of their production powers. They pick up new techniques, combine them with their experience, and that makes them extremely versatile.

• Advances in health care mean that older people offer many years of active, reliable employment. Statistics also show that older workers have better attendance and lower turnover than younger employees.

• Automation, safety devices, and improved working techniques have made many jobs much easier than they used to be. Don't automatically eliminate older people because of physical requirements.

Building with Role Players

In 1967, I picked up Bailey Howell and Wayne Embry, both thirty and both five-time all-stars who had been considered expendable by their former teams. I knew Embry would be an ideal backup for Russell, the best since Conley left in 1961. Howell was a power forward in the Heinsohn mold, providing scoring and rebounding strength.

I picked up Paul Silas, one of the greatest offensive rebounders to ever play the game, from the St. Louis Hawks. We never would have won those championships in 1974 and 1976 without Silas sweeping the offensive boards clean. I jumped at the chance to get Bill Walton from the Portland Trail Blazers in 1985. A lot of basketball people thought he was finished because of his bad feet, but Bill showed them otherwise. Watching him play with Larry Bird, Kevin McHale, and Robert Parish was something to behold. His "bad feet" helped us to a 67–15 mark during the regular season, and a world championship when we beat Houston in six games.

Now Risen, Howell, Silas, and Walton had been starters for their previous teams, so I sat down with them individually and explained exactly what their roles would be with the Celtics. "I'm going to pay you the same money you were making before. But you have to understand you're going to be a role player. I can't say how much or how little I'm going to use you. But you have to be ready to go full-tilt when I send you in. If you can play for the Celtics under those conditions, we'd love to have you. If you're going to have an ego problem, we'd better forget it right now."

All those players responded magnificently. I never had a complaint about playing time or anything else. We never would have won that 1968 championship without Embry and Howell. Phillips was a good addition, and Risen helped Russell get off to a great start. There are three championship flags hanging over Boston Garden that wouldn't be there without the contributions of Silas and Walton.

The real key to using an older person in those roles is to be completely honest. If I had given them the impression that they were going to be starting players, it never would have worked.

Red Sez: Every department, every organization, every manager needs role players. Every employee can't be a superstar. By setting up a strong role-playing system and communicating exactly who is to play what roles, you enhance your own chances of becoming a superstar manager. Start by:

• Building a bench made up of your older employees. There's a wealth of experience there, with many of them capable of playing more than one position. These people can be invaluable, particularly when you have to fill a slot on a temporary basis. Don't buy that argument that older people can't accept change—I once made the statement that I would never deal with a player's agent. Now look who I spend most of my time dealing with!

• Taking a close look at your retirees when you're having trouble filling empty job slots. They are familiar with your operation, so training would be minimal. Ask them at the time of their retirement whether they would be interested in filling in at busy times. Even a "no" answer at that time shouldn't eliminate them from consideration. An awful lot of people get bored after retirement. I got a lot of mileage out of players who had "retired" from their previous teams.

• Hiring retirees as part-time employees. This has paid off for a lot of companies in terms of lower payroll and benefits costs, as well as reduced absenteeism and turnover. By offering flexible hours, you may attract a lot of your former employees.

Age No Impediment

Some companies seem to view age as a handicap. The theory goes that as managers get older, it necessarily follows that they're going to lose a step and make bad decisions. I can tell you that theory doesn't hold in the world of sports. Take a guy like Branch Rickey, the late general manager of the Brooklyn and Los Angeles Dodgers. He made great deals for the Dodgers long after he turned seventy.

I think I made a few good deals for the Celtics after passing normal retirement age, trades that brought me guys like Robert Parish and Kevin McHale. If age does slow the decision-making process, you'd think a lot of general managers would be on the phone to me trying to get front-line ballplayers for nothing. Take advantage of the old man in Boston. It hasn't worked that way at all. In fact, my age has worked against me where trades are concerned.

Some general managers won't make any kind of deal with me. I put a legitimate offer on the table—one that would help both clubs—and they don't want to touch it. Then they turn around and make a trade that gets them less than I was offering. I guess they see me as the "old Yankee hoss trader" who always has to get the best end of the deal. A reputation that isn't deserved, I might add. Sure, over the years I've made some good deals. But I've always believed that if a trade is to be successful, it has to help both clubs.

Let me give you an example. I traded Paul Westfall, an off-guard, to Phoenix for Charlie Scott, a point guard. I really liked Westfall, both as a person and a ballplayer. But at the time I had JoJo White, another off-guard, who was slightly ahead of Paul. I needed a point guard and that's why I made the deal.

Scott helped us win a championship in 1976. So short-range, I got the better of the deal. Meanwhile, Westfall developed into a real star with Phoenix and went on playing a number of years after Scott retired. So long-range, Phoenix got the better of the deal. I think it's fair to say that both teams made out in the trade.

That was fifteen years ago. I was dealing with general managers who were in my age group, guys who didn't worry about writers saying ''Auerbach did it again.'' These younger guys today don't even want to talk to me, at least about trades. So I guess, in a different way, I'm a victim of age discrimination.

It's not the type I can do anything about, however. There's nothing in the age discrimination law that says that general managers of basketball teams have to make trades with older general managers. Come to think about it, I think that provision should be added to the law.

At any rate, this reluctance to deal with me is one of the reasons Dave Gavitt, former Providence College basketball coach and Big East commissioner, joined the Celtics' management in 1989. Meanwhile, anyone who follows the Celtics knows that I never believed in building a club through trades. In fact, I once went twelve years without making a single body-for-body exchange.

Special Situations

A player, no matter how young or old, experienced or inexperienced, didn't have to be a star or starter to get my attention. For instance, in 1966 I got Don Nelson, a forward who had kicked around for three seasons in Chicago and Los Angeles, when his name appeared on the waiver wire—no other team wanted him. The rap on Don was that he was too slow, that he didn't have the speed to play in the NBA. I knew that Nelson wasn't going to outrun anybody. But with guys like John Havlicek, K. C. Jones, Tom Sanders, Bill Russell, and Larry Siegfried, the last thing I needed was more speed.

So I sat Don down and told him not to worry about how fast he ran. I needed a smart basketball player who could come in a game at crucial times and score points. That's what Nelson did for eleven straight seasons, becoming one of the greatest sixth men in Celtic history. I took some early heat from the writers because I could have taken Jackie Mooreland, a taller, faster forward than Nelson with better stats. There was never any doubt in my mind, though, that Nelson was the right selection. He made major contributions to five Celtics championship teams.

In most companies, older employees have to choose between two extremes: full-time work and full-time retirement. Many of these people—as well as their employers—would benefit from a program that let the retiree continue in temporary part-time work. Look at it this way: The age discrimination law says that you can't replace an older worker with a younger one, and you can't force most employees to retire before they reach a specific age. If you have to keep these people, why not keep them under the best possible terms: Design part-time and temporary jobs for them. This would give you skills that you couldn't buy anywhere and allow you to provide more flexible scheduling of your work force.

Most people today can expect to live into their eighties, healthy and active. All those myths about older workers—that they can't learn new skills or that their mental processes deteriorate rapidly—will become even further off the mark in the future than they already are today.

Creating temporary and part-time job openings can help older people maintain social contacts, a sense of self-worth, and financial independence. These are all good reasons from the employee's point of view, but there are benefits for the company, too. One of the biggest is that the older employee might just be the best person available for the job.

Structured Flexibility

Make sure you spell out the conditions under which you accept older workers for part-time or temporary help. Don't allow so much flexibility that they can dictate their own schedules without regard to your needs. If you make clear your requirements up front, you shouldn't have any problems. *I spelled out exactly what I expected when I picked up a veteran ballplayer, and I never had anything but positive results.*

A few of my business friends tell me that a full-time employee would be jealous of the flexible hours offered to part-time workers and ask for similar treatment. I don't think that is true at all. First of all, part-time employees are in a holding pattern. In basketball terms, they're not going after a starting position. That means that my full-time players don't have to worry about being bumped or cut. A lot of full-time people will appreciate the fact that the older employee is not competing with them for promotions, pay raises, and the like.

Second, if my full-time players/employees are thinking team-first—as I demand—they'll realize the positive contributions of older part-time workers.

Third, if you've done your job as manager, you've created a shared work ethic between your older, experienced "players" and your newer regulars. You've done that by:

> • Developing the kind of working environment that encourages employees of all ages to exercise their intelligence, to look for new opportunities, and to be ready to accept them when offered.
>
> • Trying to provide a variety of challenging jobs, particularly in the early stages of the employee's career. Many employees tend to become specialists in certain fields or operations. Years later, though, that entire area of an employee's specialty can become obsolete. But they have their general skills to fall back on.

The Older, the Better

There's a big difference between the work ethic of an older and younger person today. A lot of young people don't have the time or the dedication to learn how to do the job the right way. They want to be successful overnight. They don't want to go through the stages and pay the price.

Some professional athletes are the same way. They look for long-term contracts and big dollars, but they're not willing to work for it. Of course, there are exceptions. Guys like Magic Johnson, Larry Bird, Michael Jordan, and Kevin McHale work hard all the time. Put a young player with any of those guys and he's going to work, whether he likes it or not. He's also going to learn.

In 1990, McHale ran a "big man's" camp trying to teach other Celtics like Joe Kleine and Michael Smith the moves that make him one of the best in the game. No one told him to do it. It's just another example of Kevin's dedication to winning, and a reflection of his leadership capability.

Leading by Example

I'm asked frequently about what constitutes leadership, like Kevin McHale demonstrated with his teaching camp, and what I consider my style of leadership. Actually, I never used just one style. Leadership to me is a blend of the different methods I've observed over the years. Each has its own set of strengths and weaknesses.

1. Bureaucratic. This type of manager usually does things by the numbers and bases his or her decisions on rules, regulations, and policies. In basketball terms, they live by the Xs and Os and spend hours watching videos of their players. STRENGTH: It's an effective technique if you're dealing with rookies or a team that needs to work on fundamentals or show more discipline. WEAKNESS: It's least effective when rapid changes take place or new problems develop. For instance, if a coach calls a set offensive play at a crucial point of the game and a defensive change makes it almost impossible to work, the players will be afraid to make an adjustment and end up turning the ball over.

2. Hands-off. This type of coach flows with the tide, letting his players do their thing without a whole lot of managerial interference. STRENGTH: It works if you have a lot of highly motivated, veteran players who don't require a lot of supervision. WEAKNESS: It can be disastrous in situations requiring quick decisions or specific directions. Anytime you see a group of players arguing during a time out at a crucial point of the ball game, you'll know the coach is taking a hands-off approach.

3. Democratic. This type of coach focuses on encouraging and developing players. He recognizes the importance of two-way communication and rewards good performance. He is confident in his own abilities and doesn't feel threatened by any of his players. STRENGTH: Players are not afraid of making mistakes or offering ideas. WEAKNESS: This approach may be less effective in a crisis situation or with rookies who require close supervision.

4. Autocratic. This coach demands that the players do exactly what she says without question or comment. She feels that since she is responsible for all the end results, she has to have all the answers and total control of the players. STRENGTH: It works best in a crisis situation where prompt and decisive action is necessary. For in-

stance, a team trails by a point and has to inbound with two seconds on the clock. This is not the time to debate over who should take the final shot. WEAKNESS: This style lowers player motivation and performance. The players realize that this type of coach will make the final decision anyway so they decide not to offer any input. It can also lead to coaches continually creating "crisis" situations so they are always in demand.

Which Method Is Best?

I've used parts of every one of these methods, depending on the circumstances. I've been bureaucratic when dealing with rookies or teams that need discipline. Veterans who are self-motivated—guys like Robert Parish, Larry Bird, and Kevin McHale—get a lot of freedom. I listened to players during a game and acted on their suggestions.

But when the game was on the line, when we got down to the final time-out, I became a complete autocrat. I decided who should take the shot, who should put the ball into play, who should set the pick, who should stand in such-and-such a spot, and what to do if the play didn't work. Just check the records and see how many games the Celtics won in the closing minutes.

In short, there isn't any "best" leadership method as far as I'm concerned. Each can be productive in some situations and totally disastrous in others. An effective manager has to be able to read situations and people so he can select the style that will work best for him at that particular time.

Loyalty Works Both Ways

Do you think it's an accident that Bird is one of the greatest foul shooters in the history of the game? If you watched him practice hour after hour, shot after shot, you'd realize why he's a winner. The same is true of Magic Johnson. When he entered the NBA, he was not a good shooter. A lot of work has turned him into one of the best in the game. Johnson, Bird, Jordan, and McHale will do whatever it takes to win, including passing on their knowledge to other people.

How many Birds, McHales, and Johnsons are on company payrolls right now? *People who have been in the trenches and paid the price have experience you won't find in any training manual, and a work ethic that can't be taught.* Instead of setting these people up as role models for younger employees, companies are laying them off or pushing them into early retirement. What kind of message does that send to young employees? Work hard, stay loyal, and, if you're lucky, you'll have a job until someone who doesn't even know you decides to let you go? That's bad for workers, bad for managers, and eventually bad for companies themselves.

Ask any executive to list the requirements he or she expects from employees and I guarantee that every one of them will put loyalty near the top. It's only natural. We want to surround ourselves with people who are loyal to our organization and ourselves as managers. But I think that some managers have forgotten that loyalty goes both ways—if we expect it from our employees, we have to give it back.

A lot of executives who demand absolute allegiance from their employees think nothing about announcing "downsizing" moves that put a lot of people in their forties, fifties, and sixties out on the street. In fact, you can't pick up a paper today without reading an article about another big layoff, plant closing, corporate merger, or other employment-threatening activity.

Now, I know that a lousy business climate leads to unemployment. Employees have to be let go, just as basketball players have to be cut or traded. I'm not talking about that. I'm referring to the planned "downsizings" that some companies use to boost stock prices and push earnings up.

Most of these individuals being cut have been with the same company for twenty or more years. They made their last change during a period when jobs were a lot easier to come by, and they were a hell of a lot younger. Things were different when they entered the job market than they are now.

There used to be a mutual loyalty that existed between an employee and an employer. In exchange for good and loyal service, an employee was given a sense of security that his or her vital needs would be taken care of: working a full week, getting regular raises in pay and promotions, having friends among coworkers, feeling that the company was part of the family—those were the expectations that most employees were led to believe they were due when they entered the job market in the fifties and sixties. If the company asked them to move, they did it, knowing they'd be taken care of.

Companies just don't seem to give that kind of loyalty to employees any longer. The result is that they're not getting loyalty back, even from the employees who survive the cutting. These people aren't blind or stupid. They see what's happening to older employees now and recognize what will probably happen to them in the future. So they develop the attitude that you can't trust top management, then continually peek over their shoulders waiting for their suspicions to be confirmed. It's certainly not an atmosphere that promotes loyalty—or productivity.

Some of these management consultants who recommend the layoffs promise that they won't have any effect on the capabilities of the companies to produce. I say baloney. How can the company replace the knowledge and expertise of the managers it lets go? What about the loss of loyalty on the part of the employees who remain? Both morale and productivity are bound to sag. For years now, the Japanese have proved that loyalty among employees is a key to productivity.

Loyalty Double Standard

Let me give you an example of what I consider to be a double standard when it comes to loyalty. The National Collegiate Athletic Association (NCAA) has a strict rule concerning student transfers. A student athlete who transfers from one college to another must forfeit a year of eligibility. The idea, of course, is to discourage a student from walking out on a coach who has spent a lot of time recruiting him. Coaches insist they need this kind of protection to prevent their teams from being seriously hurt by transfers.

But the student isn't given any protection at all from the coach walking out on him. It happens time and again. Kids are given a big sales pitch as to why they should attend a certain college. Their only connection to the school is through the coaches who recruited them. So they sign letters of intent fully expecting that they will be coached by the guy who told them what a wonderful experience they were going to have as key members of the basketball team. Before they even set foot on the campus, they start reading the papers about their coach being recruited by another school.

Usually there are denials from all concerned parties, and the stories are blamed on a few imaginative writers. "Nothing to be concerned about," the kids are told. Meanwhile the papers are filled with stories about contracts, the possibility of broken contracts, financial offers, and counteroffers.

While the auction is going on, a seventeen- or eighteen-year-old, who may be leaving home for the first time, is wondering what the hell is going on. His only connection with the school is with a coach who has made a lot of promises about how great everything is going to be. Even if the coach ends up staying, the kids go through an uneasy period where they feel a real security blanket may be taken away.

But sometimes the stories are for real and a few weeks before school starts, a coach announces he has an offer he can't refuse. Where does that leave the kids who expected to be playing for him? Usually confused, bewildered, and more than a little angry. Now they have to sit back and wait patiently while another coach is selected. Who knows whether their style of play will fit in with the philosophy of the new coach.

There's another side of the story that bothers me. What kind of message does it send out to all the kids—not just athletes—concerning "contracts." A lot of them have the idea that contracts are worthless pieces of paper that mean nothing. A person signs a long-term contract, gets a better offer, and he's gone.

What's the solution? Get rid of the double standard. Impose the same penalty on a mature adult that is thrown at a seventeen-year-old. If a coach transfers from one college while still under contract to another, he should be given the same one-year suspension that a player must serve.

Giving and Getting Loyalty

No one ever had to tell Bill Reinhart, my coach at George Washington, that a person has to give loyalty in order to get it. The best thing I could ever say about Bill is that he never forgot his people. A lot of his players appreciated him much, much more after they left him than they did while they were still in school. When you left GWU, if you had kept your nose clean and done your job, you were prepared to coach and coach well. That was true of Gordon Ridings, Matt Zunic, Howard Hobson, and a lot of other guys, including Red Auerbach.

Reinhart taught us the way to build up a program. He saw to it that every single ballplayer who stayed eligible ended up with his degree. Every single one of them. I'm not sure that any other coach can point to a record like that. You always hear of guys who are redshirted, or left school needing a few more hours to graduate. But Bill kept an eye on every one of his boys, making sure they were getting the job done in the classroom.

Another thing I noticed was the fact his players kept coming back to see him again and again. GWU used to play its games in local high schools or in the old Capitol Arena. We had no home court or fancy campus. As a result, recruiting could be a problem.

There was a time when you could sell a kid on the idea of playing in the nation's capital. But once these guys began getting a peek at Maryland, Duke, North Carolina, and places like that, forget it. The big campuses were a strong attraction. So most of Bill's players came to him through former players.

The message was always the same. Kids were assured that Reinhart would treat them fairly. Not only would he give them an excellent knowledge of the game, but he'd also be their friend and advisor. That's a promise you could give a kid, because Bill Reinhart was that kind of a guy.

I remember my first conversation with him when he offered me a scholarship to GWU. "Mr. Reinhart," I said, "there's only one question. I'll be a transfer student from Seth Low Junior College of Columbia University and I know you've already got a lot of top ballplayers on your team. If I don't make the club, will I lose my scholarship?"

I've never forgotten what he told me.

"Red," he said. "I'll make you a promise. Keep your marks up, stay eligible, and whether you play a game for me or not, I'll see to it that you remain in school and leave with your diploma. You have my word on that."

"Mr. Reinhart," I replied, "that's good enough for me."

I never forgot that feeling of trust I had after that conversation. It had a tremendous impact on all of my dealings, both on and off the basketball court.

Close, but No Cigars

Reinhart could afford to be a friend to his players. And a lot of companies seem to push the idea that the best way to build employee loyalty is to make "friends" of their employees. So they tell supervisors to bowl with them, take them into their confidence, give them advice when they're having personal problems.

I have to draw the line on a lot of that stuff. I mean, it's great if employees feel free to go to their supervisors about business problems, or even a drug or booze problem. It says something positive about the supervisor and the company *But I think there's got to be a limit as to how much involvement a manager—or a company—should have in an employee's personal life.*

I never allowed myself to get too close to my employees. You've got to realize that there's close and too close. What do I mean? Well, you can get close to a player by trying to understand his problems, if he has any; by being aware of his financial situation; by sharing thoughts on the game itself with him. But while he is a player, I've always felt you must be careful not to become too emotionally attached to him.

That's why I never went to parties with my guys, and I never cared to get close to their wives and kids. If the time ever came that I decided to trade a player, I didn't want to be thinking about things like how much his wife loved her home or his kids loved their school.

The most distasteful part of coaching to me—by far—was having to tell a guy he was being traded or released or cut from training camp. That aspect of the job bothered me right up until the day I retired. Maybe that's one of the reasons so few Celtics were ever traded. It was a traumatic experience—for me. How do you suppose I'd have felt dealing away a guy I was buddy-buddy with?

Okay, I recognize that industry doesn't trade employees. But there are a lot of other reasons why managers shouldn't get too close to employees. For instance, managers have to conduct performance appraisals. Can managers do an objective job when they're trying to evaluate an employee they went bowling with the night before? They'd damned well better, or charges of favoritism are going to wreck their departments. Or what happens in a layoff? If other employees get the impression that people kept or lost their jobs based on their relationship with the boss, a real problem is going to develop.

Bill Russell, Tom Heinsohn, Satch Sanders, Dave Cowens, and Chris Ford all moved into coaching with the Celtics after playing for the Celtics. I gave them all the same speech. "Now you're going to be coaching people who used to be your teammates. You probably like some of them more than you do others. If your players are able to pick up on this, you're going to be in trouble in two ways. The ones who don't think you like them are going to live up to your expectations. The ones who know that you do like them are going to take advantage of the situation. Chances are good that you'll lose them both.''

If you watched Ford yelling at Bird, McHale, and Parish during the course of our 1990 season, you know that my message got through.

Loss of Loyalty

As long as I'm connected with the Boston Celtics, we'll never have one of these management consultants around the office telling us who we should let go. They're the guys who really bother me. I always liked the way Robert Townsend, the former chairman of Avis, defined a management consultant in his book *Up the Organization*. He said a consultant ''is a guy who borrows your watch to tell you what time it is and then keeps the watch.'' Of course, I have to be careful about quoting Townsend. He also said that a company should never hire a graduate of the Harvard Business School. I used to teach a course in sports law at Harvard Law School.

I see the results of this loss of loyalty in the thinking of some of my students. They have a different attitude about forging ahead in business than my generation ever did. Their strategy seems to be to job hop. Spend a few years here, a few years there, then jump to the next—at a big increase in salary.

Security is not a top priority for these individuals. Neither is loyalty. Expensive to companies in terms of training and turnover? You bet. But isn't that what management leaves itself open to when it looks at loyalty only from a company point of view?

Gaining Loyalty

Of course, you can talk about loyalty, motivation, psychology, and everything else. To me the word which best explains the loyalty that ex-players feel for the Celtics is integrity. My guys knew that I'd never lie to them. When they came in to see me they knew they were going to get the truth. And they knew the Boston Celtics organization stood behind them 100 percent. They were people. We tried to treat them like men, not like parts of a machine to be discarded when we felt like it.

Look around Boston Garden during a Celtics game and you'll see the results of the family feeling we try to build up. Almost every ex-Celtic living in the area will be in the stands, cheering us on. Guys like John Havlicek, Tommy Heinsohn, Jim Loscutoff, Rick Weitzman, Hank Finkel, Bob Brannum, Mal Graham, and Gene Conley. Former players now living out of town will always call up ahead of time to let us know they're coming. No one who ever played for the Celtics has to pay to see them now. It's our way of telling players that their relationship with the Boston Celtics doesn't end when they hang up their uniform.

Believe me, we get this loyalty back in a lot of different ways. If I have a question about a player, I can pick up the phone and get a report from a former Celtic anywhere in the country. A lot of my former players let me know about local talent that might have gone unnoticed. Just before the draft in 1958, Bones McKinney, who was then coaching at Wake Forest, called me about this "kid at North Carolina who can really shoot and has great speed." No one knew who I was talking about when I drafted him, but Sam Jones turned into one of the all-time great NBA scorers.

Actually, ex-players formed the nucleus of our talent search in those days. I didn't have the time to hop a plane for a first-person inspection of the leading college seniors. And the Celtics didn't have the money to hire full-time scouts. Besides, my ex-players knew better than any scouts what I looked for in a kid. Guys like Freddy Scolari and Don Barksdale helped scout Russell while Bobby Donham recruited Loscutoff. I always feel free to ask any of my former players for help, because they know I'll always be there for them. That's what loyalty is all about.

CHAPTER 8

Managers' FYI: How to Handle a Full-Court Press by the Press

IT NEVER CEASES to amaze me how a lack of common sense can get owners in trouble with the media.

Take the 1990 World Series, a four-game sweep for the Cincinnati Reds over the Oakland A's. It should have been an unparalleled moment in the history of a great franchise. But look what happened with Eric Davis.

In the fourth game in Oakland, Davis, the Reds' left fielder, was diving for a ball and was hurt. It turned out to be a lacerated kidney, a very painful and serious injury. He was actually in critical condition for a couple of days.

While he's in the hospital, his team wins and goes home. Then the doctors tell him he can go back to Cincinnati if he hires a private plane. For days he tries to call Marge Schott, the owner of the team, about who is going to pay for the plane. She never called him back.

He spent fifteen thousand dollars for the plane. His feelings were hurt. When he got back he said he was treated worse than a dog by the team, then stuck it to them by taking out a newspaper ad thanking the fans for supporting him.

They all made up at a press conference a week or so later, but the incident gave the whole organization a black eye.

It would have been so easy to avoid the problem. First of all, the owner shouldn't have been involved. What does she pay the front office for? Someone else should have arranged for some teammates to stay with Eric, and fly back with him. They could have had a little party for him at the airport, and it would have played great with the media. More than that, it would have meant something to Davis, who, as far as I can tell, is a quality player they want to keep. Common sense.

Close Shave

Let's look at another case, that of Victor Kiam, the guy who made a fortune with Remington shavers and went out and bought the New England Patriots football team a couple of years ago.

You remember how that story went. A reporter by the name of Lisa Olson from the Boston *Herald* was in the locker room interviewing one of the players. Some of the other guys allegedly made lewd remarks and gave her a real hard time. Real gentlemen. It was a bad scene that never should have happened.

But what does Kiam say? He says he doesn't disagree with the players and criticizes the paper for sending a woman to cover the team. Then, according to the news reports, he calls her a name that rhymes with ditch.

A couple of days after that he tries to apologize and says he never called her that name. He even took out a full page ad in the *Herald* to try to set things straight.

But the damage was done! I don't know Kiam, so I'll assume he was trying to support his guys. But the way he went about it was all wrong.

First of all, the league rules allow women reporters in the locker rooms, so he has no argument with the paper or anybody else. The Celtics have had women in the locker room for years. The players shower, usually change in the training room, and wear robes in the locker room. It took some getting used to for us old-timers, but we had to do it, and we did.

I once asked Lesley Visser, then a reporter from the Boston *Globe,* to give the players a little privacy in the locker room right after a game in 1984. She understood completely and came back after the players showered and changed. It wasn't a big deal, really no problem at all. Hell, I'd even gone to her wedding the year before.

Every owner wants to support his (or her—remember Cincy's Marge Schott!) players. But there's a point where you can't close your eyes to the obvious. At least one—and maybe more—of Kiam's players was clearly out of line. (The NFL commissioner eventually fined three.) But Kiam had a very sensitive issue. To say something that would support, or even appear to support, such crude harassment of women is not only wrong, but public-relations suicide.

Remember, the guy owns the Patriots as a partial hobby. In his business, he makes a little item called the Lady Remington shaver. How many women are going to buy that product from now on? I'm not sure. Also, if many families are like mine, wives buy electric razors for their husbands. Victor got national women's organizations on his back as well as a league investigation.

There are better ways to deal with the press.

Red Sez: You're probably never going to have to worry about women reporters going into your locker room to interview employees. But the chances are good that you're going to have to deal with the media sometime during your career. Here are a few rules that can help you have a positive experience with the press.

1. Be positive. The wrong kind of story or remark can hurt your company's (and your own) reputation. On the other hand, the media provide a great outlet for you to correct a negative story or broadcast your company name and message.

2. Be prepared. Make sure you talk to everybody in the company who has any involvement in the story. Get the facts. Nothing looks worse than executives in a company contradicting each other in the media.

3. Set objectives. Try to pick out a few good points that you want to make. If the reporter doesn't lead you in the direction you want to go, use a bridge phrase. "Something you may not have thought about" or "What I really think is important" gives you the opportunity to make your points.

4. Don't be afraid to question a reporter. You have every right to find out what a reporter plans to cover, the story angle, what he or she knows so far.

5. Don't make casual, off-hand remarks. Those off-the-cuff statements can come back to haunt you when you read them in black-and-white.

6. Be careful of humor and sarcasm. What may sound like a funny comment can take on a different meaning in print or when somebody else says it.

7. Buy some time. A lot of managers get in trouble because reporters catch them off guard. You don't have to respond to a reporter's questions unless you're absolutely sure of the answers. There's nothing wrong with saying, "I don't have the answer for that right now. Let me get the information and get back to you. What's your deadline?" Most reporters will accept that. A well-organized and clearly focused interviewee makes the reporter's job that much easier.

8. Don't make off-the-record comments. Reporters can get confused about what's on and off the record. How many times have you heard the comments "I thought it was off the record" or "it was taken out of context." You saw a perfect example of that when Bud Carson was fired in 1990 as the Cleveland Browns' football coach. I read in *USA Today* some negative remarks he made about his former employers. He had a deal where he wasn't supposed to be critical or else his severance paychecks would be stopped. He claimed what he told the writer, Gordon Forbes, was off the record. It almost cost him $450,000!

9. Don't ever say "no comment." It gives the impression that you're trying to hide something. Simply saying "I don't know but I'll get back to you" is a lot stronger.

10. Don't argue. I don't care how offensive or stupid the question, you can't win an argument with a reporter. Smile, even when the tough questions come at you, so you don't appear angry or flustered.

You Can't Avoid the Media

Whatever business you're in, someday you're going to have to deal with the press. A lot of managers think they can just say "no comment" and get away with it. Sometimes that works, but, as Dick Nixon learned the hard way, sometimes it doesn't.

The game is changing in business. Years ago there wasn't much business news. Now the business page is getting to be like the sports page. In the old days, a guy could be president of a company for thirty years and only get his picture in the paper if he ran the United Way campaign. No more. Now business leaders are written about almost as often as coaches or athletes. Donald Trump and Lee Iacocca are better known than most of the players in the NBA.

So the odds are that sooner or later you're going to get a call from a reporter. It seems kind of funny to me, since I've been talking to these guys (that's generic for both male and female reporters, according to my use of the language) for so long, but some business people panic when they get the call. They freeze. That's ridiculous. These guys aren't the feds. Reporters are like lawyers, or coaches, or most other people. There's a few really good ones, a few really bad ones, and a lot in between. Most are trying to do a good job.

So first of all, don't let them intimidate you. There isn't one reporter in ten thousand who knows anywhere near as much about your business as you do. If they did, they'd have your job. But they don't. You do.

I get this all the time. When we're not in first place, they take shots at us. We don't make enough trades, we should do this, we should do that. We're not right 100 percent of the time, but our average is a lot higher than any of the sportswriters'. I can't think of one thing that any of them has ever suggested that we hadn't already considered and probably eliminated for a lot of good reasons. *So we don't panic when the press calls, and we certainly don't let them run our ballclub.* If we did, I'd have been gone long ago. We don't let the press dictate, and you shouldn't either. So what should you do?

Be a Teacher

Teach them your business and you'll get better, more positive coverage. When I started with the Celtics, none of the Boston writers knew a thing about pro basketball. But they all thought they did. Cliff Keane used to zing me all the time. He was known as "Poison Pen" Keane, with good reason. His most famous line was about a shortstop with the Red Sox who made a lot of errors. He said the guy's license plate should be E-6.

Anyway, Keane was on me constantly, claiming I couldn't beat a good college team. Until, that is, I showed him that the pro game was at a different level. I educated him. He was still tough, but not nearly as tough as he had been.

It was a long time ago, but the principle is still the same. A friend of mine in the aerospace industry, working for a big company with a lot of government contracts, was having trouble with a reporter. The guy assumed the company was cheating the government and kept slamming away. My friend did the right thing. He kept talking to the guy, kept teaching him about the industry and how government contracts and government procurement worked. Whenever the reporter would write a critical story, they'd invite him to the plant and make everybody available to talk about the situation.

That's smart. *First of all, it puts a human face on an abstract problem.* The reporter can see actual people working, people he now knows. Human nature says you're friendlier to people you know than to people you don't know. Also as the reporter learns more about a complicated subject, his reporting gets better. So assuming the company is on the up-and-up, as it was in this case, the bad publicity turns to either neutral or good publicity.

Red Sez: There are some cardinal rules you can follow as a manager dealing with the press, especially when it comes to preparation. Try to:

1. Get the information out as soon as possible.
When bad news is hidden, bad stories usually follow.
The faster you can identify a story and get it out, the better. Reporters who have to uncover the facts take a much different approach than when the information is given to them freely and completely. Sure it's tempting to sit on a story for a few days, hoping the situation will change.
But sooner or later everything will come out and it's that much worse if it looks like a cover-up.
2. Don't let your boss find out from the media what he or she should have been told by you. I found that out in my dealings with Celtics owner Walter Brown. I'd level with Walter completely and he'd end up saying something like, "Look, what's happened has happened

and we'll have to work through it.'' His message always was, ''Okay, we have a problem. Now we have to come up with a solution.'' If he had read about the problem in the papers, I don't think he would have been quite as understanding.

A friend of mine who runs a factory had to call his boss and tell him that the company had been dumping unauthorized chemicals in a local river. They called a press conference immediately, explained the situation, and outlined a plan to stop it from happening again. They also made provisions to clean up the river. So they ended up looking like a public-spirited, honest company that had made a mistake and was willing to pay for it. Imagine how much different this story would have been if a local investigative reporter had uncovered it.

3. Have all your facts ready for the press. Try to understand exactly what happened and why it happened. Then present the story as calmly as you can. Remember, an emotional delivery usually results in an emotional story. I've been known to lose my temper on occasion, but I never lost it in a press conference. Try to give straight answers but don't speculate. If reporters hit you with ''what if'' questions, don't answer them. You can never win in a conjecture game with any reporter.

4. Keep your personal opinion out of it. I'm not being quoted as Red Auerbach, private citizen. I'm Red Auerbach of the Boston Celtics. You're in the same position when you're being quoted in a story involving your company. Remember, your personal opinion may contradict your company's position.

Managers Talk, Nobody Walks

When there's a negative story about you in the paper, the tendency is to think the world just ended, that none of your friends will talk to you anymore. Forget it. Life will go on. Some managers say they'll never talk to a reporter again. Usually that's a mistake. It will just make things worse. If misinformation is part of the problem, and it usually is, how are you going to get it straightened out if you don't say anything?

The people who deal with the press will let the critical stories roll off their backs and keep talking. I've had my share of problems with Bob Ryan, the columnist for the Boston *Globe,* but I keep talking to him. I'm convinced it's done me more good than harm. And I respect his writing ability.

In the old days, guys used to buy reporters lunches and dinners and pay for travel to get good publicity. Those days are over, thank God. Now the papers and other media pay for their own people, so they'll be more objective. That's the way it should be. But there are little things companies can still do to keep good relations with the press.

We play four games a year in Hartford, where all the insurance companies are located. I was talking to one of the business writers there several years ago, and he said one of the insurance companies makes its business library available to reporters. If a writer has a question about the insurance industry, he calls and gets an answer.

Pretty damned smart. It makes the press better informed and it's unlikely that a reporter is going to be too critical of a company where he's using the library.

Red Sez: Individual managers can use similar tactics for "informing" the press. Whatever you do, strive to:

1. Show personal integrity. Would you believe a story from someone who has been known to lie? Of course you wouldn't. All your statements should be based on fact. When you give your word, keep it.

2. Be knowledgeable. Know your job and be able to pass on what you know to the people around you. If you can't answer a question, admit it. Then find the answer.

3. Be enthusiastic. The more you know about the subject, the greater your interest and enthusiasm will be. This is true whether you're talking to members of the press or your employees.

4. Stay in control. A calm voice and a steady hand are confidence builders in difficult situations. Try to speak plainly and simply, no matter what has been said or asked. Be decisive. Don't apologize or act defensive.

5. Be loyal. Back your company and your employees when they're right. Try to correct them when they're
wrong.

Damage Control

Personally, I was never big on interviews. I'd stay around the
locker room for about five minutes after each game, figuring I owed the
writers answers to any legitimate questions. Then I'd get out of there.
"Talk to the players," I'd say. "I didn't score the points. They did."
   I let most of the critical stories about the Celtics slide off my back.
I don't pay attention to them. If you start issuing denials or challenging
the accuracy of the story, you just make it worse. Forget about it and
it will die a natural death. But sometimes when a particular story is
damaging and completely wrong, I have to speak out.
   We had an example in 1990. Dave Gavitt, our director of basketball operations, and I were doing some preliminary screening for a
new coach. We were talking—just talking—to some people around the
country.
   One of the people we talked to was Mike Krzyzewski, the fine
basketball coach at Duke University. Frankly, we didn't think Mike
wanted to leave Duke, and we weren't sure it was the best move for
either him or the Celtics. But we figured that whether he wanted to
leave or not, his basketball input was always good.
   But one of the North Carolina papers went crazy. It was reported
that we offered him a job (we didn't), that it was part of a big power
struggle between Gavitt and me (it wasn't), that Gavitt was going to
resign (he wasn't), and a lot of other things. It was ridiculous, and it
could have undermined the authority of Chris Ford, who we eventually
named head coach.
   We went public. We denied every point in the story and wrote an
angry letter to the paper. Mike wrote a letter denying the story as well.
The thing finally died out, but it could have hurt us.
   As I said, most reporters are trying to do a good job. But when
you get one who is so far out of line that he or she is hurting your
business, you've got to do something. When that happens, take your
case to their boss. If you're right, 98 percent of the editors will do
something about it. They're usually trying to be fair and they don't
want some writer who isn't.

All at Once, Always

I don't think I have to tell you to tell the truth. If you don't, you're going to get killed in the press in the long run. Cover-ups have a way of becoming public blow-ups. The Patriots had a drug problem a few years ago which they tried to pretend wasn't there. They questioned the integrity of the reporter who broke the story, then tried to shut him off from any news sources. Of course, it turned out that everything he said was true. So the reporter comes out looking like a martyr and the Patriots end up with a huge credibility gap.

So the first rule is to tell the truth. But the question remains: How much truth? In other words, how much of the story do you release at once.

"Everything" is the only answer. Say you've got a bad situation that is going to reflect poorly on your company. Sometimes it can't be avoided. Let's say you run a factory like my friend and some chemicals were accidentally spilled into a nearby river. The environmentalists are raising hell and the media is sniffing blood. What do you do?

Call a press conference. Get every possible detail of the story together. I mean the history of the company, how many times this has happened before, the records of inspections, what you're going to do to prevent it from happening again, any lawsuits that are pending—the whole ball of wax.

Why? Common sense. If it's all in the paper in one day, you'll get one day's worth of bad publicity. If there are, say, five things that are bad, they'll all be in the same story. If you're lucky, it will be the same day Russia drops communism and enters a basketball team in the NBA.

But if you just release a little information, then there'll be another story the next day, and the next day, and the next day, until it's all out. Then, in addition to getting several days' worth of negative stories instead of one, you look like you're trying to hide something. You might even end up in some of those publications they sell in the supermarkets.

The Italian Connection

Of course, there are certain situations that turn into soap opera serial stories no matter what you do. We had one with Brian Shaw, a rookie who jumped to the Italian basketball league after playing a year for the Celtics.

Brian was with us in the 1988–89 season. He had a real strong rookie year. He's a six-foot-six-inch quick guard from Cal–Santa Barbara, a great penetrator, the prototype new NBA guard. We had high hopes for him.

Anyway, in the summer of 1989, while he's away at basketball camp, his agent arranges for him to sign a huge contract, almost a million dollars a year, with an Italian team. All I'll say about that move was that it was certainly in the agent's best interest. It was also a case of bad timing. I didn't get a chance to sit down with Brian. If I had, we might have avoided the whole mess. It was a screw-up all around.

We liked the kid, and never lost interest. In the next year, he indicated to us that he wanted to come back to the NBA. Fine. In January 1990, Alan N. Cohen, the Celtics' vice-chairman of the board and treasurer, went to Italy and signed him to a four-year, $5.45 million contract. We thought everything was okay.

Then before camp starts, he says he's changed his mind again and wants to go back to Italy. We like the kid, but this is getting ridiculous. So we go right to court. The judge orders him to honor his Celtics contract and fines him five thousand dollars a day until he does. Eventually, he agrees.

By this time the Boston papers were killing him, calling him greedy and a lot of other names. Brian looked bad, we looked bad. But damn it, we were right.

What could we have done differently? We should have been familiar with his situation in 1989. Maybe we could have kept him on the team. What we did right, I think, was keeping the lines of communication open and telling our side of the story as it happened. The story didn't make us look good, but it could have been a lot worse. Now I hope it's over. Brian stepped in to start in the Celtics' backcourt and we got off to a great start in 1990–91 partly because of his play.

But right now, I don't even want to see Brian going into an Italian restaurant.

No Favorites

Once you are dealing with the press, you have to be careful not to play favorites. I don't want other writers to think I'm buddy-buddy with this reporter or that one. I have a bit of a problem. One of my best friends is Will McDonough, the *Globe* columnist and NBC commentator. He's primarily a football expert but writes about everything, including basketball.

Some of the other reporters won't believe this, but the reason we've been so close for so long is that I don't give him any major scoops. This is a social and personal friendship, but as far as stories go, I try to act the same way with Will as I do with any other reporter. That way, no one can accuse me of playing favorites.

I don't do it, but there are a lot of guys who do. They get close to certain writers, go out to dinner with them, give them hints, and even feed them the whole story. I remember one time we had a league meeting in New York. Very hush-hush, very private. Then all of a sudden, the New York *Times* reported what happened at the meeting verbatim. Somebody wanted to get in good with the *Times* so he gave them a story after being pledged to secrecy. Those things happen.

When you're in business you've got to be careful about having a confidant in the media. The reason goes back to human nature. In the long run, it will cost you more than it's worth.

Infernal Internal Affairs

You can never ignore a story that can seriously hurt the morale of your company. Let me give you an example of something that happened when I was still coaching. Bob Cousy was injured just before an important road trip. All the papers asked the same question: CAN THE CELTICS WIN WITHOUT COUSY? The consensus seemed to be that we'd be lucky if we returned to Boston with one victory and our jocks intact.

Those negative stories had a very positive effect on my team. The guys really sucked it up and we went out and won every game. So how much of an impression did that make on the Boston "Knights of the Keyboard," as Ted Williams used to call them? Not much.

When we arrived back in Boston, loose and happy, one of the papers had a huge headline: WILL COUSY PLAY TONIGHT? The story went on to say how essential Cousy was to the success of the team. No mention was made of the fact that the team had risen to the occasion and won every game on the trip.

I could feel a mood swing right there at the airport. Of course,

Cousy hadn't done anything wrong, but I could feel the resentment toward him building. So I called a meeting right there at the airport.

"This story reflects the opinion of one writer who doesn't know much about basketball," I told them. "He's also not responsible for evaluating your performance and setting your salaries. I am. I know what you guys just accomplished. Cousy didn't have anything to do with that article. So let's just forget it and do what we do best—play basketball." The whole chemistry of the team could have been hurt if I hadn't acted right then.

Not that the problem ever went away completely. You see writers form their own fan clubs—there'd be pro-Heinsohn stories, pro-Ramsey stories, pro-Cousy stories. Forget the game—they were too busy writing about their heroes. They didn't know what was happening out there. So they'd write, "The Celtics streaked to another victory last night, with Ramsey scoring twenty-four and Cousy rolling up twelve assists." No one would mention that Russell dominated the boards or K. C. Jones shut down the other team's high scorer.

You see, Cousy, Heinsohn, and Ramsey were easy to interview and always made great copy. Russell and K. C. were quiet, reserved "workers" who just didn't have much to say.

I'd try to make a joke out of a lot of those stories. "Did you fellows see the paper this morning?" I'd ask. "Was that guy really at our game? He sure didn't see what I saw." Then I'd tell them about the time Webby Morse, the sports editor at the *Christian Science Monitor,* called Lynn Patrick, the Bruins' coach, and told him he was sending a young writer over who had never seen a hockey game before. Webby asked Lynn if he'd teach the kid a few of the basics. So Lynn spent several hours with the kid, explaining things like offsides, icing, and penalties. *Within two weeks, the kid was writing stories criticizing Lynn's line changes.*

No matter what I did, I couldn't head off a strain on the relationship between Cousy and Russell. At one time they were very buddy-buddy. Russ even used to go to Cooz's basketball camp. Cousy kept getting a tremendous amount of publicity, while the papers never played up Russell, even though I always went out of my way to point out the things he was doing. Bill had a great respect for Cousy as a passer, a playmaker, a fast-break guy, and Cooz had an equal amount of respect for the things Bill could do. The problem wasn't that they were mad at one another or that they stopped talking. Their social relationship just cooled off. I'll always feel that rift was a direct result of reporters writing authoritatively about a game—and its players—that they really didn't understand.

No Deep Throats

I had only one rule regarding the press, and I was very tough on this. Certain reporters would cater to certain players, hoping to develop a pipeline into the team. This still goes on today. Whenever I'd find out who the player was who kept feeding the writer little scoops, I'd call him into my office.

"You want to be buddy-buddy with him? Keep it up and you'll have him paying your salary instead of me, because you won't be here. Let's get one thing clear. You are part of the team. The next time we have a team meeting and something leaks out, it's going to be your ass. I don't give a damn who you are or how important you think you are to this ballclub. You're not going to air your grievances with the press or be a stooge for anybody. No way. This is a team and we stick together. Have I made myself clear?"

That would usually end the problem.

Getting the Bad News

Of course, you have to get the bad news before you can give it. Some coaches—and managers—complain that they're the last to know about what's going on. A big story breaks, a lot of people are in trouble, and they don't know anything about it. The sad thing is that many of them are telling the truth—no one gave them the bad news. Their argument is that they shouldn't be held responsible for something over which they had no control.

Why didn't they know? Usually there's one reason why players or employees are reluctant to bring bad news to the coach or the boss: They're afraid of the reception they're going to get. Try to put yourself in the shoes of one of your employees with a big problem. Maybe he's not going to make the deadline for an important assignment. He knows that there are going to be serious consequences if he doesn't speak up. So what does he do? The answer depends on you. How do you accept bad news from the people who work for you? If you rant and rave, your chances of getting bad news early, while there's still time to do something about it, aren't very good.

Red Sez: I learned early in my coaching career that if my players got the impression that I didn't want to hear negatives, I wouldn't. Here's what I used to do to make sure I got the bad news before it hit the newspapers:

1. Be accessible. This means giving the employee my full attention even if it means dropping something else. If the problem is major, obviously I'd stick to it until it's solved. If it's not, I might be able to postpone action for a while. But I would never put the person off with a statement like "I'll get back to you." If I delay getting back to them, I give them the impression that I don't care. So they simply won't tell me if another problem develops

2. Reward the messenger. It's difficult to bring bad news to the boss, especially when you might be the cause of the problem. That's why I always made a point of trying to reward people for bringing me the bad news. It could be something as simple as saying, "Thanks for calling that to my attention. I know it took a lot of guts to do it."

3. Ask for solutions. It's important to ask for solutions, because obviously the employee has given the problem a lot of thought. I would always ask, "What are your ideas? What alternatives do you think we have?" Whenever players or employees come to me with problems, they always know they'll be involved in the possible solution.

4. Turn setbacks into learning experiences. I always asked an employee to critique his or her behavior that led to the problem in the first place. What could have been done differently to prevent the problem? What have you learned from this experience?

CHAPTER 9

People to People: The Business Issues of Drugs, Burnout, and Brotherhood

THREE OF THE BIGGEST PEOPLE PROBLEMS for managers today—from both a personal and an organizational standpoint—are drug abuse, stress on the job, and race discrimination. When you add the external pressures of these problems to daily dilemmas that arise from normal operations, you've got the makings of major disasters.

No one has sure-cure answers to these problems, least of all me. But as you might have guessed, I do have some opinions on these matters.

The Disaster of Drugs

Nobody has to explain to me about what drug abuse can do to an organization. I know. The Boston Celtics had been lucky. We hadn't had the kinds of problems with drugs that plagued a few other NBA teams. That all changed one night. June 19, 1986. I'll never forget it. Larry Bird called it the cruelest thing he ever heard of.

He was talking about the death of Len Bias.

We had won the NBA title the previous season with a veteran team, but we knew we had to start building for the future. If there was one weakness we had, at least one point of vulnerability, it was team speed. The Lakers gave us fits with Michael Cooper, Magic Johnson, and

James Worthy. If we were to continue to contend for the championship, we had to match that kind of speed, or at least get close to it.

Through some luck, some dealing, and some plain hard work, we got the number two draft choice in 1986. This was a big deal for us. We just didn't get too many picks that high, ever. The kid I wanted was Bias, a six-foot-eight-inch forward from the University of Maryland.

Bias was very fast, a great, pogo-stick leaper with a marvelous soft shooting touch. He could play in traffic, and proved it one night when he got thirty points to lead Maryland to a major upset of Villanova, even though Villanova was sagging all over him. He had been at my basketball camp the year before, and Bird agreed that the Celtics would be set for a number of years if there were some way of getting him.

Double Disaster

His skills weren't everything. He was also a good kid. He came from a nice family. He liked to draw. He was a little flamboyant, but mostly he was down-to-earth. We tested him for drugs two weeks before the tragedy. He was clean. The Knicks examined him, he was clean. Golden State examined him, he was clean.

But, damn it, he had this friend from the old neighborhood who drove an expensive car and never seemed to have a job. He was one of those damnable leeches who hung around the team and dealt drugs. Lenny couldn't—or wouldn't—shake this guy.

Two nights after the draft, they're having a party, because Lenny was so happy to have been drafted by the Celtics. They apparently had some high-grade cocaine, and Lenny's body couldn't handle it. His heart failed and in a couple of hours, he was dead.

This obviously was a great tragedy for his family, and his family has always been my first concern. I see his mother, Lonice, going around, speaking out against drugs, and my heart goes out to her.

But since we're talking here about the effects of drugs on business, let's take a look at what this drug disaster did to the Boston Celtics.

I lost a key man for the team's future. I didn't get the front-court speed I needed to compete with the Lakers. And I still haven't, at least not the way I would have liked. At the same time, my team has been too strong to get another number two draft pick. Only four years later did we start to get the speed on the court we needed to beat teams like Los Angeles and Detroit.

There's no getting around it. Drugs dealt a serious blow to one of the best organizations in professional sports. We were victims, not as much as his family, but victims nevertheless.

Drug Homework

We thought we had done our "drug homework" in this case, but it didn't get us to the head of the class. As a manager you'd better be ultraperceptive in these matters. Beyond testing, there are some telltale signs to be on the lookout for.

Of course, Len Bias wasn't under our direct supervision when he took that fatal dose of cocaine. What's surprising to me is that so many managers are not even aware that employees are taking drugs until there is a serious accident or a person turns himself in as an addict.

I'm told that some of these people go to their cars or lockers during breaks to get drugs. Pushers have been arrested in parking lots, yet many managers remain oblivious to what's going on. Either that or they simply don't want to get involved.

These are usually the same managers who look the other way when an employee starts to develop a drinking problem. A guy starts coming in late, or missing days after a tough night—bloodshot eyes, trembling hands, poor job performance—all the signs are there but the manager does nothing. Maybe he thinks he's doing the guy a favor. So a year later, an employee with a serious drinking problem has to be fired. Some favor.

The same signals are there for drug problems. All the testing in the world isn't as effective as one manager doing his job well. Who's in a better position to spot the signals early, to take action before an employee gets seriously hooked? When can a manager reasonably suspect that an employee is using drugs? Here are some reliable early warning signals:

1. Physical symptoms, such as glassy, bloodshot eyes, slurred speech, erratic behavior.

2. Abrupt changes in performance level, absenteeism, lateness, poor judgment, memory lapses.

3. Off-the-job arrests, convictions, investigations for drug-related offenses.

Business Victims

Most companies don't have a case as dramatic as the Len Bias incident, although many have lost employees to drugs. But dramatic or not, drugs are hurting your company. Just look at the numbers. The government says that there are twelve million regular marijuana users and three million or more regular cocaine users in this country. Here's the kicker. Of those users, 70 percent are employed. That means that there are almost eleven million drug users in the work force. If you don't think some of them are working for you, you're dreaming.

I've never been able to understand the ambivalence some executives have about drugs. Some of them say they don't want to interfere with what their employees do on their own time. Boy are they missing the point.

The U.S. Chamber of Commerce did a survey of drug users seeking help and came up with some interesting statistics. Three out of four of those admitting to the problem said they had actually taken drugs right on the job. Almost half of them said they had sold drugs to other employees, and about a fifth supported their habit by stealing from their employer and other employees.

That's not all. Employees with drug problems have higher absenteeism rates, produce lower-quality work, get involved in more accidents, and create higher worker's compensation and medical insurance rates. They certainly don't do much for the company's image, and they hurt morale throughout the company.

The numbers go on and on. One estimate says the drug problem costs industry $184 billion a year. A major telecommunications company estimates that 40 percent of its health-care costs are attributed to substance abuse. Roger Smith, former head of General Motors, said drugs cost his company $1 billion a year. GM has had hundreds of employees arrested for drug-related crimes. And it's not alone.

Enlisting in the War

Damn it, when are we going to start fighting back? There's supposed to be a war on drugs in this country. *Why doesn't somebody declare martial law? You know where I'd start? Random drug testing in the workplace.*

Most states allow preemployment drug testing. Fine. Most allow testing if there is a reasonable suspicion of drug use. As far as random testing goes, it is mostly limited to certain public-safety jobs, such as pilots or bus drivers.

This is crazy. What's the difference between a bus driver and the individual who drives his or her car to work and then starts operating machinery? Aren't the other drivers on the road or the employees on the job at risk if that employee is using drugs?

I don't even completely agree with the position the NBA takes about drugs, although it is a step in the right direction. As of now, a player with a drug problem can turn himself in and he'll continue to get his salary while he goes through treatment. If he turns himself in a second time, he'll be treated again, with counseling and medical treatment, but this time he won't be paid.

If a two-time loser doesn't come forward, but his team has a reasonable suspicion that he's using drugs, it can contact an independent drug expert. If the expert agrees, he can authorize a urine test of that player. If the player refuses to test or fails to pass it, he supposedly is banned for life. I say supposedly, because these lifetime bans can be appealed after two drug-free years.

Turn Up the Heat

This is a good policy. It just doesn't go far enough. Don't get me wrong. If a guy turns himself in, that's great. I'm in favor of doing whatever can be done to help him beat the habit. *But beyond that, I'm in favor of random testing of everybody. Players, coaches, employees, managers, and, yes, even company presidents.*

Our athletes are especially vulnerable to the weasels who push drugs, as the Len Bias incident showed. It starts in high school and college. There's always some guy who's got a fancy car, who is arranging parties, who knows women. They're after the athletes with the names. Maybe it will start with alcohol, but then the hard drugs come out. These drug dealers love to hook a name athlete. I guess they feel it helps their image. Most of these young athletes, many of whom have been pampered because of their athletic abilities, can't handle this. And they don't.

Once they get on the stuff, they don't respond to "just say no" or anything like that. The only thing they respond to at this point is fear.

Fear, period. At least, that's what John Drew, a former NBA player, told me. I think he's right. John was a very talented player who admitted to his addiction and got help. He said the only thing a junkie respects is the fear that he'll run out of drugs, or the fear that he won't have enough money to buy more drugs.

Fear as a Factor

So, okay, use that fear. Give them the fear that their primary source of income will be shut off if they use drugs. I think this will prompt many of the users—and I'm sure there are some who've managed to avoid detection right on your payroll now—to come forward and get help. Fine, we'll help them. Those who don't come forward should be banned, although I'd let them reapply after they've come clean.

If we tried this in the NBA, I'm sure the players' association would shout "invasion of privacy." That's wrong! This game, which has been very good to all of us, relies on public trust. If a guy has a drug problem, here's what might happen. He could get hooked up with gamblers who might suggest he start manipulating games in return for drugs. Pathetic, but it could happen. And if it does, the goose that laid the golden egg will be dead. If the public starts thinking the NBA or any other sport isn't on the up-and-up, we might as well give the balls away and close the gyms. We're finished.

I realize, believe me, that private industry is somewhat different from professional basketball. I know it's harder for you to fire or even discipline someone than it is for me. But that doesn't mean that you should give up on the goal of a drug-free workplace. A few states have taken positive steps to make sure random drug testing policies are both fair and legal. These steps include:

1. Fair and accurate tests. Obviously, testing is only as good as the test itself. Extremely accurate testing procedures are available now.

2. A written policy. This way each employee knows what the score is and there won't be any surprises if it's violated. Most employees aren't drug abusers and they won't object.

3. A mandatory treatment program. If you thought

enough of someone to hire him, you will want to do everything you can to help. There are agencies in every city today that offer treatment programs.

4. No firing for the first offense. Some people are going to help themselves. Let them. Look at what John Drew has accomplished.

Other Weapons in the War

Look what happened in the U.S. Navy. In 1980, the Navy took a survey of young enlisted people and the outcome was shocking. It showed 48 percent of the sailors had used illegal drugs in the month before the test.

The Navy put in a ten-point system, including random testing, and cut that 48 percent figure to less than 5 percent. Interestingly, one thing the Navy did was increase its emphasis on physical fitness. This is something I've always believed in. Fitness and drug abuse are opposites, they contradict each other. *Companies that send a message to employees that fitness is a positive goal tend to be the companies with fewer substance-abuse problems.*

It's common sense. People who are jogging or playing racquetball on their lunch hour aren't going to be using drugs. Progressive companies now provide gyms, showers, and genuine encouragement to their workers to get in shape. These companies aren't stupid. They are making money on this type of program. The Navy estimates that it saves thirteen dollars for every dollar invested in antidrug programs.

Red Sez: If your company doesn't have a formal wellness program, get the ball rolling yourself with some moves like:

1. Checking with your local YM-YWCA, high school, or any of the health clubs for weight reduction programs, aerobic and exercise programs, and smoking cessation programs. I read recently that smokers cost employers about four thousand dollars more per year than nonsmokers. No, I'm not a hypocrite. Remember, my smoking is limited to cigars. Even today, I still play a pretty good game of racquetball and tennis.

2. Rewarding employees who maintain healthy life-styles or reach fitness goals with gifts or cash prizes. For instance, employees who reach their weight goal or quit smoking may be given sporting goods such as athletic shoes, gym bags, or Boston Celtics warm-up jackets.

3. Encouraging employees to have health-risk appraisals, such as glucose testing, mammograms, and blood cholesterol work. Just being able to catch health problems before they become major illnesses is effective from a cost-savings standpoint.

4. Recognizing that employees will be able to achieve their personal best on or off the job through nutrition, exercise, and a healthy life-style. An out-of-shape worker can be just as much of a liability as an out-of-shape athlete. Both are going to have lower production, decreased quality, and will seriously hurt team performance.

Organizations such as the Institute for a Drug-Free Workplace in Washington, DC, are valuable sources for strategies in this war against drugs. It's a war we have to win. We must do it, in memory of Len Bias and the thousands of other youngsters who've been murdered by drugs, the thousands of employees who have been hamstrung by drugs. So let's ignore this argument that random drug testing hurts anyone's privacy. I say that most of the people who use this invasion of privacy argument are trying to hide something. I'll be glad to roll up my sleeves to get a national random drug testing program under way.

The "Other" Drug

Until now, we've been talking about hard drugs. Alcohol abuse is still the biggest drug problem industry faces, but it's a different problem. Alcohol is legal and has a level of social acceptability that hard drugs don't have, and hopefully never will.

Legal or not, alcohol remains a major problem. I think the best thing you can do is set a good example. In other words, establish a consistent policy that discourages alcohol abuse and then follow that policy every time.

You've read the story about Arnie Risen, and the day on a train he ordered a cocktail. I sent my no-cocktails message through the trainer, because I didn't want to berate the guy for violating a rule he didn't know about. But at the same time, I needed to get the message across. I wanted a team that looked like champions. I didn't want an overgrown college frat party.

I felt that way then, and I feel that way now.

Red Sez: Getting the message across is important. Early in my career I learned that most messages don't get through because of listening problems. Either the person I was giving the message to didn't listen properly or I was so intent on what I was saying that I didn't hear the clues that would have told me about the misunderstanding.

I honestly think that contributed to my problems with Ben Kerner and the St. Louis Hawks. When I joined the Celtics, I vowed that I would become a good listener.

There are two very good reasons why every good manager should try to improve his or her listening skills. The first is that becoming a better listener will mean fewer misunderstandings. The second is that good listeners have less stress because they force themselves to slow down and think about what is being said.

How good a listener are you right now? The average manager would probably rate himself good to excellent. But if those assessments were accurate, we wouldn't have all the employment lawsuits and productivity or quality-control problems that are the direct result of poor communications. There are lots of "listening techniques" to try, but remember:

> • Try to ask questions appropriate to what the other person is saying. Don't ask questions that simply change the subject. You'll move the conversation away from the area being discussed and both of you will end up confused.
> • Even if you disagree with a statement, try to keep your response in check. I didn't always do this, particularly when dealing with agents, and sometimes I think it cost me. Now when I disagree with something a person says, I let them know about it without making it sound

like a put-down. So try to take a few deep breaths to relieve the tension before you open your mouth.

• Try to make the best of a no-win situation. During
the 1976 season, Dave Cowens, our great center, asked
for a no-pay leave of absence. Now, we needed Dave on
that team, but when he told me the ''fire'' wasn't there, I
let him go. Sure, I could have argued about contracts and
commitments, but it wouldn't have mattered in the long
run. So we lost Dave for thirty games, while he drove a
cab in Boston and got his act together. But he came back
to us. If I hadn't listened to him, I might have lost him to
the taxi industry forever.

• Keep your temper in check. Sometimes you have
to listen to a person who has come into your office angry.
Or maybe you have to discipline someone or deliver a
bad performance review. All the ingredients are there for
a real confrontation. Actually, this is the best test of a
good managerial listener. If you lose your temper, you
lose, period. Rationality goes out the window, you both
end up saying things you don't mean or that have nothing
to do with the original problem, and feelings get hurt.

Leading by Example

I've never been much of a drinker myself. I'll have a social drink
once in a while, but that's pretty much it. When I was coaching, I
never took a drink on the day of a game. I didn't want to walk into the
locker room and have the players even suspect that I'd been drinking.
That would have been a disaster.

Anytime an employee thinks a manager has been drinking, there's
an immediate loss of respect. The employee thinks of ways to humor
the manager, but probably won't pay much attention to what the manager says.

To this day, I won't drink on the day our team is playing. *I want
to send a message that when we go to work, we go to work in the best
shape we can be in.* The best shape is not to be impaired by alcohol or
any other drug.

I think that's the message you've got to send to the people in your company. I could never understand the companies that say they're against alcohol abuse, then allow middle- or upper-level managers to drink at lunchtime. Are they crazy?

What kind of message does that send? These people come back from lunch smelling of booze and they're going to manage? Some of them can barely manage to keep their eyes open. Or how about the company that claims it's against alcohol abuse, but puts out plenty of alcohol at the company picnic or the Christmas party? Quite a mixed message, isn't it? You're not supposed to drink, but it's okay to get sloshed at the company picnic or holiday event. It doesn't make sense.

Just as with hard drugs, the costs of alcohol abuse in lost time, medical claims, poor production, accidents, and everything else are staggering. Drunks aren't funny—they're major liabilities.

Progressive companies make employee assistance, treatment facilities, and organizations such as Alcoholics Anonymous available to workers. What's happening now, with the public attitude toward drinking, with the beer companies telling people to watch themselves, to "know when to say when," is good. You can drink and drive— unfortunately—but you can't drink and run ten miles or play an hour of basketball.

For managers, the best thing you can do is to set an example, and create an atmosphere where alcohol abuse is unacceptable. Then keep that atmosphere in place. No exceptions.

Putting the Damper on Burnout

One thing I've always wondered about burnout: Was there less of it before someone invented the term?

I don't know the answer to that, but I know burnout exists, and I have a couple of ideas why. It has to do with repetition, boredom, and overmanaging.

Why do so many coaches in every sport, at every level, get fired after five or six years? A lot of them are average or even good coaches, but suddenly they have one or two bad years and they get fired. Why is that?

All of a sudden they don't know the game, they can't motivate the players? That's nonsense. To me, they get fired for one reason. *They didn't change with the times.* People say a generation in life is twenty years. A generation for coaches is six years. So they have to adjust their coaching styles accordingly.

The people who are coaching don't always see that. They won't accept, or even realize, that there are changes in the players every six years or so. Whether it's the type of haircuts they want, the amount of money they get, the sort of contracts with the no-cuts and all that kind of stuff, if a coach doesn't understand his new players, they're going to get turned off. If he doesn't change his approach to his veterans, they're. going to get bored.

Red Sez: The same holds true for managers, although my six-year theory may not be so exact. But the need for change certainly is there. Just how flexible is your management style? Consider these factors for improving it:

1. Consult with your employees about decisions that will affect them. I always made it a point to talk to my players about possible trades or acquisitions. Nothing is worse than being left in the dark about changes that can affect a person's livelihood. Like the time John Y. Brown traded three draft choices for Bob McAdoo. I promised myself that I would never put myself in that position.

2. Encourage your employees to develop themselves. I could have spent every practice screaming about boxing out or getting back on defense or any of the basic fundamentals that good teams must have. But I didn't for several reasons. First of all the players would have gotten tired of the sound of my voice and tuned me out. Second, they might never accept the responsibility for developing and applying those fundamentals themselves.

3. Establish goals and performance standards jointly with your employees. Make sure you both have a clear idea of what's expected and when.

4. Recognize a job well done. We all need a pat on the back when we do a good job. Sometimes, it's the little things no one else notices that can be most effective. In basketball terms, this could be a nice pick or blockout that leads to an important score. Look around your department for the nonglamorous jobs that have to be done but which usually result in very little recognition. Let those people know that you appreciate their efforts.

5. Be empathic. That doesn't mean that you have to

agree with everything the employee says. It does mean that you really have to listen and show that you understand the employee's position.

Attacking the Syndrome

When I was coaching, I ran my practices differently than most of the other guys. They used to run two practices a day, then have long meetings, then have players look at films.

I don't think all this time accomplished much. When it was too long, players got bored. It wasn't fun, and it was that much harder to get them up the next time. And going to boring, repetitive practices day after day leads to burnout as quickly as anything I know.

I believed, and still believe, I could get more done in one good forty-five-minute practice than I could in two two-hour practices. I had to motivate these guys to play eighty-two games. That's where I wanted their best efforts, every time. But I knew they couldn't keep the same level of intensity in practice. I used practice to get them ready to give this effort, not to spend themselves on the gym floor.

My players knew I wasn't going to keep them for longer than I had to, so they were attentive. They knew we needed to get down to work and get out of there. We'd start with warm-ups, such as a three-man drill, then do a long-pass drill, something you have to practice. Then we'd go to a scrimmage.

"Practicing" Discipline

I had one very important rule regarding practices. When I came through the doorway and walked onto the court and blew my whistle, I didn't want to hear another sound. I didn't want to hear any balls bouncing, any shots being taken, not even any laughing and joking. I wanted immediate attention. They were to stop whatever they were doing and come over and gather in a semicircle around me. And I didn't want anybody sitting down on a basketball or stretching out in some crazy position. I wanted them to stand there, shut up, and listen to me.

If they didn't do it, we had problems. One day I came out to start a practice at the Cambridge Y and nothing went right. Everybody seemed to be loafing, especially Bill Russell. So after about ten minutes, I blew my whistle and said, "All right, everybody out of here! Get downstairs and get dressed. I don't want to see another shot taken. Now go!"

For three days I never said a word about it. I kept them wondering what I was going to do. So I did nothing. Absolutely nothing. If it wasn't there, it wasn't there. They just didn't feel like practicing that day. Then we met for another practice, the first one since I kicked them out of the gym three days earlier.

"Gentlemen," I began, "we will not discuss what happened the other day. All I want is a good, tough practice today. Now let's get started."

Right away Russell starts giving me false hustle again.

So I blew the whistle.

"You destroyed practice the other day but you're not going to destroy this one," I yelled at him. "I'm going to get four cigars and go up there and sit in those seats and we're going to stay here until I see a good twenty-minute scrimmage."

They started to play and after about eight minutes I had to laugh. I walked back down, blew my whistle again, and then said a dumb thing. "I didn't mean for you to play that hard," I said to Russell. He wouldn't give anybody a shot within eighteen feet of the basket. Nobody. He'd block the shot, get the rebound, throw the pass, beat Conley to the other end, stuff the ball, run back on defense, and start all over again. It was like his best playoff game ever!

I knew that if I didn't stop him right away, he was going to leave his next ball game right there in the YMCA. So I tried to make a joke out of it. "Russell, you give me a coach's dilemma. I want you to hustle and play hard so we can get our timing down. What happens? You screw around and nobody can get anything done. Then you get mad at me, tear up the practice, and ruin it the other way. You're making my job tough. Can't you just give me a happy medium?"

In Bill's defense, he had the type of skills that really couldn't be practiced. Plus we knew he was going to give us forty-eight minutes of playing his guts out during the games. But every once in a while, I'd really get on him. "When the rest of these guys see you loafing, they want to loaf, too. You're ruining it for everybody. Now start moving." He'd stand there and give me that famous Russell look, but in all of our years together, he never once answered me back.

Practice Makes Perfect

Now, I didn't just scrimmage. I scrimmaged with a purpose. I wanted to put in a new pattern or a new play. I'd speak in a soft, slow manner, explaining what I wanted to do. I'd ask if there were any questions.

Communication is everything. *It's not what you say, it's what they hear.* I wanted them to hear, "Do it, concentrate, get it right, get out." Same goes for your employees. So I kept practices tight and focused, but I also tried to make them interesting.

At least 95 percent of the time, when I scrimmaged I simulated game conditions. "Green team, thirty seconds left, ball at half court," or something like that. I tried to recreate every game situation I could. I wanted my teams prepared for anything, and I think they were. I was amazed at how few coaches took this approach to practice. For athletes already well-conditioned, what's the point of running laps around the gym?

A distance-running coach was telling me the other day about marathon training and how the theory is to make runners do one long run a week rather than a lot of short ones. Why? Because what they are training for is a long run. Game conditions. It makes sense, and it cuts down the boredom that leads to burnout.

Sometimes, to make it interesting, I'd play with different combinations, different players at different positions. The players, at least most of them, would imagine they were in a real game and did what they had to do to succeed. Plus they had the incentive of a shower when they did it right. I believe in incentives; it's amazing what a small bonus will do to get people motivated.

Game Conditions at Work

I know I was working with only twelve players who were well motivated to begin with, and that business is a little different. But keep the general principles in mind when you consider your own situation.

Are you wasting time in pointless meetings or training programs that don't approximate "game conditions"?

Are you doing everything you can to make it interesting? The way to do this most of the time is to challenge people. If they are plodding along in the same job, making the same decisions and dealing with the same people, they may be getting stale.

Shuffle the cards. See if a salesman would like to get into marketing. See if a secretary wants to try personnel work. The people may find it a challenge, a chance to learn, and it works to your benefit in another way.

The more cross-training you can do, the better prepared you are when you suffer an unexpected personnel loss. You've already trained someone for the job you need to fill.

If you can make it interesting, if you can keep challenging your people, if you communicate—tell them what it is you're trying to do—chances are you won't have a major burnout problem, or suffer one yourself.

Personal Burnout

So many coaches in the NBA tell me—maybe *boast* is a better word—about how many waking hours they spend coaching, watching film, making calls, and so on. It's like a macho thing. If they're not working eighteen hours a day, they're wimps.

What bull. It's a pressure-packed job, but that's no way to approach it. Someone working a hundred hours a week isn't going to be any good over the long haul. Even if they're on their feet, they aren't going to be thinking clearly.

Ambition is good as long as it's in check, tempered by reasonableness. I always make sure I have a life outside basketball. I go to plays or movies on the road, spend time with my wife Dot and my two daughters whenever I can. The job can't be your whole life.

Think about it. If all you've got is your job, and something goes wrong, what else have you got to fall back on? What's going to help you through the problem? It doesn't make sense, and it isn't good for your company. I'll take a person any day who's got a family, who spends time with the kids, who visits schools and talks to other parents. Because this is an individual who is in touch with reality, who knows how to interact in public. This is the person who can sense what the public wants. In other words, this is a valuable employee.

Red Sez: Here are a couple of other job-specific moves you can make to avoid personal burnout as a manager:

1. Be visible. A lot of managers become invisible because of work pressures. They bury themselves under computer printouts and, as time pressures mount, they see less and less of the people they are supposed to be supervising. As they become more isolated, they lose the ability to manage effectively. The best way to fight this problem is to make it a point to walk around your department every day. Let your employees know that they can always see you about any problem at any time.

2. Criticize with care. The purpose of criticism is to get improved performance, not necessarily to hurt someone in reference to past performance. For instance, I never criticized a player who missed a shot in the last second of a ball game that resulted in a loss. Now if he had ignored my instructions or used poor shot selection, I would have let him know about it. I always tried to criticize the person's behavior, not the person. Sometimes I even got my message across by criticizing the wrong person. One night I took a peek at Wayne Embry and then yelled to trainer Joe DeLauri, "Damn it, Joe, you're letting Embry get fat again." Wayne got the message.

3. If you offer an open-door policy, live up to it. Nothing turns players or employees off faster than a manager who says he wants their suggestions or complaints, then fails to listen to or act on them. There's a famous story around Boston about the president of a supermarket chain who announced that every Friday afternoon he would be available to anyone who had a complaint or suggestion. One of the employees went to him one Friday afternoon with an idea as to how the company could be run better. If the president accepted the idea, the guy never knew about it, because he got fired the following Monday.

4. Don't let an open-door policy undermine the authority of your own managers and supervisors. It's one thing to make yourself accessible to employees. But you should never give them the impression that they can simply go over their supervisors' heads to get something from you that they couldn't get from them.

Contract Contretemps

Let me give you an example. Walter Brown was the greatest Celtics owner in the history of the franchise. But the fact that he was so accessible to everyone created a lot of problems for me. Anyone could just walk in, sit down, and gain his ear, including my friends in the press, who never got over that Cousy thing. So they'd walk in and say something like, "Well, I see you've lost four in a row. Shades of the old Celtics!" That would stir Walter up and create some minor problems for me. But nothing I couldn't handle.

The real trouble started when Walter let himself get involved with salary decisions. For instance, when Gene Conley asked for a tryout with the Celtics in 1958, I was dubious. So I wouldn't even pay his travel expenses to the gym. But after watching him for a short time, it was obvious he could still play the game. All we had to do was work out a contract.

Before I even got around to discussing money, Gene stopped by to see Walter. Their conversation got around to money, naturally.

Walter came up with the worst question that anyone can ask a professional athlete: "What do you want for a salary?"

"How about twenty thousand dollars?" Gene asked.

"You've got it," Walter said.

Not even the stars were making that kind of money in those days. But by the time I heard about it, the damage had been done. So I had to cut Gene a few weeks later, then hire him back a few days after that for half that requested salary. There wasn't any resentment on Gene's part, because he knew he wasn't worth that kind of dough. It was just another case of Walter trying to look like Santa Claus and Auerbach having to act like Scrooge.

Walter and I had most of our confrontations over contract negotiations. He was in love with his players and dealt in emotions rather than hard business facts. He wanted to make decisions, and yet he realized he didn't know enough about the game. So he'd talk with me about the club and we'd go over the contracts together. Then he'd get to talking to one of the guys and his heart would take over. He'd figure, Red wants to pay this man ten thousand dollars so if I pay him fifteen thousand and make a mistake, I'm really blowing just five grand.

The ballplayers were no dummies. They'd wait until I left town, then get good old Walter out on the golf course. It happened all the time. Then I'd get back to my office, expecting to resume salary discussions with somebody, and Walter would come in and say, "Gee, Red, I just did something and I know it was wrong." He never had to tell me what it was that he did.

Finally I brought it to a showdown. "Walter," I said, "this is ridiculous. Every time a ballplayer has a little bit of trouble getting something from me, you step in and give him whatever he wants. Now, besides ruining everything I'm trying to accomplish with this club, you're also making me look stupid. So let's have an understanding. Either I sign all of them, or I sign none of them!"

He said, "You're right, Red. I'll keep my big nose out of it from now on."

We never completely solved that problem, because right up till the day he died, Walter loved the Celtics much more than he could afford to love them.

Stressed Out on Stress

Just before the 1965 playoffs started, I picked up a paper and saw a picture of myself. It kind of shocked me. My God, I thought, do I look that bad? I had a dead cigar stub in my mouth, bags under my eyes, and a look of complete exhaustion on my face.

Until that moment I hadn't fully realized what I had been doing to myself. That was the year Walter Brown died. I was general manager, coach, scout, everything. I worried about the team's transportation, I ran the front office, I sat in on all of the NBA's board of governors meetings, I negotiated our lease with the Garden, I supervised ticket sales, I worked out the deals for radio and TV coverage, and I kept as many speaking dates as my schedule would allow. Emotionally and physically, I was drained.

About that time I got a phone call from Frank Ramsey, who had retired in 1964 and moved back to Kentucky. "Red," he said, "there's no way you can continue this. You're going to kill yourself. Something's got to give. So, look, if you ever need me for anything—if I can help and carry that load for a while—you put in a call to my home and I'll be right up to do whatever I can."

Frank was right. I was going to hurt myself. Even if I didn't, I was going to hurt the ballclub. And that was even worse.

Beginning of the End

I decided right then and there that the following year would be my last one as coach. About that time, I also decided that I'd better start doing something that I had never done before—delegate. When I told Walter Brown that I wanted complete control of the team in 1950, I meant just that, but I had Walter around. Now Walter was gone, the league was expanding, and a lot of our newer fans were wondering where I ever got that name "Red."

Delegating my coaching job to Bill Russell was easy. There wasn't any question that he was the best person for the job. A lot of the Boston press predicted that I'd never be able to keep my hands completely off the coaching reins. But I never interfered with Bill or any of my other players who coached the Celtics, including Tom Heinsohn, Satch Sanders, Dave Cowens, K. C. Jones, and Chris Ford.

I can't say that I agreed with everything they did. Russell relaxed the dress code that I had enforced all those years. And he didn't practice any harder as a coach than he did as a player.

But once I was relieved of the everyday coaching duties, I had more time to be general manager. I traded Mel Counts to Baltimore for Bailey Howell and got Wayne Embry for cash and a draft choice. I wasn't just dealing for something to do. Sharman, Cousy, Heinsohn, Loscutoff, and Ramsey were all retired; Sam Jones was thirty-four, K. C. Jones was thirty-five, and Bill Russell was thirty-three.

I'm not going to say that I was never tempted to return to the bench. But whenever the urge hit me, I'd take a good look at that 1966 photograph and forget it. You didn't have to be a psychologist to see the stress written all over it—and me.

Recognizing Stress Situations

Stress can hurt you in many ways. It can even be a killer in certain circumstances. Here are some leading causes of job-related stress to be aware and beware of:

1. Exorbitant work loads. This was my problem in 1965. I had to do more than I could possibly do, no mat-

ter how hard I worked. There's nothing more frustrating than steadily slipping behind in your work, knowing there is nothing you can do to correct it. If this is your problem, do something about it while you can. Get help.

2. The job. Being a professional coach is a stressful job in itself. A coach may have to deal with temperamental players, interfering owners, fickle fans, incompetent referees day in and day out. Maybe that's why as I write this, there are only two coaches—Lenny Wilkins of Cleveland and Chuck Daly of Detroit—who have been with the same team for as long as four years. Many jobs in industry are so stressful. Take an air traffic controller who has to make instant decisions where there is no margin for error. Or how would you like to work at the return desk of a department store after the Christmas season?

3. Time pressures and deadlines. Any professional coach of any team has to handle these two leading causes of stress. Granted some do it better than others. Managers also have to be able to function when they are under pressure to get an order out or meet a deadline. There are always going to be times when the best schedules are going to be changed for a rush order. Just make sure you're not creating artificial time pressure by refusing to make or delaying decisions.

4. Information overload. Information is the lifeblood of any manager's job. Not having enough of it can force a manager into shaky decisions that create stress. But having too much information can also lead to stress, because it forces a manager to delay or postpone a decision while he weighs all the alternatives.

5. Role ambiguity. When employees or managers don't have a clear understanding of their responsibilities and duties, they get placed in stressful situations.

6. Underachieving. A manager who's placed in a job that makes only minimal demands on personal abilities is heading for problems. The frustration of having little to do or accomplish produces real stress.

7. Job insecurity. This is a built-in kind of stress for certain jobs, such as professional sports, advertising agencies, or the entertainment industry. High pay is supposed to make this kind of stress easier to deal with, but it

doesn't always work that way. Defense cutbacks and a slowdown in the economy have forced many companies to lay off employees in industries that had always been considered secure. Uncertainty over whether an individual will even have a job next month or next year is a major stress factor over which the manager has little control.

Developing a Stress Management Program

If you take a close look at the leading causes of stress, you'll see that they are either external or internal. The exterior causes are easier to pin down. For instance, if your work load is too heavy or you're being buried by a mountain of unnecessary paperwork, you can recognize it fairly easily and plan to do something about it. If the job itself is creating the stress, you should consider a transfer or career change. A lot of good coaches have retired or moved into management because they can't handle the stress any longer.

Internal stress is a lot harder to identify. This is where the "type A" and "type B" personalities come into play. I'm not a doctor, but you don't have to be a medical person to understand the difference between the personalities.

Type A's are aggressive, dedicated to achieving more in less and less time, extremely competitive, and likely to set unrealistic deadlines. They are also more achievement oriented in terms of dollars or awards. Type A's are outwardly confident, but usually have to hide a sense of insecurity. They are also more likely to develop heart disease at an early age.

You don't have to be a brain surgeon to describe type B's. They are just about the opposite of everything described above. Doctors say they should lead good, long lives, but I don't think they have much fun. I wonder how many other people they put to sleep or drive into early graves because of their laid-back behavior. I don't think too many professional athletes—at least the good ones—fall into that category. One former Celtic does come to mind—Curtis Rowe. Bill Fitch, at his first practice as the Celtics' coach, cut him after watching this type B jog around the gym.

If you take a look at the flags hanging over the Boston Garden or watch any of the films from my coaching days, you'd probably say that

I'm a classic type A. That doesn't explain why I've never had any heart problems (knock on wood!) and can still play racquet ball with guys half my age. I think, like most people, I'm a combination of both types.

My real answer is that I've found ways to handle stress. There are as many ways to handle stress as there are causes. Here's a collection of stress-relieving techniques that work for me. Pick out the ones that might work for you.

1. Exercise. Go for a walk, jog, swim, or play golf, tennis, or any other outside sport.

2. Take a hot bath or get a massage.

3. Talk out your frustrations with someone you know and trust. Make sure this person is not the cause of your stress.

4. Give yourself a positive reward after accomplishing something.

5. Don't look back. Second-guessing yourself is one of the major causes of stress.

6. Try to help someone else who is having a problem. I always try to be there when one of my former players needs advice. It gets my mind off whatever is bothering me and usually makes me feel a lot better.

7. Make a decision. Procrastination is another leading cause of stress. Sometimes making no decision can be worse than making the wrong decision. Learn the steps in good decision making and use them.

8. Try to put more variety in your life. Concentrating on the job twenty-four hours a day is counterproductive. Stop and smell the roses once in a while. Go to a basketball game (especially if the Celtics are playing). Get involved with a charity or community project. The satisfaction you get out of it is a real stress buster.

9. Keep an open mind. Don't assume you know everything. Resistance to change has forced many good managers into loss of health or jobs.

10. Start a regular physical-fitness program. I don't care if it's a fifteen-minute walk or a two-hour Nautilus program. The important point is to do it on a regular basis. You can actually feel that stress washing away in your postworkout shower.

Racism and Sports

Racism is illogical and counterproductive, yet it persists, mostly because of ignorance and fear. We don't know one another, so we're afraid of one another.

Sports has helped break down racial stereotypes. Intelligent fans go to watch Michael Jordan, Dr. J., Larry Bird, or Magic Johnson, and they don't care what color they are. What could be less important? All they care about is the performance. At the same time, they see a team, the original rainbow coalition, made up of blacks and whites, Catholics, Jews, Protestants, agnostics, what have you, all working together and enjoying it.

There's almost a magic to the way sports brings people together. I've been in so many towns where white people will tell me the only place they regularly interact with people of other races is the YMCA or other athletic facilities. How bad would things be in our society without sports?

Racism and Business

Clearly, it's time for business to "pick up the intensity," as Tommy Heinsohn puts it.

We in sports had to have what they now call a "multicultural work force." (If you stay around long enough, there will be a name for everything.) Eventually we had more "minorities" than nonminorities. *We were looking for what every business looks for—success.* So we put together the best teams, which made people from different races, creeds, backgrounds, and parts of the country get along and work together.

It wasn't a matter of choice for us, and I'll tell you this straight out. If you're a company of any size at all, it isn't a matter of choice for you either. Where are your workers coming from? What groups make up more and more of the potential work force? I'll tell you. Women, blacks, Latinos, Asians, Central Europeans, everybody. That's who is going to be coming in the door. You've got to be ready for them, they have to be ready for you.

Red Sez: It's not easy to set up a system to assimilate a multi-ethnic work force. But it's a necessity. No matter what size business you're involved in. You can start preparing by:

1. Building a favorable climate for acceptance. Make it clear that you are interested in employing the best-qualified person for the job, period. Nothing else matters. Once your employees understand your commitment, a lot of those discrimination problems that have been hitting other companies simply won't develop.

2. Using a buddy system when possible. Try to have one of your veteran employees take a new minority worker under his or her wing. A simple act like taking them out to lunch the first day or introducing them around the department can help get everyone off to a good start. I'll never forget the day that Bones McKinney approached me and said, "Red, I hear you drafted Cooper."

"That's right," I told him.

"Well, how about letting me room with the kid?" he asked.

Cooper and McKinney roomed together and became good friends.

What made the story significant was the fact that McKinney was a dyed-in-the-wool white Southerner from North Carolina while Cooper was black. No action on my part could have made Cooper feel more welcome than what McKinney did.

3. Getting help from key members of your department. Some people are natural leaders who are looked up to by other employees. Ask them to welcome new people, filling them in on how things are done and where they can go for help if they have a problem. If your veterans put out the welcome mat, other employees will follow.

4. Identifying and stripping away myths and stereotypes about minorities. Eventually all your employees will learn that talent is color blind.

5. Making sure that all your employees understand that they shouldn't worry about cultural differences, such

as accents. Unfortunately, some managers give employees low marks because of the way they talk. People can't be expected to leave their culture at the company door and become Americanized overnight.

Breaking the Barriers

Back in 1950, there was still an unwritten rule in the NBA—don't draft black ballplayers. Hogwash. I've already told you how I went to my first draft with Walter Brown. I wanted Chuck Cooper of Duquesne in the second round. Walter agreed. Some clown goes up to Walter and says, "Mr. Brown, are you aware Mr. Cooper is a Negro?"

Walter, the best owner I ever met, turns to the guy and says, "I am aware that Mr. Cooper can play basketball. If that is the case, I don't care if he's plaid."

Walter and I didn't have any trouble with this decision because we both agreed on one thing—we didn't give a hoot about what color some guy was, or where he was from, or anything else. *All we cared about was whether he could perform, whether he could help us succeed.*

That's probably why the Celtics had the first all-black starting five in the NBA in 1966: Willie Naulls, Satch Sanders, K. C. Jones, Sam Jones, and Bill Russell. Later Russell became the league's first black head coach. Hire people who can perform. Period.

As a manager, you've got to do a few things. When there is an incident with one of your people, you've got to stand up and speak out.

But just being willing to take a stand after the fact and speak out isn't enough. You've got to attack problems before they happen. How do you do this? One way is to talk to your people. Another is to make sure your company is represented in the major civic organizations in your community. I'm talking about organizations such as the National Urban League, the NAACP, whoever in your community is doing the job of making a better life for less fortunate people and trying to find jobs to get them up the ladder. I think most companies are aware of this. But if you merely sign up to join a group or buy tickets to a few dinners, that simply isn't enough.

Red Sez: Conduct a quick discrimination self-audit on your own management style and the atmosphere of your work area. Here are some specific areas to probe:

1. Your own behavior. *The single greatest influence on integration of the work force is the attitude of the manager.* Employees quickly learn how far they can go by observing what the manager does, not what he or she says. Managers who laugh at sexist or racist jokes and then try to lecture about brotherhood are going to be seen for the hypocrites they are.

2. Employee selection. What's the cultural background of your employees now? Are you selecting employees to fit in with your existing structure or are you trying to get the best "players" available? Have you set qualifications that are not necessary for a person to do the job? Not only are these requirements illegal, they can prevent you from hiring a lot of good people.

3. Discrimination charges. Have any racism or sex discrimination charges been filed against your department? Don't get too confident even if you can answer this question with a definite no. Many people who are being discriminated against say nothing until they finally reach the breaking point.

4. Attitudinal surveys. Compare the responses of white males with the responses of minority and female employees to see where discrepancies exist.

5. Retention rates. Some companies do a good job of hiring minorities and women, then find they leave because they are not comfortable with the organization. If you are losing a lot of these people, conduct exit interviews to get a handle on the problem.

Two-Way Communication Is the Key

What we in sports have seen for years business is seeing now. Blacks who come from inner-city housing projects, Hispanics who haven't lived in this country all their lives; these people are isolated. Many of them haven't had extensive schooling, haven't had the advantages others of us take for granted. When people have these backgrounds, they don't know the rules. They don't know how business works or how you play the game. That's why companies should have orientation programs introducing people and explaining the rules. *The key is that people must understand how the game is played.* What is expected of them? How do they relate to their supervisors? How will they be rewarded for good work? What will happen in response to subpar performances?

Some companies take it a step further and have remedial education programs for employees. I have to think they will pay off in the long run.

Also, the more communication you have with employees, the better off you are. Not only do you get to know them, they get to know you. This, too, can change some preconceived notions. One consultant took a survey at a company and found that many new minority employees thought their white male supervisors all went home and kept their suits and ties on until they went to bed.

Actions Speak Louder than Words

When Boston was going through its school-busing crisis, I was asked to publicly condemn racism with speeches and public appearances. I was reluctant to do that for several reasons. First of all, I didn't want to give anyone the impression that I had all the answers. I don't and I'm not aware of anyone who does. There's nothing easier than to run around preaching about brotherhood and understanding. Usually you end up speaking to, or being read by, people who support your position anyway. So what do you really accomplish with a lot of generalities and theories? I'd much rather deal with specific situations.

Don't get the impression that racism starts and ends in Massachusetts. It's a national problem and it seems to me it's getting worse, especially among our youth. I don't want to sound like I'm preaching. And you might not see a direct connection between your job as a manager, racism, and how today's kids are evolving. But bear with me.

More than half of the teenagers surveyed in a national study said they had witnessed racist acts. One-fourth said they had been victims of bias. And incredibly, about 30 percent admitted they would be likely to commit racist attacks.

The study, conducted by a respected national polling firm, focused on teenagers' attitudes about race relations. The results showed that racial intolerance has crept into every corner of the nation, in urban, suburban, and rural communities and among every racial and ethnic group. We read about racially motivated attacks like the ones in New York's Howard Beach and Bensonhurst neighborhoods. But the survey shows that racism is no worse in Boston or New York than anywhere else in the nation.

The most surprising finding in the survey was that only one out of every four teenagers said they would tell a teacher or other school official about a racial episode they had witnessed. This shows the lack of confidence schoolchildren have in the school's ability to respond to racism. That's no knock on educators. Racial intolerance among teenagers is a reflection of racial tension among their parents. We can't expect teachers to alleviate the problem, especially without the cooperation of parents. So what is the answer?

Heroes and Villains

The survey found that former collegiate and professional athletes are the role models most respected by youngsters. So Northeastern's Center for the Study of Sport in Society, along with Reebok, is doing something—a nationwide human rights campaign aimed at schools across the country. Former athletes will help raise the awareness of human rights and improve relations.

For the past forty years, I've tried to make every member of the Boston Celtics aware that he's a role model for the young fans who follow the game. I've tried to instill a work ethic, I've insisted my players carry themselves well in public, and I've encouraged them to participate in community activities. Nearly every other executive in the NBA has done the same thing.

The athletes have responded. If I listed every organization our players have worked with, there'd be no room in this book for anything else. But in a crazy kind of way, they've done too good a job. And that's where you come in.

The kids in the inner cities, the kids we really need to reach, are isolated. Who do they see for role models? They see the drug dealer on the corner with his fancy car and gold chains. They see the crap that passes for entertainment on TV.

Chances are they also see the athletes, the Jordans, the Birds, the Magic Johnsons. Now I submit that our guys are good role models. Dr. J., Julius Erving, one of the best players of his generation, is now making a public-service message in which he talks about never letting drugs, tobacco, or alcohol get in his way as he worked toward his goal of being the best player in the world.

That's great, and it's the right message. But it's only part of the answer. As sociologists have correctly pointed out, pro athletes shouldn't be the only role models for kids. Why? For the obvious reason. Only one kid in a million is ever going to play in the NBA. And if a kid puts all his eggs in one basket, and doesn't make it, he's going to be disappointed and have nothing to turn to.

What do these kids need? They need to see the rest of the world. They need to see people making it in other fields besides sports, entertainment, or crime. In other words, they need to see the people they never see, those from all facets of the business world.

It's important that you get your people in touch with all types of kids. Kids are thirsty for this kind of contact. It opens a new world for them. It shows them there are ways to make it, to have rewarding careers that they never knew about.

Business Role Models

How do you do it? There are a lot of programs, from Big Brother/Big Sister to YM-YWCA volunteers. One I particularly like is tutoring. The CIGNA Corporation in Hartford, Connecticut, to name one, buses hundreds of kids to its offices in Connecticut for an hour a week, where employees tutor them in math or English.

What kind of role models are best? I like people who made it to the top the hard way, playing it straight. For example, take Bill Cosby, the great entertainer. He exudes class. He achieved the top ranking in television without using foul language. Most of today's humor isn't funny—it's nasty, sexual, or crude. Cosby doesn't need that kind of garbage. He proves that you can set high standards for yourself and meet them, if you're willing to pay the price.

This guy got a doctorate from the University of Massachusetts.

Not a phony one from a mail-order school, but a real one. He made up his mind that he wanted to learn how television could help the lives of children and things like that. So he set a goal and achieved it. Bill even has a professor from Harvard review the scripts for the Cosby show to make sure he's portraying the black family in the proper light.

I saw him get off a plane in Cleveland once, although he didn't see me. As he started walking from the gate, two little kids went up to him and offered a piece of gum. He'd never seen the kids before, and a lot of people would have blown right by them. Pretty soon, though, the two kids were laughing and Cosby was laughing, too. They were having a hell of a time, like they were family. That's my idea of a role model.

Now obviously you don't have Bill Cosby working for you. But I guarantee you've got people who have many of the same traits, who've set goals and met them, who know how to communicate, who care about kids. People like the CIGNA tutors. Get them in contact with kids, particularly the minorities in your community. Employees will enjoy it, the kids will love it, and your company will get more good-will out of it than it would out of any advertising or public-relations campaign.

Red Sez: The business world is full of consultants who will help you conduct a human resources audit to discover important talent in your organization. How about conducting a quick one of your own to see what kinds of teachers or role models you have under your command? People who could work to help others both inside and outside your organization. Start by asking questions to uncover such personal capabilities as:

1. Ability to handle change. Some people are greatly stressed by change while others seem to thrive on it. These are the people who see change as a challenge, not a threat. They have a strong sense of control of both their jobs and personal lives. Their goals and priorities are well defined and they have no concern about the color or religion of the people they deal with.

2. Self-confidence. Many discrimination problems result from a lack of self-confidence. People fear they will lose their jobs to minorities because they don't have the required skills. Employees with self-confidence don't feel threatened by anyone.

3. Ambition. Not everyone with some or all of these positive traits wants to be a role model. Encourage the ones who do to contribute. Try to make the others informal helpers in your department.

Then, figure out how to utilize those talents for helping others, with strategies like:

1. Making them trainers. Use them to break in new employees, supervising their orientation and integration.

2. Using them as consultants. Reduce the amount of routine work they do so you can best utilize their skills.

3. Making them project managers. If you can't relieve them of their regular duties, try to utilize them for special duties. Minority employees are going to feel a lot better if they know they have someone to talk with in case of a problem.

4. Giving them additional feedback. If you're going to assign these employees to new or uncertain situations, be prepared to give them more feedback. No matter how confident they are about accepting change, there's bound to be some concern about their performance. Tell them the things they are doing right and be prepared to offer help and additional feedback.

CHAPTER 10

Bonehead Plays: Learning from Our Mistakes

EVERYONE MAKES MISTAKES, from the savviest business manager to the neophyte NBA coach. You don't have to read more than a couple of headlines in any section of your daily newspaper to uncover the latest bonehead move by someone in authority.

The worst thing about making a mistake, though, is not learning from it. If you're a manager, and you haven't made a mistake, you're not living up to your management responsibilities.

Like I said, everyone makes mistakes. I'm no exception. But I learn from mine. So should you.

Bonehead by the Redhead

In 1963, we won our fifth championship in a row. That was also the year we lost Bob Cousy and gained John Havlicek. There's another special reason why I'll always remember 1963. It's the year I made one of the biggest bonehead plays of my Celtics career.

It involved the drafting of a player by the name of Billy Green from Colorado State. In those days, I did everything, including scouting, so I had watched Billy play on a few occasions. I also had some lengthy conversations with him, checked him out with other coaches and some retired Celtics, and liked what I saw. He was a good kid with the right attitude and seemed like he would fit right in with the Celtics.

So I made him our number one choice. Nothing he did in camp made me second-guess that decision. He was fast, had a nice scoring touch, and was coachable. No problem at all, I thought. Then just before we're ready to break camp, he came into the office to discuss his special "travel arrangements." I explained that the Boston Celtics always travel as a team, so there wouldn't be any need to make separate arrangements.

Then he hit me with the bombshell. "I don't fly," he said.

Billy thought he'd be able to travel by train and meet the team in the various cities. Maybe in the early years it might have worked, when we only had a few teams centered in the Northeast. In fact, Bones McKinney, who played for me with the Washington Caps, was another guy who refused to fly. Bones could get away with it, because all the teams traveled by train in those days. But there was no way I could send a player to the West Coast by train and expect him to be in playing condition when he got there.

I thought I might be able to talk Billy into changing his mind. There was no way he could, I guess. I mean the kid really wanted to play for the Celtics, but this fear of flying was just too much to overcome. So I had to cut him.

Jackie Jensen, the late outfielder for the Boston Red Sox, had the same problem, but the team was able to work it out. It was easier for baseball where a team is in a city for three or four games, although it wouldn't work now with all the expansion. Basketball then, as now, was a series of one-night stands.

So the bottom line was that I blew a number one choice on a kid who could never play for the Celtics. To make it even worse, there were a few kids I could have drafted that year who turned into outstanding ballplayers. About the only thing I can say about that episode was that I learned from it. When a scout or ex-player told me about a kid who could "fly," I always made sure he did it both on and off the court. Bill Green wasn't the last first-round choice that I've had to cut, but I guarantee he's the first and last for that reason.

Bill Reinhart, my coach at George Washington University, used to say there were only two things wrong with making a mistake: *not admitting it, and not learning from it.* Bill's philosophy was that mistakes are not usually due to negligence; they happen because a system or process needs improvement.

Sometimes an admitted mistake can turn out for the best. I never saw this demonstrated better than in our 1965 playoff game against

Philadelphia. We had the ball and a one-point lead with four seconds to go. Russell attempted to put the ball into play, but his pass hit a support cable and Philadelphia was given possession. Russell walked into the huddle, admitted his mistake, and used the admission to urge: "Somebody bail me out. I blew it." So Havlicek went out and stole Hal Greer's inbounds pass and we won.

Red Sez: Too many managers—both in and out of sports—view mistakes as failures. Their attitude is: "Let's put this behind us, fast." Or they spend a lot of time trying to find someone to blame for the mistake. They haven't learned that mistakes can be opportunities to make improvements in whatever process produced the error.

Here's what I do when a mistake has been made:

1. Approach it in a nonthreatening way. Too many mistakes are covered up because employees are reluctant to admit them because of the reaction they might get from the boss. A good coach or manager promotes a feeling of trust and openness so people are not afraid to come forward when they make a mistake. Focus on *what* went wrong, not on *who* went wrong.

2. Not try to find a quick fix. It's always tempting to come up with fast solutions to limit the embarrassment flowing from a mistake. The hope is that the problem doesn't crop up again, at least until the manager has moved on to another job. Finding out what really went wrong and involving everyone in the solution is a lot more effective.

3. Ask the right questions to try to get to the root of the problem. A lot of people worry so much about the consequences of a mistake that they offer a lot of rationalizations to make their actions look better.

A question like "Why did you do this?" is going to put the person on the defensive. Try to get the information you need in steps. For instance: "When you took that action did you expect this result? What's another way to accomplish the same job? If you had to do it again, what would you do differently?"

4. Admit my own mistakes. There were some losses which I felt I was partially to blame for. Who's to say

every loss had to be the team's fault? Common sense will
tell you that can't be true. Maybe I made a bad move, or
called for the wrong play, or made a poor substitution.
Or maybe my attitude was bad and the players picked it
up. I'd tell them after the game that I did a lousy job and
promise that we'd all do better next time.

Bonehead Owners

Walter Brown was the greatest owner the Boston Celtics ever had.
Even though he died more than twenty-six years ago, his spirit remains
with the Celtics and it always will. The players missed Walter because
he was their friend and their very best fan. But no one will ever know
how much I missed him, nor will anyone fully appreciate the difficul-
ties the Celtics faced with future ownerships.

In the ten years following Walter's death, the Celtics had seven
owners. One was Marvin Kratter, the head of a big conglomerate with
offices in New York's Pan Am building. He was a brilliant man, but
like most geniuses he was convinced that a little bit of studying and
application could make him an expert in somebody else's field.

He had a direct line installed in my office that connected to his
headquarters in New York. I knew he'd be on that phone five or six
times a day if I didn't do something about it, so every time it rang I
made believe it was out of order! Finally, I simply told him to get the
phone out of there because it was bugging me. He removed the phone,
but I knew that wouldn't be the end of his interference.

The whole thing came to a head when I was summoned to New
York to discuss whether we should protect Don Nelson and Satch
Sanders during the 1968 expansion draft. After listening to several of
his directors discussing whether we should protect either or both of
them, I finally exploded.

"Listening to you guys discussing the skills and future abilities of
ballplayers is like letting civilians run a war. It's a joke. Would I pick
out a piece of real estate and tell you people how much it's worth and
what you should do with it? Of course not.

"But that's what you're doing now with the Celtics, and I want
no part of it. If you're going to make these kinds of decisions, then you
can take over the ballclub. I want nothing to do with it and I'll call a
press conference to say so."

Eventually, they came around to my way of thinking. In fact, Kratter and I became good friends after he sold the team.

Bonehead Companies

The worst of times—at least economically—came in 1970 when a company called Trans-National Communications, based in New York, bought the club. Everything was handled out of New York. They took all of our money and then never bothered to pay our bills. We owed money to hotels in every city. So the Celtics had to travel COD all over the league! They wouldn't let us stay unless we paid in advance. One time I had to lay out nine thousand dollars of my own money before our guys could board an airplane!

We were making a profit at the gate, but we never saw a penny of it. Not only that, I didn't have access to any of our financial records. There were people on the payroll who I never heard of. It was just awful.

Then one day we were notified that our office telephones would be shut off if we didn't pay our bill. On top of that, the phone company insisted on a two thousand dollar deposit, just to make sure we didn't default again. I had to personally visit the business office and ask for an extension of our credit. Embarrassing? You bet it was. It was an indignity the ballclub didn't deserve. But what could we do about it?

Finally, Trans-National went bankrupt and ownership of the team reverted to the Ballantine Brewing Company. When Ballantine sold us to Bob Schmertz in the summer of 1972, we had our first real security since Walter Brown died. Schmertz made a fortune in developing retirement communities, and he bought the team as an investment. Then he fell in love with the players, just like Walter did, and it was nothing to see him hop a plane and meet the club on the road to give moral support. When he died in 1975, we decided to wear black patches on our uniforms, just as we did after Walter's death.

Bonehead Swaps

I didn't think things could ever get worse for the Celtics than they were under Trans-National, but I was wrong. Irv Levin became

Schmertz's partner in 1975, then took over the team completely. It wasn't that Irv was so bad, but he was instrumental in bringing the Celtics the worst owner we ever had. I'm talking about John Y. Brown.

In 1978, Levin swapped the Celtics to Brown for the Buffalo Braves and moved them to San Diego, where they operated as the Clippers. The Celtics sent Kevin Kunnert, Freeman Williams, Kermit Washington, and Sidney Wicks to Buffalo and we got Billy Knight, Nate Archibald, and Marvin Barnes in return. We also got Brown, former owner of Kentucky Fried Chicken, who had already run the Buffalo franchise into the ground.

I didn't know one thing about the deal until it was completed. It was the first time in Celtics history that a player transaction was made without my knowledge. About this time, the New York Knicks asked me to become team president at the highest salary ever offered an NBA executive. I was very touched by the outpouring of support from the Boston community asking me to stay with the Celtics. My wife, Dot, also had very definite ideas that I should either stay with the Celtics or come home to Washington.

Brown also gave me his word that I would be included in all basketball decisions. He probably also promised Colonel Sanders that he'd never change the original Kentucky Fried Chicken recipe either. Unfortunately Brown had this ego and thought he knew a lot about everything. He'd call other general managers around the league and ask them ridiculous questions. Of course, they all gave him crazy answers, then told me about his calls. In that one year, he almost killed the franchise.

Let me give you an example. Brown told me that a player by the name of Earl Tatum was available. I said that he had some talent and that if we could get him for a third-round draft choice, it would be worth it. A few days later Brown came into my office with a big smile on his face. We got Tatum for a first-round choice!

The worst deal he ever made was trading three first-round draft picks to New York for Bob McAdoo, without even consulting me. That did it. I gave him two weeks to sell his interest in the team or I was gone. Luckily for the Celtics, Brown was making plans to run for governor of Kentucky, so he agreed to sell to Harry Mangurian, Jr. My last comment about Brown made the Kentucky newspapers. "Watch out for that guy," I warned. "He'll trade the Kentucky Derby for the Indianapolis 500."

Harry Mangurian reminded me a lot of Walter Brown. He was low key and didn't have a giant ego. So we were able to rebuild the

Celtics, starting with the drafting of Larry Bird in 1978. Then we signed M. L. Carr, a Detroit free agent, and offered McAdoo as compensation in return for two 1980 first-round draft picks. Then we worked a deal with Golden State that essentially gave us Robert Parish and Kevin McHale in return for Joe Barry Carroll and the eighth pick. We also talked Danny Ainge into giving up his baseball career and traded Rick Robey for Dennis Johnson.

We won the world championship in 1980–81 and 1983–84. Meanwhile, Harry sold the team to the present owners, Don Gaston, Paul Dupee, Jr., and Alan Cohen, in 1983. These three are also in the Walter Brown tradition, supportive but not interfering, dedicated fans who care more about winning than anything.

I'm not saying that owners should simply stand in the corner and nod obediently every time a management decision is made. They have invested millions of dollars in a franchise, and are entitled to have some input in team decisions. As far as I'm concerned, the chemistry has to be right between owners and management in order for a team to be successful. Right now the chemistry between management and ownership of the Boston Celtics couldn't be any better.

We're lucky to have three owners like Gaston, Dupee, and Cohen. All three of these men are fans first and owners second. They said they were going to spend money to improve the ballclub, then they went out and did it. They are great businessmen, but they are also wise enough to listen to Dave Gavitt, senior executive vice president, Jan Volk, general manager, or myself for decisions involving players.

Sure they give us input, but never in an obtrusive, interfering way. When we need them, they are there. Alan Cohen went to Italy to sign Brian Shaw last year. They love the sport and the bottom line to them is winning. I wish that all owners could be like these three.

Bonehead Business

Let me tell you another story about ownership and business. An American subsidiary of a Japanese automobile company produced three to five times more defects than its Japanese counterparts, according to an article in the Los Angeles *Times*. A sampling of Honda Accords made in Ohio had more squeaks, rattles, and mechanical defects than imported models, according to an article in *Business Week*. The Ohio models counted 162 problems per car versus 93.1 glitches in imported models. In basketball terms, that's a real blowout.

Now consider this. Chevrolet closed an assembly plant in Fremont, California, because of poor quality and high production costs. The next year, Chevrolet entered into a joint venture with Toyota and reopened the Fremont plant. It is now the best-performing plant in the whole Chevrolet organization, even though the previous work force was rehired almost intact.

So what happened in Fremont, California? The only real change was that management of the plant was turned over to the Japanese. The employees were divided into small teams, allowed to define their own jobs, and were held accountable for their own quality. The teams conduct their own quality audits and even have ''stop-line'' cords that allow them to shut down the assembly line if a problem is encountered. Want to bet Henry Ford is turning over in his grave?

The bottom line is that the system works. For a lot of years, we've been giving the Japanese credit for developing this emphasis on the quality-control process. *Actually they deserve as much credit for that as the Russians do for inventing basketball.*

The Deming Solution

Dr. W. Edwards Deming, an American, went to Japan to teach statistical quality to the Japanese. He came up with the following fourteen-point program that is still used in Japan today. I'd love to claim these points as my own and make them a ''Red Sez.'' But all I can do is agree with them:

1. Create constancy of purpose toward improvement of product and service.

2. Adapt the new philosophy that we can no longer live with commonly accepted levels of delays, mistakes, defective materials, and defective workmanship.

3. Cease dependence on mass inspection. Require, instead, statistical evidence that quality is built in.

4. End the practice of awarding business on the basis of price tag.

5. Find problems. It is management's job to constantly work on improving the system.

6. Institute modern methods of training on the job.

7. Institute modern methods of supervision of pro-

duction workers. The responsibility of foremen must be changed from numbers to quality.

8. Drive out fear, so that everyone may work effectively for the company.

9. Break down barriers between departments.

10. Eliminate numerical goals, posters, and slogans for the work force, asking for new levels of productivity without providing methods.

11. Eliminate work standards that prescribe numerical quotas.

12. Remove barriers that stand between the hourly worker and his right to pride of workmanship.

13. Institute a vigorous program of education and retraining.

14. Create a structure in top management that will push every day on the above thirteen points.

Dr. Deming taught this program to the Japanese more than forty years ago. Maybe if he had gone to Detroit instead of Tokyo our automobile industry would be in better shape. You can read all about his theories in *Out of the Crisis,* published by the Massachusetts Institute of Technology for Advance Engineering (1986). Meanwhile, in the U.S., it's estimated that 25 percent of a typical factory's operating budget is spent on finding and fixing mistakes. That means that one out of every four people isn't producing anything. They spend all their time looking for and fixing things that aren't done right the first time. That's a bonehead way to operate a business.

Bonehead Communications

One of the most expensive mistakes I ever heard of is the Hubble Space Telescope. The thing took years to build and cost $1.5 billion. They spent millions blasting it into space, and then found out it didn't work.

Obviously, I'm not an optics specialist, but what upsets me about the Hubble fiasco was that some technicians at Perkin-Elmer, the company that built it, suspected that something was wrong but never got the word to anyone who could do something about it. According to an investigation of the incident, Perkin-Elmer built a huge mirror for the telescope, a very delicate instrument. They only had one test instrument to make sure the mirror was shaped and polished correctly. What happened was that the test instrument was assembled incorrectly, and nobody noticed until the telescope was already in space. I'd say that $1.5 billion is a tough price to pay for not checking your work.

The scary thing is that the company had everybody working on the mirror project squirreled into one division, one corner. They didn't let other people from the company into the area; they didn't even let people from NASA in some of the time. When some of these guys discovered there might be a problem, they never notified NASA or people from the rest of their own company. They just ignored their own findings and plowed ahead.

The mistake was, apparently, a monumental lack of communication. Why wasn't the process open enough so that legitimate differences of opinion could be aired with senior management? Look at the results. I understand it will cost tens of millions of dollars to fix the mistake—if it can be done at all—by using the space shuttle.

Bonehead Building

I've been in arenas all around the country, and I can't understand why so many of them are built so poorly. The roof of the Hartford Civic Center crumbled after a snowstorm, just hours after a college basketball doubleheader. It could have killed ten thousand people if it had occurred a little earlier. That really hit home for me, because the Celtics play a few league games there every year.

But when it comes to pure bungling in arena construction, it's hard to top the Nassau Coliseum on Long Island. They put the main exits right at center court! The one place where they can sell the most expensive seats, and all they have there are stairs! That's not the half of it.

They built the building with no box office. Didn't anybody on the building committee ever hear of tickets? They put the training room across the exit corridor from the locker room. That meant that an athlete who needed to go to the training room for treatment had to wrap a towel around himself and fight his way through the crowd. They even had the electrical outlets in the wrong places.

They spent millions building that place, then spent millions more fixing it. They finally moved the exits to the corners. Okay, there was public money invested in the project and that can introduce problems. But how smart do you have to be to think through how a sports arena will be used? Why couldn't they have gone to some successful arenas to see how it was done? Unbelievable!

Bonehead Marketing

You don't have to be an economist to realize that we are getting killed in the foreign markets. Some of the problems don't have anything to do with price or quality. We just don't take the time or put in the effort to do the job right. Or we make stupid little mistakes that hurt us.

I remember a big laugh some Mexican friends of mine had when Chevrolet introduced its Nova model in Mexico City. Newspaper, television, and radio ads attracted a lot of attention, but not the kind General Motors was looking for. No one had taken the time to realize that "no va" in Spanish means something like "it doesn't go." So GM spent a lot of money on an advertising campaign that was doomed to failure. It would be like naming an NBA team in Mexico the Spanish equivalent of "can't win." I don't think too many season tickets would be sold.

Some other big companies have made similar mistakes. I never really understood the strategy of Coca-Cola in creating a new formula. For years and years, consumers had accepted the idea that the original recipe couldn't be improved. So they ended up antagonizing consumers and even had to bring the old formula back as Coke "Classic." It seems to me that they only divided their market instead of expanding it.

It also gave competitors something to talk about. I'll never forget Pepsi's full-page ad in many newspapers immediately after Coke made its announcement. Five words that created a real impact: "The other guy just blinked."

Other companies get into trouble by trying to go into areas where they don't belong. Take a company like Texas Instruments, which has a great reputation for inventing digital equipment and applying engineering breakthroughs. It helped create the market for hand-held calculators and digital watches. Then they opened retail stores to sell them. They closed the stores almost immediately, then jumped into the home computer market, where they lost over $300 million before bailing out. Now, Texas Instruments has great engineers and scientists capable of inventing and manufacturing quality products. Marketing geniuses they are not. So why don't they stick to inventing and let someone else do their selling?

Some companies get in serious trouble by not listening to employees. Sperry Corporation came up with a new computer, called Sperry IT, which was compatible with the IBM AT personal computer but delivered more performance for a lower price.

Sperry marketing managers went to MicroD, Inc., and came away with an initial order of three thousand units. But Sperry management turned the deal down, saying that it already had two distributors. MicroD answered by developing its own computer and went into direct competition with the Sperry IT. MicroD sold $40 million of its computers the first year, while Sperry lost money on the IT. Actually, Sperry's loss wasn't only financial. A number of its top managers left to find jobs where management would listen to them.

Bonehead Plays and Risk

A lot of bonehead plays I've talked about in this chapter could have been avoided if a manager had decided not to do something. If I hadn't drafted Billy Green, I never would have known or cared about his fear of flying. But supposing Billy had been able to overcome it and had turned into a productive player. Any manager who never takes a risk will never make a mistake or pull a bonehead play. He won't do much of anything. *So making a bonehead play is not the end of the world. It's what you learn from it that is important.*

Every decision you make involves some risk. You have to be able to determine when the risk is reasonable and when it's not. I probably didn't make the best decision when I punched Ben Kerner, the St. Louis owner, in the mouth. But I wouldn't second-guess myself about challenging six-foot-eleven-inch, two-hundred-fifty-pound Moses Malone to a fight one night at Boston Garden.

That incident occurred when Larry Bird got into a fight with Philadelphia's Marc Iavaroni and both were thrown out of the game. It's an old trick. You get a mediocre player to pick a fight with the other team's star and you get a big advantage when they both get thrown out. I lost it completely, and ended up in Malone's face. The only casualty turned out to be Sixer coach Billy Cunningham's torn sportscoat.

After the game, Larry commented on my action: "That showed me he was a true Celtic. He makes sure everyone is treated fairly and brings out the best in everybody. He knows where his heart is, what he's made of. He'll be part of the Celtics till he dies." No locker-room speech would ever have accomplished what that little confrontation with Moses did.

So even if you don't end up challenging Moses Malone with fisticuffs, you do need to take risks. The secret is to limit them to reasonable risks. I always start by asking myself two questions before making a rash decision:

1. What's the worst thing that can happen to the Boston Celtics if my decision is wrong?
2. What's the worst thing that can happen to me personally if my decision is wrong?

I asked myself those two questions before I gave John Brown my "him or me" ultimatum. The answer to question one was for me to leave and Brown to stay. The risk was worth it because if we had both stayed, the organization would have been destroyed.

The answer to question number two was that I would be out of a job. Of course, the Knicks had already offered me a job at a lot more money. And remember, I had another "offer" on the table that I wouldn't have been allowed to refuse: My wife, Dot, told me that I was a Celtic and that I should come home to Washington if I left the organization.

The Next Risk Step

The point I'm trying to make is that if your company can survive the answer to question number one and you can live with the worst outcome of question number two, the risk is worth taking. *Remember that the downside of risk taking—failure—is only half the possible outcome. The other possible outcome is success.* So I then ask myself two more questions:

1. What's the best possible thing that can happen to the Boston Celtics if my decision is right?

2. What's the best possible thing that can happen to me if my decision is right?

The answer to question number one in the Brown case was that I would get rid of an interfering owner who knew little about the game, and I could take steps to bring the team back to what it used to be. For me, personally, it would mean that I could regain control of the team and start going after the players we needed.

Use this upside–downside formula for analyzing and evaluating risk in all of your major decisions. It will help you look at failure and success, and decide whether or not the risk is worth it.

How important is the ability to make decisions to a manager? Here's what Lee Iacocca, Chrysler chairman, says about it: "If I had to sum up in one word what makes a good manager, I'd say decisiveness. You can use the fanciest computers to gather the numbers, but in the end you have to set a timetable and act. And I don't mean rashly. I'm sometimes described as a flamboyant leader and a hip-shooter, a fly-by-the-seat-of-the-pants operator. But if that were true, I could never have been successful in this business."

CHAPTER 11

The Celtics Mystique: One Ingredient in a Successful Organization

I RECEIVED A LETTER from a Louisiana schoolteacher a couple of years ago that I got a big kick out of. During a geography lesson, she asked her kids to name the capital of Massachusetts. The class was silent, until one little boy suddenly raised his hand and said, "Celtics."

There are probably a lot of places around the world where kids would have the same reaction. There isn't any question that the Boston Celtics are one of the best-known sports teams throughout the world. People who know hardly anything else about our country can usually tell you who the Boston Celtics are.

Why? A lot of it has to do with the game itself. To my way of thinking, basketball is the number one game in the world. It doesn't require a lot of expensive equipment or elaborate stadiums. A ball and a couple of hoops will do the trick. The rest of the answer has to do with a question I usually get when I speak to a business group: "Is there such a thing as 'Celtic pride' or 'Celtic mystique'?" The answer is yes and no.

The Little People

For years, people have claimed there was a leprechaun who lived under the floor of the Boston Garden and popped out to guide the winning basket into the hoop in the last seconds of a game.

Well, for one thing, no self-respecting leprechaun would live down there, with the hockey ice and what have you. Anyway, the North End of Boston is an Italian neighborhood, not Irish. The Irish live in South Boston. So there's no leprechaun.

But when people start thinking you've got a leprechaun working for you, they are acknowledging that you've got something going, something that perhaps could be called a "mystique."

Here's what I mean. For years, the Yankees were at the top of baseball. People used to say they had an almost magical quality, "five o'clock lightning," which helped them win those late-inning games. (Back then baseball was played in the afternoon—but don't get me started on television and night baseball and the World Series.) And look at college football's most famous team. People think Notre Dame's "Touchdown Jesus" on the library actually helps them win football games.

Actually, there's no magic or supernatural help, at least none that I know of. If you do the fundamentals a little better than the next guy, you have a way of getting the breaks late in the game. Not every time, but often enough.

It's the same in the business world. Companies such as IBM, Xerox, and Polaroid have had, at various times, a similar mystique. How did they get it? Imagination and hard work. Doing it better than anyone else in their "leagues."

When I think of what makes up the Celtics mystique, I think of it as an organization that worked like a machine but felt like a family.

Teams and Family

If you're going to have a "team mystique," obviously the first thing you have to have is a team. That's harder than it sounds.

Too many organizations—ballclubs and offices—break into cliques. Nothing can kill a ballclub faster than cliques. Every year, my first priority was to avoid cliques. There can be black cliques, white cliques, old-school cliques, even wife cliques.

The old Knicks had a problem with cliques years ago. One guy would only pass to one other guy, then two other guys would only play with each other. The fifth guy got the ball by accident. I want to tell you something: It's very easy for five guys to beat two guys, and we did it, time and again.

The idea is to have a team, and to make it known that the team is bigger and more important than any individual. If some guy can't live with that, I'd try not to get him in the first place. But if I had him, my philosophy was to let him go and ruin the chemistry of some other team.

I always appreciated something Wayne Embry said after we got him in the sixties. He'd been an all-star and captain with Cincinnati, but they'd let him go. His ego was crushed. He was only thirty years old, and he had some very good games left in him.

"The first thing you noticed was the way you were treated in Boston," he said. "You were now a Celtic, one of Red's guys, and you knew he'd bust his butt to do anything in the world for you. Even if you weren't, he made you feel like you were the greatest player in the world. In his own mind, he believed anyone wearing the green and white was special. If I played two minutes and grabbed one rebound, he'd be sure and mention the contribution I made."

That was nice of Wayne. Of course, he went on to become the general manager of the Bucks and Cavaliers, and has used that same philosophy to beat my brains out more times than I care to recall. That's because he knew instinctively what I always tried to do—to have a twelve-man team, not a series of two- or three-man teams.

Most of my players were leaders when they joined the Celtics. I tried to lead them in a way that didn't destroy those leadership qualities and tried to teach them a concept: Everybody is an individual and all individuals must be treated differently, yet treated exactly alike in a team sense.

I like to think they got more than just basic knowledge of the game here. They learned how to control a team, and they learned that a team is more effective when each of its members concentrates on the particular phase of the game in which he excels. They learned that winning is the only statistic that matters. And I think they learned the importance of honesty and openness in player relations. On top of all that, they learned what it means to have pride in an organization. All of which are business basics as well.

Caring Makes a Difference

Almost every single one of my former players keeps in regular contact with me. My phone's always ringing. Sometimes they just want to say hello, or tell me some news about their families or careers. Sometimes they want advice. It gives me a good feeling inside to know they still value my opinions, and that I've apparently had a good influence on their lives. Call it respect, if you want to, or call it friendship. In my mind, it's just their way of letting me know they're still my guys, and I hope they always feel that way.

That's it. It's caring. I'm still in touch with guys who played for me thirty-five or forty years ago, such as Bones McKinney, Frank Ramsey, and Ed Macauley. I know where they are, what they're doing, when they'll be in town. That's a family feeling, and the newer guys sense it and want to be part of it.

Paul Silas, the great rebounder who was called the "chairman of the boards," was an old veteran when he came to the Celtics. One day he came to me. "Red," he said, "I heard a lot about this Celtics pride and thought it was a bunch of crap. But I was wrong. I feel part of it now and this has been the happiest part of my career." It was one of the nicest compliments I ever got from a guy who told it like it was.

Trust Plus Communication

I believe that pride and tradition are built on trust. The players always trusted in the Boston Celtics organization. Too many business leaders expect the trust of their employees, but aren't prepared to give it back. I have a system. I have some guys score a lot, and some guys I want rebounding, and some who give everything they have in guarding the other team's best players. Not everyone can lead the team in scoring. I tell everybody that I need the rebounding, the defense, the passing as much as the scoring.

The trust kicks in when I'm true to those principles. In other words, I have to reward people for doing the grunt work as well as the scoring. And I try my best to do just that. As I've said, I don't believe in statistics. What's more important, a rebound in a tie game with thirty seconds left, or ten points at the end of a blowout? But the stat sheet will have one guy with ten points and the other guy with none! The solution is easy—throw out the stat sheet.

I try to reward what I think is valuable to the team. You've read how Bill Russell came to me as a rookie worried he couldn't score enough. And I told him I didn't care if he ever scored a point; that I had some of the finest shooters in the league, and his job was just to get them the ball by rebounding and playing defense.

Thirty years later, here comes another Bill with the same complaint. I'm talking about Bill Walton, who came to the Celtics because of team chemistry. Then one day, he's down in the dumps because he isn't scoring. So I dust off the Russell speech and take Bill No. 2 aside. "I'm not interested in how many points you score. I'm interested in what you contribute. Did you rebound? Pass? Run the floor? Play defense?" Since he did all those things—he did everything a guy with two bad feet could be expected to do, even walking four miles to practice to try to strengthen his ankles—his face lit up. He was a different guy after that.

Is all that trust and pride part of the Celtics mystique? Sure it is.

Best Foot Forward

I've always been concerned with the image of the Celtics. I don't want our people getting in brawls or behaving poorly in public. I've communicated this in no uncertain terms, because a champion looks and acts like a champion. My guys responded and so will your people. It's a funny thing—people want to be part of a class organization.

When it gets down to it, mystique is a combination of a great product and people willing to give it everything they have. The players who've been part of it usually say something about people when they're asked about the Celtics mystique.

Tommy Heinsohn said the team's success was due to groups of men who could check their egos at the door and put the team first. This isn't just talk, it has to be a way of life. Satch Sanders called it "realizing the big picture is so much brighter than our own little picture."

"Why were we so good?" Bill Russell asked rhetorically. "Because we were a team. That's it, we were a team. We all recognized that and understood it, and when you do, you find that all the other things just aren't that important. My concern was the Celtics, period. That's it. We were the Celtics. I wasn't playing for Boston or playing for the NBA. I was playing for the Celtics. And the only thing that counted with me was the Celtics. We were a family. Maybe I could have made another million dollars playing someplace else, but I couldn't imagine playing anywhere else. I was a Celtic."

Lenny Wilkins, great player and coach of the Cleveland Cavaliers, said the key was our balance. "I used to laugh when I heard 'Celtic mystique' because that wasn't it. It was just that Red was smarter than everybody else. He could never get a top draft choice because his team always drafted last. So he'd find a guy like Bailey Howell, a quality player, and pick him up for a year or two at the end of his career. That would give him depth. Every year he had the deepest team in the league, with great balance.

"Of course, it's easier to motivate people on a winner. Everybody wants to play for you, so all you do is send out the message to shape up or ship out, and people shape up. But Red was smart with people. He knew when to give them free rein. If you have creative people, you have to let them create some of the time, think for themselves. It's what prepares them for what they need to do when the clock's running down in a close game. Red knows how to give people some rein."

Hey, Lenny, I appreciate the compliments, but my "smarts" aren't unique—nor is our mystique, for that matter. That technique of tapping each individual's strengths and preparing him to do what he does best can be applied to any—and every—organization, from business to sports.

I can't say that I agree with everything Lenny said, especially that comment about my being smarter than everyone else. I like to think that maybe I just worked harder. And I always tried to encourage people to do things on their own.

Mystique Sparks Success—And Vice Versa

M. L. Carr—talk about a guy who was great for chemistry—said the mystique was "experience gained over the course of years, that people could come together, face all kinds of adversity, and still come out on top. So Larry Bird goes out and scores fifty points and you look in the stands and there's John Havlicek who did it before. Robert Parish grabs twenty-five rebounds and then you look at Bill Russell, who got forty. Brian Shaw makes one of those great passes and then you look over at Bob Cousy, who made the same pass a thousand times before.

"Then you look up at all those championship flags and realize that the Celtics always came together when they had to. That's why the system has withstood the test of time. Big contracts, players' egos, television exposure, no-cut contracts, it doesn't matter.''

Chris Ford, former Celtics player and subsequently coach, connects the mystique with the number of fans—all over the country and world. "If you play for the Celtics, people think of you as a Celtic forever. They forget that I played for the Pistons for almost seven years. When you travel with the team, you notice the wave of green out there at the hotels, arenas, and airports. I can only compare it to the Yankees or Notre Dame.''

Dave Cowens says that teams like Los Angeles, Milwaukee, Philadelphia, and the Knicks also have traditions to fall back on. "Boston just happened to win eleven out of thirteen [NBA championships] and no one is ever going to do that again. They can all win one but it's hard to keep on going. There are always more people at Celtics games. We always enjoyed that. Even away games. Then you want to beat them even more when they really want to beat you.''

I liked the way Johnny Most, the Celtics' broadcaster for thirty-five years, described the mystique. "It's quite simple,'' Johnny said. "The Celtics have always been able to instill in their players the idea that the ultimate victory belongs to the group, not the individual. And so they take pride in themselves as a unit. There's nothing sophisticated about what these guys have done. It's the oldest formula for success in the world: They function with pride.''

I don't think Johnny will ever realize how much he contributed to that pride. When he arrived in Boston to be the play-by-play man in 1953, we were a struggling team that had never won anything. We needed someone who could help us sell basketball to a city filled with baseball and hockey fans.

A conventional play-by-play man would never have done the job. Johnny could make a Cousy pass, a Russell rebound, or a Loscutoff pick sound like a work of art. He came up with such terms as "fiddling and diddling,'' and "stop and pop.'' Johnny Most gave life to all the Celtics' greats of the past thirty-seven years for hundreds of thousands of fans throughout New England.

Sure he was an excitable character who saw things only the Celtics' way. But in his prime he called a fast and accurate game. He always gave you the switches, picks, block-outs, shots, assists, and rebounds. We retired his microphone in December 1990, and it's now hanging up there next to the championship flags and retired numbers. But his spirit will never be retired. That spirit was a big part of our mystique—and our success.

Commitment to Excellence

Some people have said that the ''mystique'' is a physical thing, that my teams won because they were in better shape than other teams. I don't think that was the whole reason. Players still talk about the time we acquired Willie Naulls, and on the first day of practice, he threw up and passed out. He ended up having a great year for us.

The point is that in basketball, you run for forty-eight minutes. If you can condition your guys to be just as fast after forty-seven minutes as they are after four minutes, then fatigue won't beat you. It may well beat the other guy. That's knowing your product and your people. It's basics, and basics, I keep saying, are important—in business and in sports.

To Kevin McHale, the Celtics mystique is simply a good thing for the media to write about. ''But as a player you realize that it doesn't mean anything,'' McHale said. ''John Havlicek or Bill Russell or Bob Cousy aren't going to win any games for the Celtics today. The Celtics mystique is simply the experience that's been gained over the years. It's guys like M. L. Carr and Bill Russell, who taught me about sacrificing, about playing hurt, things that never show up in the box score. It's living proof that no matter what adversity you confront, somehow the team always comes together and makes it happen.''

Kevin never complains about his sixth- man role, a huge concession that many superstars would not make. He always talks to the media, never misses a team function, and leads the team in donating time to charities. Something happened on December 19, 1990, that illustrates what Kevin means when he talks about egos not getting in the way of team goals.

In the closing moments of a Celtics win over Philadelphia in the Boston Garden, Kevin scored his fifteen thousandth career point. The game wasn't stopped. The ball wasn't given to McHale. In fact, the milestone passed virtually unnoticed. To make matters worse, only a short time before, the Celtics had stopped a game in the Garden to allow the Denver Nuggets to award a game ball to Orlando Woolridge for scoring his ten thousandth point.

We screwed up. There isn't any other explanation. Our front office was embarrassed, as well as a few members of the media. Some of our players were upset. But not Kevin. He simply laughed the whole thing off. ''The fact that they feel so awful about it means I'll get that much more mileage out of it,'' was Kevin's only comment. Here you have the guy who would be the franchise on any other team, but happens to have spent his whole career with Larry Bird, one of the five best players in the game.

Trading Places

Another important ingredient of the "mystique" is communication. I don't make many trades, but if I had one in the hopper, I'd ask some of the guys, "Hey, I've got a chance to get so-and-so. What do you think?" I had very bright guys in Russell, Cousy, Sharman, Havlicek, K. C. Jones, and many others. People who have something to offer like to offer it. It's human nature. And if I took their advice, they'd invariably make an extra effort to help the new guy pick up the Celtics system. If you take a look at your own management style and find that true trust is lacking, you're missing an important tool for creating your own "business mystique."

Sometimes, in my case, the feedback would be to not make any trade at all. For instance, after the New York Knickerbockers knocked us out of the playoffs in 1990, a lot of people started saying that our front line of Robert Parish, Larry Bird, and Kevin McHale was too slow, that we might never make a serious run at another NBA championship unless we traded for some young blood. Bird came right out and said it would be a mistake to break up that line. Of course, there was no way I was going to trade Bird, McHale, or Parish. What good would it do to bring in young guys if they didn't have anybody to play with?

So we got Brian Shaw back from Europe, drafted Dee Brown, and hired Chris Ford as coach and Dave Gavitt as senior vice president. I hired Dave because he knows the game and he understands human nature. Those are the two ingredients that separate winners from losers as far as I'm concerned.

Halfway through the season we had a strong lead over Philadelphia in the Eastern Conference, even though we went through a losing streak while Bird was out with a bad back. With Larry back, we were considered legitimate contenders for another NBA championship.

It's nice to be back in the hunt. Since 1956–57, the Boston Celtics have never gone more than four seasons without a championship. The Bruins have won five Stanley Cups in their sixty-five-year history, the

Red Sox have won one World Series in seventy-two seasons, and the Patriots have been in the Super Bowl once in twenty-five years. I'm not saying that to embarrass any other teams. I just want to make it clear that Celtics fans expect more—and so do I.

Mystique a Misnomer?

In basketball, and in every line of work, you want to prepare your people as well as you possibly can. If your people sell, what are the basics of sales? Are your people better at them than the next guy's? If your workers are landscapers, do they know more about landscaping and work harder than the others? That's where the mystique comes in. Not with luck or leprechauns.

The Celtics mystique—I think *tradition* is a better word—starts with selecting the right people and convincing them that team goals always take priority over individual accomplishments. It's concentrating on the fundamentals and giving players the competitive edge that makes them want to win. It's instilling a sense of discipline so that every player realizes that he will be treated fairly and not according to some rigid formula that doesn't allow room for individual interpretation.

It's recognizing how important older employees can be to an organization and why loyalty has to go both ways. It's acknowledging the importance of product knowledge and avoiding areas where this expertise is lacking. It's constantly comparing your operation with the competition's and, if they're beating you, doing something about it. As far as I'm concerned, any team—and any business—can create a winning "mystique" by following these same principles.

For instance, when Greg LeMond won the Tour de France in July of 1989, he had a cheering section in front of a TV set at an industrial plant eight thousand miles away. LeMond had pedaled to the world championship wearing a Giro helmet and employees at Giro Sports Design in Santa Cruz, California, were allowed to leave their work-stations to watch his victory.

Jim Gentes, CEO of Giro, explained that he tries to keep his people excited about what they are doing. He even tracked down the serial number of LeMond's helmet and held a party in honor of the two production workers who had put it together. For Gentes, communicating his company's vision and image to employees is a way of providing them with guidelines for taking initiative and making decisions.

"We pick symbols and role models in order to set both the goals and the tone of the company," Gentes said. "For example, during our annual review, we list the companies that we recognize as being great. It's a way of making people aware of the kind of organization that we want to be. We want to emulate their creativity, their reputation for quality, and being people-oriented," Gentes said.

Red Sez: Instilling pride is a big step toward winning employees' enthusiastic commitment to their jobs. Some others:

- Explaining your organization's vision and strategy. The more they know about the progress of your company, the more they can help. When people are informed, they begin to think, and that's when they come up with ideas. Take quality, for instance. A well-trained employee who understands the larger picture of the company and of the product itself builds better quality into it. You can't inspect quality into a product. If employees know what they're looking for as they build it, they're far better off.

- Encouraging an open exchange of ideas throughout the organization. Try to get to the point where employees are exchanging ideas with one another on a regular basis and treating each other with mutual respect. For instance, an employee comes up with an idea to improve a product that simply won't work. Instead of dismissing it as a dumb idea, an explanation should be given as to why it won't work. It's all a matter of attitude and communication.

- Training employees to identify and prevent problems, not just solve them. If all your people do is solve problems, they're doing their jobs wrong, because they obviously are not taking steps to prevent them in the first place. Before they can prevent problems, of course, they have to be able to recognize and identify them in the first place. It's up to management to give them the training and motivation to do it.

Us versus Them

I once made the comment that the Celtics aren't a team—they're a way of life. I just can't think of another way to describe the feeling that players on our team have for each other. Every player supports his teammates in so many ways. We understand each other. We feel that, as Celtics, we belong to the most exclusive club in the world. We're proud of each other.

That pride affects everything we do, both on and off the court. I remember a team meeting we had to divide the money after we won the championship in the 1965–66 season. Woody Sauldsberry had missed half the year because of an injury, and John Thompson, now the great Georgetown coach, hadn't played much as Bill Russell's backup.

Someone suggested that Woody and John should receive half shares. I just sat back and kept my mouth shut. Bill Russell spoke up, as I knew he would. "The hell with that kind of stuff," Bill said. "Everyone gets a full share." End of meeting.

There's no better example of family pride than the feeling that comes over the Celtics organization when one of its players is elected to the Basketball Hall of Fame. In 1991, we had two Celtics admitted, Dave Cowens and Nate (Tiny) Archibald. Dave showed what a player can do with desire, determination, and dedication. He was a small center at six feet nine inches. Yet he played big and held his own against the best, including Kareem Abdul-Jabbar.

Tiny Archibald is one of the great guards of all time. One year he led the league in scoring and assists. But it was one of his off-the-court moves that made the biggest impression on me. Tiny insisted that one of his contract bonuses would be for a hundred extra pairs of new sneakers to be distributed to kids from boys' clubs around New York. You can't help but be proud of a guy like that.

I'm always asked to compare Celtics players and teams. How would the 1957 championship team have done against the 1981 championship team? Would Havlicek be able to handle Bird? How would Parish do against Russell? Could McHale handle Heinsohn? Which team was the best? Could the team of 1984 beat the team of 1974? I guess it's a natural part of sports talk to make comparisons. Sportswriters do it, fans do it, and even players do it. Of course, no one can answer those questions.

Even if it were possible to wave a magic wand and schedule a game between any of those great Celtic teams during their prime, I wouldn't want to make any predictions. Sure, this year's team is bigger than the teams I used to coach. But as big and talented as they are, our old teams would give them a helluva battle. One thing I would say for certain—every player on the floor would function with pride, a necessary ingredient for anyone who has worn or wears the Celtic green.

Debunking the Myth

John Havlicek, Bob Cousy, and Dave Cowens, all members of the Basketball Hall of Fame, have similar views concerning the "mystique" of the Boston Celtics. "I don't know exactly what the mystique is, but I think it's something that's been created by the media," Havlicek said.

"I read all these quotes from other players about how the ball takes a bad bounce on the old parquet floor or that Red turns the heat up or down and shuts off the hot water in the visitors' dressing room to give the Celtics a special edge. Red has no control over any of that stuff, but the press makes it sound like he does so they can come up with all sorts of magical reasons to explain those championship flags hanging over Boston Garden.

"We won because we had a combination of talent, management, and motivation. The mystique as far as I'm concerned is tradition and that started when Red came to the Celtics in 1950. Red is the building block, the architect putting the whole thing together. He was able to stay a step ahead of everyone by giving himself a little edge. He did it legally, and there wasn't any reason why other teams couldn't have come up with some of his strategies. They just didn't have his genius.

"Take the idea of the sixth man role that Red started with Frank Ramsey. I don't think that anyone else in basketball could have come up with that idea. When the other team substituted, they decreased their proficiency; when our sixth man went in, our skill level went up.

"The way I was taught to handle that sixth man role by Ramsey illustrates what I mean by Celtics tradition. When I joined the team in 1962, all of the papers were saying that I was going to take Ramsey's job. But Frank told me all the things I had to do, what to watch out for, how to take advantage of situations in a game. Probably the best piece of advice he gave me was to be ready when Red wanted me in the game.

"I used to sit as close as I could to Red, with my jacket over my shoulders. When he called my number, I practically rushed out onto the floor. Watch some of the substitutes coming into the game today, and you'll see the difference. They report to the scorer's table, take off their pants and jackets, then the horn sounds and three minutes elapse before they can get into the game. Those guys would have run into real problems if they had ever played for Red.

"Call it mystique or tradition or whatever you want, but the credit has to go to Red. A lot of people have speculated that Red had the best talent. It's true that he did have great players. But who was responsible for getting them? I don't think that any other coach could have handled that talent—and the egos which went with it—as well as Red did. Remember, too, that Celtics players have come and gone down through the years, but the organization is always able to regroup and make another run for the title. Red is the constant, the lifeline of the team's success. As long as he's a part of the Boston Celtics, the tradition will continue."

Many former Celtics are responsible for perpetuating the Celtics mystique, according to Bob Cousy. "Almost all of us who get questioned about it have a tendency to exaggerate or even make things up because it sounds good or is fashionable. So the stories get better and better and everything gets thrown out of proportion. Celtics tradition started with Walter Brown having the foresight to hire a basketball person who knew how to win in the most expedient manner.

"Arnold [Cousy and my wife, Dot, are the only ones who don't call me Red] recognized from the beginning the basic ingredients that were necessary to create a winner. Even during the first six years when we weren't winning championships, Arnold had a way of extracting the most out of whatever potential was available. I think that's the criterion you use when you measure success in coaching. It's simply getting the players to give the best they can in relation to their talents. I don't know anyone who was able to gauge talent the way that Arnold could, especially when it came to role players. A good example of that was when he signed Don Nelson after everyone else had given up on him.

"Arnold has never been described as an X's and O's coach, which, in my judgment, is an advantage. Basketball is the easiest game in the world to overcoach and allow the ego to get involved. Arnold never allowed that. In preseason, he stressed getting the guys in shape more than anything else. He liked to get out of the box early and he did it by keeping the theories as simple as possible. We had only six plays over the years with two or three options off each. If we never ran a play all game long it suited Arnold because it meant our transition game was effective.

"Arnold stressed good rebounding, strong defense, and a transition game whenever possible. Those are the ingredients that made the Celtics winners, not the so-called mystique. So whenever anyone asks me to explain the Celtics mystique, I point to Arnold. He personifies what Celtics mystique means. He was there at the beginning, and he's still there. When he steps down and ceases to play any part in the organization, I think the Celtics will be more susceptible to what happens to other teams. But as long as he's there, he will be the glue to hold the organization together."

"Whether you want to call it mystique or tradition, the fact is that there is something special about the Boston Celtics," Dave Cowens said. Cowens never played for me, but I dealt with him over a ten-year period, when he was both a player and a coach.

"Red always kept everything simple, easy to comprehend. Everyone was always aware of what was expected of him because Red always spelled it out clearly. His genius was in being able to deal with all of the human factors associated with high-profile athletes and to motivate those people and keep them together to sacrifice for one another and win games. He was able to keep players like K. C. Jones and Sam Jones on the bench—guys who would have been starting for other teams—without crushing their egos.

"I think the Celtics mystique is the direct result of a business plan that Red wrote when he first joined the Celtics. He was a visionary who knew what it took to win in this league, and he went out and got the players he needed to do it. He was lucky that Walter Brown gave him a completely free hand in running the team, so he was able to execute his plan without interference from the front office. But Red was the guy that made it happen and kept it going. The Celtics usually finished too high to give Boston a top pick, so Red had to be creative when it came time to draft.

"Teams like Los Angeles, Detroit, Milwaukee, Philadelphia, and New York have tradition, too. Last year Detroit got excited when it won its second NBA championship in a row. Boston just happened to win eleven out of thirteen, and no one else is ever going to do that. If you go to Europe and mention that you're from Boston, the first word you hear is *Celtics*. Only the Boston Celtics could have taken the team public and sold eighty thousand shares of stock throughout the country. Even when the Celtics are on the road, they sometimes attract as many fans as the home team.

"I do think that this tradition cost Celtics players a lot of money over the years. I remember when the American Basketball Association started and NBA players were jumping because of the large salaries being offered. Sure I could have made a lot more money with the new league, but I never even thought about it for a minute. John Havlicek passed up an incredibly lucrative contract to stay with the Celtics. I think it's a tribute to Red Auerbach that not one Celtic defected to the new league. We all stayed and took a personal hit so we could remain a part of the Celtics tradition.''

CHAPTER 12

One Man's Perspective: The Future of American Business

IN THE FALL OF 1990, a group of major league baseball players went to Japan to tour and play a series of games. There were some big names: Griffey, Gruber, Dibble, Dykstra, Fielder, and others. They lost four of their first five games and ended up 3–4–1. To put it bluntly, they got their asses handed to them.

It seemed that our guys were just there to have a good time, to goof off, to unwind after the season here.

The trouble is, the Japanese don't understand goofing off. They are as serious about baseball as we are—more serious in fact. It's tied to their national identity, and they want to be the best in baseball, just as they want to be the best in business.

So we send over a team that's not giving 100 percent, and they get beat. Bad. Like scoring five runs in the first three games. Our guys shrug it off, but the Japanese don't. To them it means, symbolically, that they are better than we are, higher on the ladder, the champions, if you will. When they start thinking that way, they become a very dangerous competitor—whether it's on the baseball diamond or the business playing field.

Yet, there are our guys, lollygagging. I'm in sports. I want this country to show its best face to the world and this kind of thing has driven me nuts for years.

Long-Term Symptoms

Back in the sixties, Bob Cousy and I were in a small town in French West Africa to run a clinic. I thought this place was in the middle of nowhere; it didn't even have radio or newspapers. But the kids knew basketball, as I quickly found out.

A few weeks earlier, the U.S. had sent a crummy AAU team to the Pan American Games. They stunk the place out. We have done this—sent lousy teams to international tournaments—so many times it makes me sick. This was another one.

Anyway, there we were, standing on the court, when a small boy came up to us.

"You're supposed to be the great American player," he said to Cooz.

"You're supposed to be the great American coach," he said to me.

"So how come the Russians beat you?"

We were embarrassed. What could we tell him? He was right.

This country apparently thinks that just because a team has USA written on the back of its warm-up jackets, it will automatically win. It won't. Nevertheless, year after year we send more lousy teams with USA on their backs to lose to the Yugoslavs or the Russians or the Brazilians or the Italians, you name 'em.

Or else we send a good team that's just goofing off. I can't believe it. *I used to push for a cabinet position—Secretary of Sports—to at least make sure we send decent teams around the world to represent this country.*

Go Back to "A for Attitude"

I think the problem is attitude. We were arrogant about everything after World War II. We thought basketball and baseball were our games, so we couldn't possibly lose. Even when we lost, we'd kid ourselves and say it was a fluke, or we weren't trying. We were better than those foreigners.

We've had the same provincial attitude in business, and to some degree, we've still got it. It's got to change, because like basketball, business is a worldwide game now. We've got to compete with Europe and Asia, not just Atlanta and Milwaukee.

Look at what's happened in basketball. The NBA used to have the rest of the basketball world at its feet, but it's not that easy any longer. NBA teams always won the McDonald's Open, an annual event between an NBA team and the European Basketball League, by an average of twenty points. Before the 1990–91 season, the New York Knicks needed a last-minute shot to force overtime in the first game. Then they kept alive the NBA's perfect record in international competition by defeating the Italian club, Scavolini Pesdaro, 119–115.

The Knicks went on to defeat POP 84 Split of Yugoslavia, 117–101, in the championship game. Toni Kukoc, the six-foot-ten-inch center for the Yugoslavian team, had a great game, with eighteen points and eight rebounds. But he was outdueled by Patrick Ewing of the Knicks, who had twenty-three points, thirteen rebounds, and two blocked shots.

I don't know how long that NBA winning streak is going to continue, though. The Soviets and the Yugoslavs have proven over the last few years that the United States could be beaten in basketball on the amateur level. There's no question that the game is taking on an international character. It's affected player development. It's affected scouting. It's affected the appearance of the sport, and it has influenced the economics of the game.

International Flavor

In 1988, we had one of our finest Olympic teams, yet we failed to win the gold for only the second time in our history. Look at that ballclub: We had players like David Robinson, Danny Manning, Willie Anderson, and Dan Majerle. It was a very good, unified, and disciplined team under a great coach, John Thompson. But we just couldn't get the job done in the final game. Russia had great players, too, and this illustrates how the balance of power has changed.

When you're building your ballclub, you look at all the factors that will make your team as strong as it can possibly be. The influence of the foreign player has already been felt in a very meaningful way. Vlade Divac was instrumental to the Los Angeles Lakers' great sixty-three-win season in 1989–90, for example. Nadev Henefeld of Israel helped lead the University of Connecticut to a Big East championship. Russian all-star high school teams have come in here and held their own against our ballclubs.

This speaks to the interest and enthusiasm in other countries for the game. It also demonstrates that the game shouldn't be viewed in purely nationalistic terms insofar as we're talking about dominance. If other countries' teams are succeeding against us at the collegiate level, then international parity on a professional level is probably already here.

Basketball, 2001

I'm not talking about how well the game's played just in the Soviet Union, either. We're seeing good ballplayers in Australia, South America, the Philippines, the Far East, Yugoslavia, and Israel, to name just a few other places. This is something that David Stern, the NBA commissioner, is acutely aware of. In fact, the Utah Jazz and the Phoenix Suns opened the 1990 season playing before a packed house in Tokyo.

I expect the NBA will be an international league in the nineties. The Celtics already have a full-time scout in Europe. We were impressed with the play of Yugoslav Stojko Vrankovic during training camp in 1990, and he made the team. The impact of the foreign player is further seen at the collegiate level, where there were over 150 foreign players on scholarship in this country in 1990. It's getting bigger and bigger every year, and again, this translates into how you plan things.

Why the rise of good, young foreign players? Wherever there's money involved, the popularity goes up. And basketball is unique because it is inexpensive to play. The rewards are great in all sports, of course. There are great golfers in Spain and Japan. There are fine tennis players coming out of Russia, like Chesnakov and Zareeva. Athletic skills—like business capabilities—offer areas of wide potential throughout the world.

Basketball has realized this for several years now, which is why more than half of the NBA teams have full-time foreign scouts. The Celtics look in the future will be affected. There are players in Europe with great size and strength. There are players with strong wills and a hunger to succeed. The Celtics are looking at this market very seriously. It's a path to success and it's a means to stay at or near the top in the nineties.

Business, 2001

A lot of companies used to think that the foreign market started and stopped with the foreign-food section in the local grocery. That's no longer true. Industry is doing the same things as basketball. American companies are forming joint ventures with European or Asian companies, opening plants together, everything.

That's a good sign. But if we're going to compete, if we're going to lead the world going into the twenty-first century, we've got to clean house, get rid of the old "we're the only game in town" attitude. We've got to stop assuming it's still 1956, and we're still on top of the world. It means taking the rest of the world seriously, seeing what they're doing, and doing it better.

That means getting back to some basics: knowledge of product, knowing what customers want, attention to detail, and aggressive marketing. Look at the auto industry. It was still turning out big, expensive, inefficient cars when the Japanese, Germans, and others had figured out that a lot of people didn't want them anymore.

Those "foreigners" took an industry that we virtually invented and beat us at it. I remember a few years ago when we were traveling in Denmark to give clinics. It seemed like everyone was driving an old car. They were, but it was a good, solid car.

These were people who didn't have the money to buy a car every other year. Buying a car was a big investment. I remember a waiter telling me he worked for twenty years to afford to buy a car.

It doesn't take a genius to figure out what this guy wanted when he finally was able to buy a car. He wanted one that was going to last, that wasn't going to fall apart after thirty or forty thousand miles. Most people in Europe are like this guy. They need a car that is going to last and be economical to run.

That's the philosophy behind Saab, Volvo, and Volkswagen, and it's what made Honda and Toyota successful today. These cars are hugely successful in the United States because most intelligent American consumers also want what that waiter in Copenhagen wanted. Nobody with any respect for his money wants to shell out ten or fifteen grand, or more, every other year just for transportation.

Red Sez: One way to get rid of that "only game in town" attitude and get back to the basics is what business today calls "benchmarking." Basically, it's getting better by comparing.

The impolite term for it is copycatting. The aim is simple. Identify winners. Identify why they win. Emulate them.

Every manager can apply the principle, whether you're studying the competition to find out about their products or services or operations, or you're studying winners among managers in order to incorporate their successful strategies into your own management motif.

Whichever is your motivation, you must:

- Focus outside your usual bailiwick, making comparisons to outside benchmarks, not the normal internal ones. If you're a financial manager, see how the best sales supervisors delegate authority. If you're a fast-breaking basketball guard, check out some training exercises from the local ballet troupe.
- Not ignore ancillary areas for investigation, so that your improvement activities may be aimed at a secondary function of your departmental or personal management program. If your most important responsibility is production, don't let that be your only target for improvement. Look at other job tasks that might offer bigger increments of potential improvement.
- Identify key performance variables, measure them, and then create action plans to attack weaknesses. A power forward may want to work on his short jumper to make his moves to the basket more respected. So he takes more jumpers during practice and tries to raise the percentage of his points that come from the outside. A manager tries management by walking around and checks the number of complaints he or she gets compared to the past. More problems that are solved means better performance.

Keeping in Touch

Those European and Asian companies figured all this out, but our companies didn't. We lost touch. We got careless. We stopped talking to the guy in the street, finding out what he was thinking and what he wanted. Some of these guys who become executives think when they get the key to the executive toilet that puts them above everyone else. Their heads get bigger than their bellies and they forget what their businesses are about.

We kept building cars for looks, not for performance or permanence. We were trying to sell cars because the seats were made of "rich Corinthian leather." Unbelievable. Who gives a damn? What was the engine made of? How long was it going to keep running? What was the gas mileage? Corinthian leather!

The product is first and foremost. Everything else is a variable that can be adjusted. Your public-relations guy can run off with the mayor's wife, your accountant can develop amnesia or sticky fingers! All of that stuff can be handled. The product is the bottom line. If the product isn't good, you can have the greatest ad campaign in the world, and all it will do is postpone the inevitable. You're going down the tubes.

Success Doesn't Translate

People say I could run any other business. They used to speculate in the paper that I would take over other sports teams in Boston, such as the Red Sox or the Patriots. They're wrong. It doesn't make sense. The reason is that I don't have enough knowledge of the products involved.

As owners in sports keep proving, a little learning is a dangerous thing. Those guys who've been successful—not to mention any individuals by name—in selling chickens or shavers, or building ships, come in and think they can be just as successful in sports. Then they don't win the championship in the first year, and they can't understand why. Ever hear the expression "It's a whole new ball game"?

The same thing happens in these mergers and takeovers. A petroleum company buys a printing company, or a food company buys a gun company, or what have you, and assumes it knows all there is to know about running the new business—any business. They go in, fire and demote people who do know this particular business, put their own people in, and the company goes to hell, more often than not.

They don't have the knowledge of the product. You can see these ads on TV for the Stanley Works, the big tool company. It's extremely successful. Why? It's run by a man out of MIT named Dick Ayers. He knows every machine in his plants, inside and out. He knows every tool he makes. And he keeps talking to builders, carpenters, and marketing people, so he knows what his customers like, and especially what they want. Knowledge of product. It isn't that complicated an idea.

Jocks as Businessmen

I could write a whole book about athletes who've gotten into all kinds of financial trouble because they thought their success as players would translate to business. So they open up a sporting-goods store or a restaurant, thinking they'll have something to go to when their playing days are over. Most of them end up playing longer than they should because they lost all of their money in some of these investments. There are players in the NBA today who are making millions of dollars but don't have a dime, because all of the money they earn has to go to creditors of some bankrupt investment. It comes back to the same thing—no knowledge of product.

I remember years ago Bob Cousy opened up a gas station in his hometown, Worcester, Massachusetts. Cousy had grown up there and had attended Holy Cross, where he had been a huge sports hero. You would think a gas station with his name on it would make sense. He did attract a lot of customers when the station first opened. But when they realized Bob himself wasn't going to pump their gas or put air in their tires, they stayed away in droves. I guess they felt he misled them when he didn't personally clean their windshields. In any case, Bob didn't keep the station too long.

A business requires a total time commitment that the average athlete simply can't make. Stan Musial, the former great outfielder for the St. Louis Cardinals, realized that when he opened his restaurant. He was in that restaurant night and day. He also selected a partner who knew a lot about running a restaurant. Most athletes don't make out too well in the restaurant business, including two former Celtics, Bill Russell and Satch Sanders. They just didn't have the product knowledge or commitment.

Be Your Own Best Customer

Let's get back to the auto industry. Detroit is beginning to turn itself around, led in large measure by Lee Iacocca, the Chrysler chairman. Lee was the guy at Ford who stopped listening to the bigwigs and began listening to the customers. He realized they wanted a sprightly little sports car, and he came up with the Mustang. It was a big success.

Another thing I admire about Lee is that he's straight with his employees and the union. He doesn't try to snow them or get them to back down. He wants to produce a car that's reliable and doesn't start coming apart after ten thousand miles. And if they do the job, everyone will share in the profits.

It hasn't been any bed of roses for Lee at Chrysler, but he saved the company and headed it in the right direction. He's emphasizing quality, he's building the kinds of cars that people want because he's listening.

How do you stay in touch? One way is to go out and be your own best (or worst) customer. I did this years ago at the Boston Garden. What I found out was incredible. The people selling tickets were telling fans they couldn't buy tickets for future games, only the very next game. Sometimes they'd even say, "What do you want to see that game for?"

At the time, we didn't control the box office. So we did the best we could. We put the word out all over town that it wasn't us making those decisions and to call us with any complaints. Or come see us. Then we'd investigate every complaint. Eventually we got it straightened out.

When you watch the Celtics on TV, you'll usually see a shot of me sitting in the stands. I could sit in a luxury box if I wanted to. But I don't. I want to be in the stands. It's the best way of staying in touch with my business.

The stands are where the customers are. If there's something wrong, I'm going to see it. If an usher is rude, or if a cable or a table is a danger to athletes, you name it, I can see it and get it corrected. I once grabbed a toddler who was headed for the floor and possible danger (but I did like his movement without the ball).

These people in the stands don't have to come to watch my team. I appreciate it that they do, and I want it to be a memorable evening, without any needless hassles. If they have a good night, they'll be back.

Best and Worst in American Business

I can't believe business people who lose touch with their customers. I've seen guys open restaurants and do okay at first. Then, maybe after a year or two, they'll start living off the fat of the land. They'll take long vacations, let someone else run the show. They might even start cutting corners, figuring to crank up the profits a little.

You know what happens to places like this. They start to slide.

Then the guy raises prices to cover the lost volume and pretty soon the customers are going somewhere else. I remember reading about some guy who opened a restaurant called Chapter 11, then went into it. Self-fulfilling prophecy, or what?

A restaurant, since we're on the subject, is a labor- and time-intensive business. In other words, you've got to be there. One of the best restaurateurs I know is a guy in Boston by the name of Anthony Athanas. He's from Albania and worked on a pushcart with his father back in the thirties. When he put some money together, he opened a restaurant.

He ended up with four of them, and Pier IV is one of the most famous restaurants in the country. Why? Anthony never retired, never took long vacations, was never anywhere except the restaurant. I remember asking him once what he did for vacations. He looked around the restaurant, smiled, and said, "Red, this is my vacation."

It helps to like what you're doing. But being there has to do with your image, how people perceive your business. If there were a problem at Pier IV, Anthony knew about it immediately and you'd better believe it was corrected that day. He was always there, getting to know customers, making sure the food was cooked to perfection. That was his product, food and a pleasant atmosphere. He made it good. He was a success.

You can read all those stress books about business and they'll tell you how you've got to divorce yourself from the office, or never take work home, or completely forget work once five P.M. hits. You can do that if you want to be a mediocre manager. But if you want to excel, you've got to use some personal time for business.

Talk Is Cheap—And Valuable

I can't talk enough about the simple act of talking to people. Some of these bosses become big poobahs and lock themselves in the executive suite. They lose touch. Eventually their company and their careers are going to begin to slide.

Once you have the good product, does it end there? Will the world beat a path to your door? You don't have time to wait and find out. You've got to sell it now.

A few years ago, I was asked to speak to a group of scientists at Hewlett-Packard. These people, I was told in advance, were real egghead types. Some of them were probably geniuses. They just wanted to stay in the laboratory and build the latest toy. They had absolutely no interest in helping the advertising or sales departments come up with marketing strategies.

So I got there and started right in.

"Scientists like you shouldn't have to waste time answering questions from the sales department. Don't listen to those clowns in the advertising department when they ask about product benefits. Forget about it. You shouldn't have to help in any of that selling crap."

Everybody is smiling.

"Of course," I said, "you don't have to eat either."

I then went on to tell them what I really thought. You can have the best computer or printer or whatever, and it doesn't mean a thing if it doesn't get to the customers, if it isn't sold. And who better to explain the marketing strengths than the people who designed and built it? Common sense.

I never tried to sell the Celtics with professional salespeople. I did it with the players. They are the ones who make my product.

On the flip side, if anyone knows they'll have to help sell what they make, they'll make it better. Human nature.

Iacocca is a master of this. He believes he is making a good car. But how does he get his message across? Before he took over, Chrysler had been in a steep slide. Its reputation was slipping badly. How does he get the customers back?

He comes up with the best warranty in the automobile business, five years or fifty thousand miles. That's a direct message to the person on the street. It says, "I believe so much in my product that I'll take a bigger chance in backing it up than anyone else will." I think his message made people want to take a shot with him.

That's the only way we're going to come back, and put America where America belongs. We need to know our products thoroughly, and make them and sell them better than the Japanese, the Germans, or anyone else.

Worldwide Performance

I remember years ago, I had an NBA all-star team touring Yugoslavia. The locals had just finished second in the world tournament, clobbering another one of the lousy American AAU teams. They didn't want us to put on a clinic or anything.

It didn't occur to them that we had different levels of play in this country and that our pros might have a thing or two to offer. Besides, they had a redheaded six-foot-seven-inch kid, the top scorer in Europe and a big hero in Yugoslavia.

Okay. In my pregame talk I had a message for Bill Russell. "Bill," I said, "tonight I don't want you to score. I don't want you to rebound. I don't want you to help out. All I want you to do is guard the redheaded kid. If he scores one basket, I'll break your neck." (My motivation technique was a little less polished in those days!)

The game opens, the kid gets the ball and goes up for a jumper. He had a big smile. Russell suddenly appears out of nowhere and blocks the shot to one of our guys. This happened six times in a row. The kid was embarrassed.

Russell was getting tired of it, but he knew he'd gotten into the kid's head. The next time he blocked the shot into the kid's face, what is now called an "in-your-face disgrace."

The kid went nuts, screams and kicks the ball into the stands. The ref threw him out of the game. We won by thirty-two points. The next night they tried to get physical with us—with Russell, Bob Pettit, Tom Heinsohn. We won that one by fifty-four points. Then they asked if we might do a clinic.

Maybe I'm old-fashioned, but that's the way I'd like to see U.S. companies perform around the world.

Personal Success

I still remember the first time a corporation asked me to talk to its employees about success and motivation. I thought at the time, What the hell can I tell these people, many of them experts in their respective fields, about anything? I'm a basketball man.

But they convinced me that the same principles that made the Celtics winners applied to companies, the same motivational tools that work for players work for employees. I guess they must be right, because I've been very busy on the lecture circuit.

Usually most of my audiences are male and familiar with names like Cousy, Russell, Sharman, Havlicek, Cowens, Bird, and all the other great Celtics. But last fall, I had a real test. I suddenly looked at my audience and they were mostly women. How much did they know about basketball? I wondered. Would they be able to understand the principles I was trying to get across?

The answer was an emphatic yes. I got a rousing reception and, judging from the questions they asked, I had no doubt they knew exactly what I was driving at. So maybe the techniques of a basketball man can be translated to business. Meeting and talking with successful executives around the country has been a learning experience for me, too.

For instance, I've noticed that most successful managers have certain characteristics in common. For one, they listen to others and let their employees in on their thinking. Some managers tell their employees only enough to get the job done. This unwillingness to share information discourages employees from accepting responsibility and working creatively. These are the same managers who listen selectively, hearing only what they want to hear. The top managers recognize that the best decisions are made by the people who have, and share, the most information.

Two, they know when to take a backseat and when to grab the wheel. Effective managers aren't pompous and full of self-importance. They give their subordinates the support to do their jobs, and then stay out of the way. They're rooting for everyone to win and have no interest in streaking out front and leaving everyone else in the dust. Their attitude is "I want to win and I want you to win."

They also know their own strengths and limitations. Real leaders know what it is they like about their work, what they don't like, what they're good at and what they're not good at. They are open to direction and suggestions and can always find the good side of a bad situation and come up with a solution.

They project a can-do attitude. Managers who are flexible enough to shift gears and help out when the crush is on will develop employees with the same capabilities. Having a can-do attitude doesn't mean managers have to be blind optimists. It does mean they have to be capable of coming up with the right questions that will lead to the right answers.

They are willing to take risks. They are also willing to make mistakes as long as they and the people they supervise learn from them. Good managers also realize that people rarely do things well the first time. A willingness to correct a mistake once it's been made, instead of trying to place blame, is the mark of a good manager.

They have a sense of humor. We all have difficulty liking the person who takes himself or herself too seriously, who has no sense of humor. The top managers I have met all have the ability to laugh at themselves. Of course it's important for managers to take their jobs seriously. But managers who take themselves too seriously tend to become stuffed shirts who feel their titles or jobs make them better than anyone else.

They are initiators. They take charge of their lives and focus on things they can do something about. They ignore things that they can't possibly change.

They train employees to identify and prevent problems, rather than just trying to solve them after the fact. If all people do is solve problems, they're in the wrong jobs because they should be concentrating on preventing them in the first place. When you see employees thinking of prevention instead of correction you can be sure they have a thinking manager.

They have the guts to say no. Too many managers are afraid to say no because they don't want to disappoint people. Having the fortitude to simply say no or to veto a suggestion is a necessary management ability. Don't feel that the price of keeping employees happy is never having to make an unpopular or negative decision.

They help employees understand how their jobs fit into the big picture. Top managers create a vision or objective for their departments and communicate it to their employees. They help people understand how they fit into their department, what their roles are, and what they're trying to achieve as a team. When people understand what they are working toward, then they can better understand how they can help.

If you ask me, the future of American business rests in all our hands—in the hands of all the managers who are striving to be successful, to get ahead, to propel their company (or team) to the top.

I don't have all the answers. But I sure hope some of my opinions can contribute to the successful achievement of that overall goal.

Fast Breaks

IN FOOTBALL it's the two-minute drill; in hockey it's "sudden death"; in baseball it's extra innings; and in basketball it's overtime. I'm talking about that time when the game is on the line, when the right or wrong decision is going to make the difference between victory and defeat. I faced this situation many times. Score tied, fifteen seconds left, time out. Crunch time, as they call it.

People used to say I was an autocrat, that I ruled like a dictator in those situations. That isn't so. The first thing I did in the huddle was ask if anybody had any ideas. I wouldn't always accept them, but if they sounded better than what I was planning, I would. The important point was that after exploring all of the possibilities, I made the final decision. When I started to speak, I demanded absolute silence and attention from each of my players.

God help anyone I caught not listening. I'd get madder than hell when someone wandered away from the circle. "Don't you think you ought to get back here?" I'd say. "If I decide to put you out there, it might be nice if you knew what the hell was going on!"

The important thing is that I had to be in charge. I'd see other teams go into their huddle and everyone would start talking at once. Or the coach would talk and no one would listen. Or some would listen while others went looking for towels and cups of water. A lot of coaches—especially in tight situations—might back off and let their stars decide what to do. That way the responsibility on them wasn't as great. I always felt that I was in the best position to make that final decision. Besides it was my job. I wasn't always right but the point was that I made a decision.

Robert Parish, a great player with a tremendous sense of humor, affectionately calls Kevin McHale "the black hole."

Why? "When the ball goes in to Kevin, it never comes out again," according to Parish.

Some managers' offices are black holes, as well. A problem goes in, or a question comes up, and an answer never comes out. For whatever reason, the manager doesn't make a decision. If you remember one thing from this book, it's just this: *Make a damn decision.* There's an awful lot of this touchy-feely stuff about management around lately and some of it is okay. Communication and feedback are important. But remember that the reason you're in charge is to make decisions. In your day-to-day life as a manager, most of the time a wrong decision is better than no decision. At least your people have some direction and an idea of what they're supposed to do.

Under some circumstances they'll even turn a wrong decision into a right one. This really happens. I remember a few times calling the wrong play, but at least my guy got a shot off, and we got the rebound and scored. By doing something, they got the job done.

In this section, I'll lay out some common managerial problems, give you some options, and then offer a rationale for your decision. That's the important thing—reaching that decision.

Situation 1.

A key employee asks for a day off and is turned down. He takes the day off anyway.

Do you:

1. Do nothing, hoping that the whole situation will simply blow over?

2. Make an example of him by issuing an unpaid suspension?

3. Take a close look at his record before making any decision?

Answer: Doing nothing is your worst possible choice. You can bet that every other employee is aware of the situation and is waiting for your response. The other extreme—setting an example to keep other employees in line—usually doesn't work either. The best alternative is to take a close look at his previous record before making any decision. If it's happened before, or if his overall record is spotty, a suspension or even discharge may be justified.

Of course, not even a perfect record justifies what amounts to gross insubordination. So you can't ignore the situation and let him go back to work as if nothing has happened. Talk to him and put the conversation in writing. This whole situation could have been prevented if the employee had been given permission to take the day off.

Bob Cousy came to me once and asked if he could miss a day of practice. I asked him why, and he explained that he had a chance to make a television commercial.

"What will they pay you?" I asked.

"Five thousand dollars," Cousy said. Now Bob was making fifteen thousand dollars at the time, so that commercial represented a third of his salary. "Sure you can go," I said to Bob. "How about taking me with you?"

Can you imagine Cousy's reaction if I had turned him down. He was a great kid and never gave me any trouble. But if I had made him pass up that commercial for one practice, he would have had the right to be resentful. I watched a former Celtics coach put himself in a tough situation over a similar request. One of the stars of the team, a great player who always gave everything he had and never asked for any special favors, requested a day off from practice to attend a friend's wedding. The coach turned him down flat. Of course, the player went to the wedding and now the two of them had a problem. If he suspended the player, he would hurt the team. In this case, he did nothing, which was his best move under the circumstances. But it didn't have to happen.

I always liked to be able to do a player a favor when he asked for it, even if it meant bending the rules a little. It accomplishes two things: First, you end up with a player who feels he owes you a favor; second, you don't put an employee in a position where he challenges a rule and has to be disciplined. Now, you can't give in to every request or you're going to end up with an undisciplined team. Flexibility is the key.

Situation 2.

As a manager, you have a department that's running okay, but could be doing better. You need a new supervisor, but there's no one qualified to take over from within. You have to bring in someone from the outside, and you find a good candidate.

Do you:

1. Just hire the guy and not say anything?

2. Tell the department you're doing it and warn them that they need improvement? Explain why the new guy is just the person to kick a little butt and take a few names?

3. Explain to the department that you're making the change and why? You might tell them that while you prefer to promote from within, you feel there's no one ready at this point to take the job. Tell them about the new person's qualifications, and suggest that his or her strengths will mesh well with those already in place. Ask them to work with the new person because everybody looks better when the department improves, and some of the people there could then be looked at for promotion.

Answer: The first choice is bad policy. When you don't say anything, people make their own assumptions. Rumors start flying, and you won't believe what some of them claim. It's best to level with the people.

The second choice is communication, but bad communication. If you berate the people already in the department, you're creating an impossible situation for the new person coming in. The people will resent the hell out of him. They won't work with him, and the situation will get worse.

This is one of the many situations where honesty and openness are the best policies. When you tell the employees that you don't feel anyone is ready for promotion, they won't like it. But they'll reluctantly appreciate your frankness, and may even try to prove you wrong with better work. By saying why you made the move, you'll squelch rumors before they start, and your people will at least know where you stand. What you want to do is get your new person a fair chance. Most workers are open toward new bosses, if they don't have some artificially created prejudices. Avoid creating those prejudices, and you create that fair chance. If you've picked the new supervisor well, he or she will take it from there.

As a matter of fact, I faced this situation in 1980, when I went outside the organization to hire Bill Fitch as head coach. I used the same technique that I'm recommending to you and it worked. We won the division championship in Bill's first season and the NBA championship in his second (1981–82).

Situation 3.

Same situation as number 2. You're recruiting an outsider to come in as a supervisor. This is someone you want. But he says he has to have six weeks' vacation. Your company policy is two weeks until an employee has reached five years' service, three weeks until ten years, and then four weeks after that. In other words, your limit is four weeks' vacation a year. He says he has six weeks in his present job and has to have six to move.

Do you:

      1. Give him the six weeks but explain that it's a violation of company policy and tell him to keep quiet about it?

      2. Finesse it? Tell him that officially he can only have two weeks of actual vacation, but you'll give him compensatory time to make up for the other four weeks?

      3. Stick to your existing vacation policy?

Answer: An amazing number of people try solutions similar to number 1 and, in my opinion, it's a big mistake. Do you think that people are stupid, and aren't going to figure out that someone who's not around for six weeks a year isn't getting some kind of special treatment? Employees don't miss things like this. And let me tell you something. People resent other people, especially new people who haven't proven themselves, being singled out for special treatment. The fact that you're being sneaky about it is just going to make it worse.

In pro basketball, everybody knows that players are treated individually when it comes to salary. You just don't find fringe players expecting to be paid like Magic Johnson or Larry Bird. But there are certain other things, travel, meals, and time off for personal business, where everyone expects to be treated equally. It's understood, and if you play favorites with this stuff, you're in trouble.

I'd try to stick to the existing policy. But if the person is the Second Coming of Lee Iacocca and you can't do without him, then you'd better level with your employees. They probably aren't going to like it, but they'll at least appreciate that you were up-front with them.

Situation 4.

A woman employee comes to you with a complaint. An old-time male employee, a real veteran, has ''girlie'' pictures up on the wall of his cubicle. You, of course, know this, because the guy has had them for years. Some employees even send him postcards for his wall gallery. The woman complains that the pictures are demeaning to women and constitute sexual harassment, and demands they be taken down.

Do you:

1. Explain to her, in your best Dutch Uncle manner, that the guy's been around forever, that he's an unreconstructed chauvinist, and that it's all quite harmless?
2. Tell her the best way to deal with him is to ignore him, that eventually he'll get the message that his behavior is no longer acceptable?
3. Go to the man and tell him to get the damn pictures off the wall?

Answer: I'm going back a few years here, but there was an old vaudeville routine where one guy passes a hand grenade to another guy and says, ''Hold this while I look for the pin.''

When someone comes to you with a complaint of sexual harassment, believe me, you are now standing there holding a legal hand grenade, and you better start looking for that pin immediately. I picked this example for a reason. It's the kind of thing that's gone on in offices and factories around the country for years.

Because of this, you might be tempted to think of it as harmless. So you might be tempted to just shrug it off, and tell the woman who brought the complaint just to forget it. That would be a very big mistake. A woman brought a similar complaint to court in California recently, and the judge found that, indeed, it did amount to sexual harassment. This is happening more and more. The rules of the game are changing and you should be aware of them. When someone brings a complaint of sexual harassment, you have to take it seriously. If it's probable, or even possible, that the person bringing the complaint is correct, you'd better do something. In this case, tell the male employee to get the pictures off company property.

Situation 5.

A variation on situation 4. But this time, instead of going to you, the woman has gone to the human rights commission in your state and filed a complaint. You've just been contacted by the commission.
Do you:

1. Fire the woman?
2. Try to deal with the problem before the date of the hearing?
3. Stonewall the whole thing?

Answer: Maybe there was a time when you could fire someone for something like this, but you'd better not try it anymore. If you fire someone for doing something he or she has a legal right to do, such as filing a complaint or reporting an unsafe or illegal activity, you're guilty of retaliation. Wrongful discharge is one of the fastest-changing areas of employment law. So firing the woman or ignoring the situation could cost your company a lot of money. Your best bet is to complete a full investigation and take whatever action is necessary. Then go see the guy with the pictures and tell him politely to make them disappear.

Situation 6.

You've got a midlevel manager whose performance, for years, has gradually gotten worse. He's now at the point where he isn't doing an acceptable job. However, he was once a good manager and got along well with his immediate superiors for years. There are no written records showing his declining performance. But it has dropped substantially, everyone is aware of it, and it's beginning to hurt production. Some of the people working for him are looking for other jobs:

Do you:

　　1. Fire him?
　　2. Kick him upstairs into a similar job with new people?
　　3. Put him on probation and start working with him to improve his performance?

Answer: You can't fire him, without risking a big hit in court, because you've got no paper trail, no written record of deteriorating performance. His records say he's a decent worker, even though that's no longer the case. Should you transfer him? Most of the time, no. Managers use this method as a quick fix. They'll take a person who's doing a lousy job, and put him in another one involving the same kinds of duties and responsibilities. What happens, more often than not, is that his performance remains poor. So they haven't solved the problem, they've just transferred it.

Maybe there was a time when companies could afford to carry someone like this by giving him a nothing job. With the competition as it is today, that's no longer possible. The best choice is to sit down with him and find out why a once successful performer is running into problems. There could be an off-the-job reason that's causing his problem. Maybe it's substance abuse, or depression, or pressure at home. Who knows? But you'd better dig in, find out what it is, and do something about it.

Situation 7.

You've just been promoted into management and one of your assistants has taken over your old supervisory job. He has the experience to do the job, but he's running into a few personnel problems. Some of the people who used to work with him are having a difficult time adjusting to working for him. The absence rate in the department is up and production and quality are down.

　　Do you:

　　1. Fire the supervisor?
　　2. Bypass the supervisor and start managing the department yourself?
　　3. Get the supervisor to do his job?

Answer: There's one rule of management that should never be broken: If you put someone in a supervisory position, you've got to give him room to manage. You've got to give him every opportunity to grow. In this case, obviously, he's having a problem. But you must have seen something positive in this person or you wouldn't have given him the job in the first place. The best thing you can do is let him work out this situation himself. If you step in now, you do nothing for him. You cut him out. He begins to think that he doesn't have to make any of the hard choices, that you'll make them for him. You've got to make him do the job. He has to get in there, find out what the problem is, and do something about it. That's the only way he'll grow as a supervisor, and the only way you'll survive as a manager.

When I turned the coaching reins over to Bill Russell in 1967, a lot of the Boston press said I'd never be able to keep my hands off the team. Coaches following Russell included Tom Heinsohn, Tom Sanders, Dave Cowens, Bill Fitch, K. C. Jones, Jimmy Rogers, and Chris Ford. I never interfered with one of them.

There's an old adage that says, If you want it done right, do it yourself. That saying has probably caused more high blood pressure, coronaries, and managerial turnover than any other combination of words in the English language. It nearly cost me big in 1966. I was handling jobs that are now covered by eight people in the Celtics' organization. Fortunately, I took a look in the mirror one day and recognized that I was slowly killing myself. Right then and there I decided to turn the coaching duties over to Russell. I also made my mind up that I would give him both the coaching responsibility and the authority to carry it out. As far as I'm concerned the ability to delegate properly is the ultimate managerial skill.

Situation 8.

A new employee has almost completed the ninety-day probation period. He's always there on time. He plays on the softball team. But his work is marginal. If you look at it honestly, it's not even as good as the work turned out by the two or three of the weakest members of the department.

Do you:

1. Let him become a regular employee, hoping that his work will improve in time?

2. Extend his probation for another three months?

3. Let him go?

Answer: In this day and age, probation is sometimes your last best chance to get rid of a marginal employee. If I drafted a guy—and I have drafted such guys—who were only as good as the twelfth man on my team, would I keep the guy and pay him big bucks? Not if I could help it. Look, you've taken a close look at this guy. His work isn't up to the level being put out by your weakest employees. What makes you think it will improve if you extend his probation? If you let him become a regular employee, it means that other people will have to carry him to some degree. They aren't going to like that.

The whole probationary process is there to let you make an objective judgment about whether he can do the job or not. By the way, if you hire someone who isn't right for the job, you're not doing him any favors by keeping him in it. You're just delaying the time when he will find something that he is good at and performs well.

Situation 9.

You work for a major company that has just bought out a smaller competitor with a lot of problems—flat sales and climbing costs. You're told to improve the numbers. It's your big chance.

Do you:

1. March in like the U.S. Marines and start kicking butt and taking names? Let those clowns know in no uncertain terms that things are going to improve or you will know why?

2. Come in quietly, don't say much, just spend a few months checking the place out?

3. Arrive, don't make radical changes, start talking to the people who work there?

Answer: One of the worst aspects of this whole merger-takeover business of the past decade is the way some companies take over others. I can't believe it. They march in like Sherman through Georgia, walking over people, firing and demoting them without even giving them a chance. It doesn't make sense and good business people don't operate that way. You never see the Japanese do it.

Think about it. Your company bought this company because it was a viable concern. Maybe it had run into problems, but it must have had something to offer. That means there must be some people in there who know what they're doing. If you blunder in and fire the competent people, you'll be making your own job that much more difficult.

So unless you've inherited a desperate situation, don't make radical changes. Find out what you have before doing anything. Talk to the people who are there. Study production records. Look at awards the company may have won. You've got to establish credibility. When you see what changes need to be made, explain why you're making them and give the reasons behind your moves.

Lead by example as much as you can. Get your hands dirty. When you are making a change, don't knock what people have already done. Be positive, but don't try to kid everybody. Don't say you're going to do "a little fine-tuning," then initiate widescale changes. You'll have no credibility. Above all, don't make any promises you might not be able to keep. The courts are filled with lawsuits from ex-employees who claim they have employment contracts because of statements made by their bosses.

The key here is put yourself in the position of a competent person in the company you've taken over. How would that person want to be treated? If you treat the person properly, you'll keep him. That's the person you want to keep. That's the person who can make you look good.

I still remember the resentment I felt when the Celtics ownership passed into certain hands. One time, I had a group of real-estate executives telling me who I should protect on an expansion list. On another occasion, I had a fried-chicken expert drafting players and making trades. He was so good at it that he ran the Buffalo basketball team into the ground, and nearly pushed me into joining the New York Knicks.

Let me give you a positive example with the current Celtics ownership, Don Gaston, Alan Cohen, and Paul Dupee, Jr. The three of them are great businessmen, experts in their respective fields. But they let the Celtics management run the team. Not one of them has ever told me who should be drafted or traded and I'm sure they never will. Yet they're always there when needed, like the time that Alan Cohen went to Italy to re-sign Brian Shaw.

Situation 10.

You have an employee with a drinking problem. You've seen it coming. For a while, it wasn't too bad. You hate to interfere in the private lives of your workers, so you didn't say anything. But now, his production has fallen off badly. He's surly and defensive. He's also having a negative effect on other employees who are tired of doing his work.

Do you:

1. Fire him?
2. Tell him he's letting everyone down and appeal to his sense of pride?
3. Give him a final warning and make sure he understands that you mean business?

Answer: I don't pretend to understand the chemistry of drinking, because I never did much of it myself. No player ever smelled alcohol on my breath before or during a game, because I had strict rules about drinking. If they couldn't do it, I couldn't either. I recognize that a coach of a professional sports team can enforce some rules that would get a lot of business managers in trouble. If you told an employee he couldn't drink off the job, he might hit you with an invasion of privacy lawsuit. There are definite steps that you can and must take when you're dealing with an employee with a drinking problem, however.

I don't think you should fire the guy, at least not before you've given him adequate warning. Usually the person who develops a drinking problem has been around for a while and was probably once a valuable employee. That's why I think you should make some effort to salvage him. But lecturing him or appealing to his sense of pride isn't going to work. What can a manager possibly say to a guy that he hasn't heard from his wife, kids, or close friends? All a lecture usually accomplishes is to make the drinker a little cleverer in hiding the disease.

I like the concept of "tough love," which is why I'd choose solution number 3. You're not a psychologist. You don't know what makes people drink, and I'm not sure that anyone else does either. I wouldn't even mention the word alcohol. Tie everything in with performance. He's not doing his job and you're not doing your job if you let him get away with it. Warn him that you're not going to put up with it any longer. Then put it in writing. No more absences on Fridays and Mondays, or the days before or after a holiday. No more excuses for declining production, poor quality, mistakes, or arguments with other workers. Make sure that he understands that his job is on the line if he doesn't change his behavior today.

Then stick to it. There used to be a coach around the league who was always giving his players "final" warnings. "If you do that once more, you're gone," he'd say. Of course, nobody was ever "gone," so nobody took him seriously. Alcoholics behave the same way when they get the idea that the boss doesn't really mean it when he says they'd better straighten out at once. If you tell him that he's going to be suspended for unexcused absences, you have to do it. Remember the biggest favor you can do for the guy is to help him keep his job.

Don't mention drinking, unless he brings it up. Even then, you should only refer him to an employee assistance plan, if you have one, or the local chapter of Alcoholics Anonymous if you don't. Be positive in the sense that you will allow enough time for recovery. But make it clear that it's this path or no path. It's not easy, but it can be done.

Situation 11.

You've had it up to here with one of your employees who's always whining. The guy is a complainer. He complains about everything. He complains about his job, the amount of work he's required to do, the people he works with, the product; he even complains about the company picnic. You know he's wearing his coworkers down and hurting morale. He's wearing you down. His work, however, is satisfactory.

Do you:

1. Fire Him?
2. Ignore him?
3. Talk to him?

Answer: We've all known chronic complainers. Nothing makes them happy, except possibly more things to complain about. People like this can wear you down. When I've got someone getting my goat, I do something. Firing isn't usually a good choice. First of all, it's unusual for this type of employee to do any one thing that justifies discharge. The average complainer is usually a person with a lot of experience who is capable of doing a good job. There's another good reason why you should never fire a complainer until you take a close look at the reason for the discontent.

A lot of companies are being hit with having to pay huge awards to employees who were able to prove that they were fired in retaliation for making legitimate complaints. These are the so-called whistle blowers, the workers who go public with safety or other violations and are fired for their trouble. So you want to take a close look at the reason for the complaint before doing anything.

First, consider that the employee may be right. Ask around. There may be a problem out there that you're not aware of. Keep an open mind. But if the complaints have no basis in fact, it's time to deal with the person. Some complainers simply want recognition. They want to be told they're doing a good job. If someone is doing a good job, and you haven't mentioned it, then do it now. Some people would rather have a pat on the back than a raise (God bless them). But don't treat complainers as squeaky wheels. Don't hand out compliments that aren't deserved. Certainly you won't base promotion or raise decisions on how much an employee squawks. If you've got a complainer who doesn't deserve additional praise and doesn't seem to have a legitimate gripe, you'd better talk to him.

Two things here. Don't take the complaints personally, and don't play his game. In other words, if he starts bad-mouthing the company, don't start bad-mouthing him. Just be straight. It's possible that just by talking to him, you'll straighten some things out. In my experience, talking helps about 80 percent of the time. If not, and if his complaining is of such a nature that it's hurting morale and production, then you're going to have to stop it. Tell him flatly it won't be tolerated, and then follow up.

But don't take this step unless you've got a really serious problem. Some people are just complainers by nature, and don't mean much by it. It's their way of blowing off steam. They'll complain, then go do a decent job. Give some credit to your other employees. They usually know a "benign" complainer from a destructive one.

One of the disadvantages of running a professional sports team today is the horde of reporters who are always ready to quote the "anonymous" source. Usually this is the person who isn't playing for one reason or another, so he bad-mouths the whole team. This type of individual can rip an organization apart, whether you're talking about athletics or electronics. I had a situation like that a few years ago when a player was leaking stories to the press. I called him in and told him in no uncertain terms that if it continued, the newspaper would be paying his salary. He got the message.

Situation 12.

There's been a screwup. You're the sales manager, and one of your sales reps has blown a major account. Your boss is demanding to know why. You're not sure what happened. When the guy made his last sales call, you had the account. Three days later, you didn't. You suspect he failed to make a sales call when the account needed new inventory. The general manager, your boss, is demanding an explanation first thing in the morning.
    Do you:

1. Tell him you think the sales rep screwed up big-time, and you're trying to find out the details?
2. Emphasize that it wasn't your fault, and that the sales rep's butt is in a sling when you find him?
3. Just find out what happened and tell your boss?

Answer: This is as much a question of style as of substance. When you are in charge of people and one of them makes a mistake, it's also your mistake. That's the bad news. The good news is that your boss understands (or should understand) that mistakes happen. What you need to do, what you need to be in the habit of doing, is finding out the whole story. Then tell your boss in an affirmative, positive way, leaving out nothing and adding nothing.
    Here's what's wrong with the first two answers. They're mealy-mouthed. You end up looking like a wimp in both cases. Part of management is image. You must project the image of a take-charge guy. A friend of mine, an executive of a publishing company, was late for work every day for eighteen years. He just couldn't get up in the morning. But he walked in every day like a tiger on the prowl, snarling and ready to take on the world. For eighteen years, everybody assumed he'd been at a power breakfast or something. His image was that good.
    Image is important, but, of course, so is substance. Put yourself

in your boss's shoes. When he has a problem, he wants to solve it. He doesn't want to hear anything but the facts, so he can make a decision and get the problem out of the way. If you just give him accurate facts, he'll appreciate it. If you try to give him a big story, he'll see right through it.

Index

34D